Southeast Asians
and the Asia-Europe
Meeting (ASEM)

Southeast Asians and the Asia–Europe Meeting (ASEM)

State's Interests and Institution's Longevity

EVI FITRIANI

ISEAS

INSTITUTE OF SOUTHEAST ASIAN STUDIES

Singapore

First published in Singapore in 2014 by
ISEAS Publishing
Institute of Southeast Asian Studies
30 Heng Mui Keng Terrace
Pasir Panjang
Singapore 119614

E-mail: publish@iseas.edu.sg
Website: <http://bookshop.iseas.edu.sg>

The responsibility for facts and opinions in this publication rests exclusively with the author and her interpretations do not necessarily reflect the views or the policy of the publisher or its supporters.

ISEAS Library Cataloguing-in-Publication Data

Fitriani, Evi.
    Southeast Asians and the Asia-Europe Meeting (ASEM) : state's interests and institution's longevity
    1.   Asia-Europe Meeting.
    2.   Asia—Foreign relations—Europe.
    3.   Europe—Foreign relations—Asia.
    4.   Regionalism.
    5.   International cooperation.
    I.   Title.
DS33.4 E8F54   2014

ISBN 978-981-4459-50-1 (soft cover)
ISBN 978-981-4459-62-4 (e-book, PDF)

Typeset by Superskill Graphics Pte Ltd
Printed in Singapore by Markono Print Media Pte Ltd

For my daughters, Hana and Zirly,
for their love and company during the steep path

And for my parents
for their love and prayers

CONTENTS

LIST OF ILLUSTRATIONS

Tables

Figures

FOREWORD

There is already a very large literature on regional institutions. Why should Evi Fitriani's new book, *Southeast Asians and the Asia-Europe Meeting (ASEM): State's Interests and Institution's Longevity*, merit the attention of readers? In my view, there are two core reasons why this book deserves attention and, indeed, is quite likely to win attention.

One is the volume's distinctive focus. Fitriani examines one of the least explored and least appreciated of the major regional bodies — the Asia-Europe Meeting (ASEM) — and she brings to it a self-consciously Southeast Asian perspective. ASEM has received relatively less attention than the other high-profile regional groupings in part because its trans-regional nature has been seen by many as having an inherent implausibility about it. Could a body that aimed to link two very large and very different regions — each of which is highly heterogeneous — really amount to anything, or even sustain high-level political engagement for more than a brief period?

Fitriani explores the reasons ASEM has endured despite widespread scepticism. She supplements her assessment of the scholarly literature with a valuable body of empirical evidence arising from an extensive range of interviews she conducted with key players across Southeast Asia. This offers a distinctive window onto the dynamics of ASEM that has not previously been available to us.

If one reason to pay attention to this book is the distinctive focus of the scholarship, a second — perhaps less immediately apparent — reason is what this author represents. Evi Fitriani is in the vanguard of a rising cohort of Indonesian social scientists who are not content to speak only to local debates inside Indonesia, but seek also to engage with global scholarly discourse. There is a determination and confidence in this cohort that cannot be overlooked.

This is an altogether welcome development. Indeed, international research ventures and funding bodies are now keen to engage with Fitriani and her cohort. We can all look forward to hearing more from this new wave of Indonesian scholarly voices, and Evi Fitriani's will be prominent among them.

Andrew MacIntyre
Deputy Vice-Chancellor International and Vice-President
RMIT University, Australia
June 2014

ACKNOWLEDGEMENTS

The study of the relations between Asia and Europe in the Asia-Europe Meeting (ASEM) that underlines this book is an actualization of my interest in and passion for the two regions. Having lived and studied in both regions, I have captured some of the pain, neglect, suspicion, and misunderstanding as well as admiration and respect of the Asian and European people towards each other. The establishment of ASEM in 1996 seemed to be a long-needed remedy for the Asians and the Europeans. However, ASEM does not shine robustly in bridging the relationship and seems to have been marginalized in global affairs. With these concerns and questions, I have studied ASEM for the last six years.

This book is the result of my learning process to which many people have contributed. My supervisors, Professor Andrew MacIntyre and Professor Jennifer Corbett, are deeply instrumental in this learning process. Rather sceptical about ASEM but very supportive of my study, Andrew has motivated me to overcome the challenges along the way. Jenny's supportive advice and trouble-shooting approach have maintained this learning process in several stages. In addition, many people from the Australian National University (ANU) have also helped me during my research. I want to thank Professor John Ravenhill, Dr Wendy Noble, Assistant Professor Yusaku Horiuchi, Professor John Uhr, Professor Richard Mulgan and Dr Sue Holzknecht. Moreover, several people and institutions need to be acknowledged for assistance during data collection. The late Dr Hadi Soesastro was instrumental in helping me formulate the initial idea of this research and gave his continued support. I want to express my sincere gratitude to all of my interviewees and resource persons, the management and staff of the Asia-Europe Foundation (ASEF) in Singapore, Professor Hiroyoshi Kano of the Institute of Oriental Culture of Tokyo University, Professor Datuk Roziah and Dr Azmi Mat Akhir of the Asia-Europe Institute (AEI) of the Malaya University, Professor Yang Farina of University Kebangsaan Malaysia, Ms Ruamporn Ridthiprasart of Thailand's Ministry of Foreign Affairs, and Ravinther and his family in Kuala Lumpur as well as Yuko Shindo and her parents in Gifu, Japan. Furthermore, Dr Ellen Mashiko and Dr Brian Spicer are my indispensable mentors. For all of them I say thank you from deep in my heart.

Several institutions have made this study possible through financial support. The AusAID through the Australian Development Scholarship (ADS) and its liaison officer Mrs Billie Headon provided generous support for me and my family. The ANU vice chancellor's office and the Crawford School funded my fieldwork and my travels to conferences in Melbourne and Kyoto. ASEF sponsored my observation in Copenhagen.

It would have been impossible to finish the research for this book without the support and prayers of my family. My parents, my sister, and my husband are very important in this learning process. My two angel daughters, Anisa Hanareswari Sukarno (Hana) and Anindhita Nayazirly Sukarno (Zirly), are the source of my spirit and strength; it was a desire to motivate them to achieve their dreams that sustained me in many hard times and challenges during this research.

Last but not least, I want to thank the Institute of Southeast Asian Studies (ISEAS), including the reviewers and editors, for publishing this book. I hope it is useful.

Jakarta, July 2012
Evi Fitriani

ABBREVIATIONS

AECF	Asia-Europe Cooperation Framework
AEPF	Asia-Europe People Forum
AEYNSD	Asia-Europe Youth Network for Sustainable Development
AEYPLS	Asia-Europe Young Political Leaders' Symposium
AEVG	Asia-Europe Vision Group
AFTA	ASEAN Free Trade Agreement
ASEF	Asia-Europe Foundation
ASEAN	Association of the Southeast Asian Nations
ASEM	Asia–Europe Meeting
APEC	Asia Pacific Economic Cooperation
APT	ASEAN Plus Three
ARF	ASEAN Regional Forum
CAEC	Council of Asia-Europe Cooperation
CAFTA	China–ASEAN Free Trade Agreement
EC	European Commission
EC	European Community
EAEC	East Asian Economic Caucus
EAEG	East Asian Economic Group
EAS	East Asia Summit
Ec. SOM	Economic Senior Official Meeting
EP	European Parliament
ESDP	European Security and Defence Policy
EU	European Union
Fin. MM	Financial Ministers Meeting
FMM	Foreign Ministers Meeting

FTA	Free Trade Agreement
Mercusor	Association of the South American Countries
MFA	Ministers of Foreign Affairs
MOFA	Ministry of Foreign Affairs
NGO	Non-Government Organization
NLD	National League for Democracy
PM UNSC	Permanent Member of the United Nations' Security Council
SAARC	South Asia Association of Regional Cooperation
SLORC	State Law and Order Restoration Council
SOM	Senior Officials Meeting
SPDC	State Peace and Development Council
TAC	Treaty of Amity and Cooperation
UK	United Kingdom
UN	United Nations
UNESCO	United Nations Educational, Scientific and Cultural Organization
US	United States
WTO	World Trade Organization
WG	Working Group

MAP 1
Map of ASEM Partner Countries 1996–2008

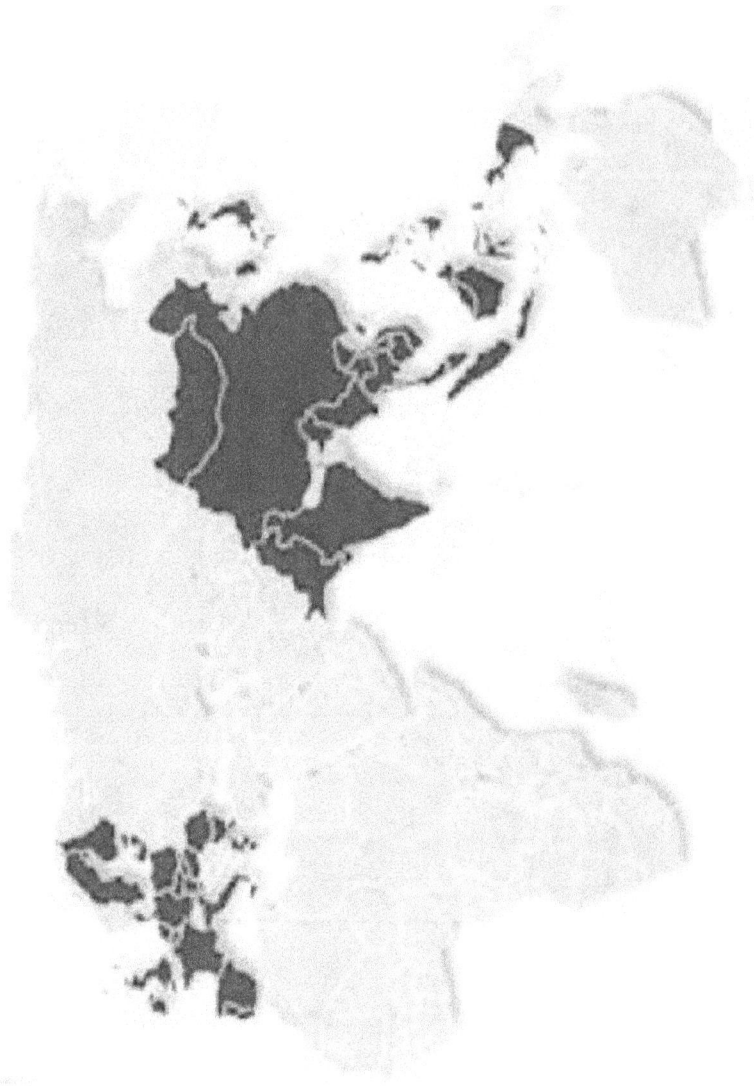

Source: The ASEM Education Secretariat 2010, Asia-Europe Meeting (ASEM), <http://www.asem-education-secretariat.org/en/12183/> (accessed 17 May 2010).

MAP 2
ASEM Countries After 2010 Enlargement

Source: Wikipedia.org, <http://en.wikipedia.org/wiki/File:ASEM.PNG#file> (accessed 6 December 2011).

INTRODUCTION

The Asia-Europe Meeting (ASEM), established in 1996, to foster inter-regional relations between Asia[1] and Europe,[2] has attracted little attention in either of the two regions, so much so that the longevity of this institution poses a puzzle. On the one hand, the region-to-region relations between Asia and Europe in ASEM are suggestive of a new pattern of interactions in international relations, which may lead to different outcomes in global affairs as compared to traditional state-to-state relations. On the other hand, that ASEM exists at all is not generally known, and ASEM Summits have attracted little media coverage. ASEM has been criticized from inside and outside as being merely a "talk shop" that considers a variety of broad topics, but has no political will to bring the talk to reality, and lacks the capacity to implement its intentions. ASEM has, however, survived until today, and one of the most important reasons for this survival is the persistent attendance of Southeast Asian leaders and participants in the ASEM forums.

For Southeast Asian countries, the region-to-region relations between Asian and European countries in ASEM have some characteristics that are unusual in terms of their engagements in regional and global affairs. ASEM does not include the United States and it was initially expected to balance the United States-European Union (EU)[3]-Asia triangle. In addition, ASEM is the first forum in which Southeast Asian countries have been able to meet and coordinate collectively with countries in Northeast Asia, namely Japan, China and South Korea vis-à-vis another partner, in this case Europe; it may therefore demonstrate the EU's influence in the formation process of (East) Asian regionalism. Moreover, the ASEM biannual Summit has a high profile as this is the only forum attended exclusively by heads of states and governments of Asian and EU countries. The climate for inter-regional discourse has also been changing. Despite some downturns at the end of the 1990s and early 2000s, the inter-regional relations between Asia and Europe in ASEM have been constructed during a critical period of world history when East Asia has been developing as an economic powerhouse, while Europe has been seeking an identity as a global actor under EU.

This book investigates the reasons why Southeast Asian countries have maintained the ASEM process,[4] despite criticisms. It uses the richness of interview data to provide broad-based insights into the cognitive processes of ASEM forums, into the pursuit of foreign policy advantage in the ASEM process, and into the flexibility of ASEM's informal institution. This investigation is undertaken wholly from an Asian perspective not only due to constraints of time and resources, but also because the researcher is an Asian national and Southeast Asia is the region she knows best. This observation focuses on the years from 1996 to 2008 when the Asian side of ASEM only consisted of thirteen countries in East Asia. An epilogue at the end of the book comprises some developments after 2008.

This chapter introduces ASEM and emphasizes the significance of this study. The chapter highlights the relevance of this inquiry into the Southeast Asian perspectives on ASEM and shows how these perspectives have contributed to ASEM's longevity. This chapter ends with the structure of the book.

ASEM — A JOURNEY INTO INTER-REGIONAL AFFAIRS

In the post-colonial era, the inter-regional relations of Asia and Europe did not gain an autonomous momentum until the early 1990s. Some efforts were made to link some European and Southeast Asian countries in the 1970s and early 1980s; the European Communities and the Association of Southeast Asian Nations (ASEAN) held several formal contacts that led to a Cooperation Agreement in 1980. However, these contacts were more rhetorical than substantial in nature (Leifer and Djiwandono 1998, p. 203; Stokhof and van der Velde 1999). It was the rapid and high economic development in East and Southeast Asia during the 1980s that drew the Europeans' attention to what was perceived as "the world's most dynamic region in the 21st century" (Edwards and Regelsberger 1990, p. 5; see also Richards and Kirkpatrick 1999; Forster 1999). Consequently, EU launched "the New Asia Strategy" in 1994 that underpinned the need of European countries to resume close ties with the Asian countries whose economic growth had been seen as a world phenomenon (European Commission 1994).

In November 1994, Prime Minister Goh Chok Tong of Singapore and Prime Minister Jacques Chirac of France proposed a summit of Asian and European leaders. Whether the meeting supposed to be in the region-to-region meeting format is disputable. Interviewee S31 informed that the inter-regional framework was not really the original intention of the Singaporean leader; the inter-regional format was something that developed in the preparation process. The proposal to create a forum for Asian and European leaders seems to have built on the momentum of two previous events: the EU's enthusiasm to strengthen relations with Asian states, and the EU's failure to obtain observer status in the Asia-Pacific Economic Cooperation (APEC) in 1993 (Forster 1999; Yeo 2000). The first meeting of thirty-five heads of states and governments from ten Asian countries and fifteen EU member states, accompanied by the European Commission (EC) President Jacques Santer, took place in Bangkok in March 1996. A senior Singaporean diplomat, Tommy Koh, commented on the ASEM inauguration (Koh 1998, p. 3), "It was a historic re-engagement of two ancient regions and civilizations". The Summit has been held biannually since 1996: 1998 in London, 2000 in Seoul, 2002 in Copenhagen, 2004 in Hanoi, 2006 in Helsinki, 2008 in Beijing, and 2010 in Brussels. The agendas and issues for each summit are presented in Appendix III. The Summits are the highest level forum and stand as the most important organ of ASEM.

The official purpose of ASEM is idealistic. The Chairman's statement at the first ASEM Summit in 1996 declares that "this partnership aims at strengthening links between Asia and Europe thereby contributing to peace, global stability and prosperity" (ASEM Infoboard 2006b). The principles of the Asian and European countries' relations in ASEM are described as informal, multidimensional, equal partnership, high-level meetings but also include non-state government forums (European Commission 2005, 2006b; ASEM Infoboard 2006e). In the Asia-Europe Framework of Cooperation (AEFC) adopted in 2000, it is written that ASEM is "to create a new Asia-Europe partnership, to build a greater understanding between the people of the two regions, and to establish a strengthened dialogue among equals" (ASEM Infoboard 2006e). The AEFC also identifies the key priorities that later develop into ASEM's three pillars of cooperation: political, economic, and social-cultural. The pillars are upheld by political dialogues, economic cooperation and social-cultural interactions.

The number of countries participating in ASEM has been growing as a result of the enlargement of the EU and ASEAN. Table 1 shows ASEM partners and the year of their accession.

ASEM has developed beyond intra-governmental forums. In the forums conducted to prepare the fourth ASEM Summit in 2002, ASEM started to include representatives of civil society from Asia and Europe and to organize consultative social forums alongside the summits (Reiterer 2002*b*). Therefore, in terms of the actors, ASEM has worked as a mechanism within three concerted channels of interactions: between state officers or government-to-government (G-to-G) level as the "first track"; between business communities as the "second track"; and between civil society and non-governmental organization (NGO) or people-to-people (P-to-P) level as the "third track". The first track is managed through inter-governmental diplomatic relations whereas the second and third tracks are organized by Asia-Europe Foundation (ASEF). Between ASEM Summits, there have been uncountable meetings and forums with various agenda focusing on the three pillars. All these are called "the ASEM process", which has developed as a multilateral, multi-field, multi-actor, and multi-level inter-regional forum (Yeo 2003; European Commission 2005; ASEM Infoboard 2006*a*). The structure of the ASEM process is presented in Appendix I, whereas the development of the ASEM process can be seen in Appendix II.

ASEM is a unique inter-regional forum in two respects: first, ASEM was innovatively built as a region-to-region forum between states and peoples from two regions. Although both sides are quite dissimilar in socioeconomic dimensions as well as in the level of regionalism and regionalization, the two regions share some commonalities, allowing partnerships to be nurtured. Europe and Asia have neither geographical proximity nor cultural similarity. Comparing Asia and Europe regionally, one could easily find those differences that have led to divergent values and interests between the countries and peoples of the two regions (CAEC 1997; Palmujoki 2001; Letta 2002; Saberwal 2004; Loewen 2007). In addition, regionalization of Europe is more institutionalized than that of Asia (Fawcett and Hurrell 1995; Palmujoki 1997; Ruland 2001; Fawcett 2004). Whereas EU regional interest and position may be formulated in Brussels, the preference and position of the Asian states have been difficult to crystallize due to the absence of a formal regional institution. Thus, ASEM is a form of inter-regional relationship that tries to link not only two unequal, diverse regional entities, but also two different regional types.

Having said that, two commonalities can be identified between Asia and Europe. First, both are made up of diverse states with a variety of cultures

TABLE 1
ASEM Partners and the Years of Accession from 1996 to 2008

ASEM Asian partners			ASEM European partners		
Founding partners (1996)	Enlargement I (2004)	Enlargement II (2008)	Founding partners (1996)	Enlargement I (2004)	Enlargement II (2008)
Brunei	Cambodia	India	Austria	Cyprus	Bulgaria
China	Laos	Mongolia	Belgium	The Czech Republic	Romania
Indonesia	Myanmar	Pakistan	Denmark	Estonia	
Japan			Finland	Hungary	
Malaysia			France	Latvia	
The Philippines			Germany	Lithuania	
Singapore			Greece	Malta	
South Korea			Ireland	Poland	
Thailand			Italy	Slovakia	
Vietnam			Luxembourg	Slovenia	
			The Netherlands		
			Portugal		
			Spain		
			Sweden		
			United Kingdom		
10	3	3	15	10	2

that have resulted in different interests (Palmujoki 1997, 2001; Fatchett 1999; Friedberg 2000; Yeo 2000). Moreover, the regional diversities existing in Asia and Europe have resulted in complex configurations and management of regional identity (Gilson 2002). The second commonality found between Europe and Asia is the fact that they have currently been facing similar challenges due to population, resource and environmental changes, and contemporary security threats.

Second, the ASEM process has grown in parallel with other engagements that had already existed before or been developed since the establishment of ASEM. Previously, despite their successful regional integration, EU member states still maintained their own bilateral relations with Asian states. ASEM was also built on pre-existing networks: mainly ASEAN-EU and ASEAN Regional Forum (ARF) linkages, as well as EU-Japan, EU-Korea, and a previous EU-China engagement (Gilson 2002; Palmujoki 1997, p. 273). According to Westerlund (1999, p. 25), ASEM is a perfect medium "for sending political signals and for the concerting efforts" whose results were settled through bilateral contacts. So, what cannot be solved at bilateral level may be perceived differently at regional level, and perhaps could be answered in an inter-regional forum, or vice versa (Reiterer 2006). Indeed, ASEM has been seen as a breakthrough in the stalemate in EU-ASEAN relations that had arisen due to some political constraints in the early 1980s and 1990s (Leifer and Djiwandono 1998; Forster 1999; Yeo 2007). Yet, instead of localizing their incompatibility in a political setting, the ASEAN countries drove the Europeans into a broader framework of interaction by involving powerful countries in Asia: Japan, China, and Korea.

Thus, the ASEM process can be considered as a breakthrough in Asia-Europe relations. It is in some ways a departure from the previous EC approaches to Asian countries that were mainly conducted at bilateral or sub-regional level such as ASEAN-EU. However, it has been claimed that these regional-to-regional relations are not meant to replace the pre-existing bilateral and sub-regional engagements (Santer 1998). It means that the inter-regional level of engagement has proceeded concomitantly with other EU relations with Asian countries but has provided a more flexible mechanism for settling issues (Forster 1999; University of Helsinki 2006; Bersick 2007). Nevertheless, on the one hand, EU interactions in two or three layers of engagement with each of its Asian partners may become a diplomatic innovation; on the other hand, this would undoubtedly result in more complex relationships[5] among ASEM participating states.

WHY A BOOK ABOUT SOUTHEAST ASIA AND ASEM?

When ASEM was launched at the first Summit in Bangkok in March 1996, it was met with soaring enthusiasm in Asia and Europe. This was the first meeting attended by so many Asian and European heads of states and governments. The attendees included twenty-five heads of state and government from ten Asian countries; seven members of ASEAN, Japan, Peoples Republic of China, and the Republic of Korea, and fifteen EU member states, accompanied by the President of the EC. Representatives of business associations and scholars from both regions accompanied the leaders to the Summits. It was a unique event as it not only brought together many leaders from the two regions in the post-colonial era (Koh 1998; McMahon 1998; Forster 1999), but also because it was initially expected to balance the U.S. presence in Asia and Europe and to strengthen the Asia-Europe axis within the U.S.-EU-Asia triangle in the post-Cold War period (Forster 1999; Hanggi 1999; Richards and Kirkpatrick 1999; Dent 2001). Aside from its uniqueness, the first ASEM Summit took place when Asian countries were enjoying very high economic growth and the EU states were highly confident after the successful ratification of the Maastricht Treaty. With the exclusion of the United States from the forum, leaders from the two continents nurtured the hope of building an alternative axis, a new economic and strategic partnership. The excitement of prospective collaborations among the ASEM partners[6] in this early period resulted in the establishment of ASEF in February 1997 to generate and facilitate people-to-people contacts among Asians and Europeans.

Towards the end of the 1990s, however, the Asian financial crisis hit many Asian countries right before the second ASEM Summit in 1998, dampening the enthusiasm of Europeans, as if the rationale for ASEM had vanished. Indeed, several officials and scholars who were interviewed for this study consider the institution an insignificant diplomatic forum. Some of them do not see its relevance in current world political settings; others have lost interest in it, and many have never heard of it. ASEM forums have been criticized as involving too much talk and no concrete outcomes (Forster 1999; Lee 1999; Soesastro 2000; Yeo 2000; Dent 2001; Pereira 2007). Sceptical observers also consider that ASEM has lost direction and has no institutional mechanism to safeguard its vision and monitor the results (Fatchett 1999; Yeo 2000; Dosch 2001; Kivimaki 2007; Loewen 2007). Apart from the diplomats in charge of the ASEM process and ASEF staff, people in Asia and Europe are rarely reminded that ASEM exists, let alone acknowledge its achievements in fostering Asia-Europe relations.

Nevertheless, ASEM has survived to this day; heads of states and governments have continued to attend ASEM Summits and the institution has been enlarged by new partners. Despite the significant absence[7] of some European leaders, the institution has maintained a high-level summit biannually and more countries are joining. The seventh ASEM Summit was successfully held in Beijing on 24 and 25 October 2008 with the theme "Vision and action — Towards a win-win solution". However, unlike previous Summits, all Asian and European leaders, especially those from the EU, attended the Beijing Summit. Why did the European leaders' enthusiasm for ASEM suddenly revive when China hosted the Summit? Why have the Asian countries, in particular, members of ASEAN, maintained ASEM despite the seemingly diminished interest from Europe? What has ASEM done for Southeast Asian countries? The last question is relevant especially because it was a Southeast Asian country that first initiated the idea of ASEM.

Previous studies of ASEM have mainly emphasized the apparent "ineffectiveness" and "obsolete role" of the forum. How ASEM is perceived by the people who are involved, directly and indirectly, has not been investigated thoroughly. In particular, the benefits and disappointments that ASEM brings to Southeast Asia have not been specifically investigated from the point of view of the relevant key actors in this area. Similarly, the reasons why East Asian leaders, particularly those from ASEAN member countries, continue to attend ASEM Summits, despite the absence of European leaders, have remained unexplained. This book focuses on the reasons for the longevity of ASEM from a Southeast Asian perspective, and also investigates what benefits ASEM has brought to its Southeast Asian partners.

The significance of observing ASEM from Southeast Asian perspectives derives from several considerations. First, this book represents the newest research on Southeast Asia and the ASEM. Its significance lies in its originality as it uses a broad range of interviews as the main source of data to support the arguments. It digs the insights gained through eighty-two direct, in-depth interviews to obtain a deeper understanding of the meaning of ASEM forums for those involved and those not involved, and the role of ASEM in intra and inter-regional relations. Opinion and reflection from interviews with diplomats, scholars, journalists, business people, and NGO activists are put side by side with secondary data on economic, political and security relations to produce insights and draw implications and conclusions. The interpretive method helps analyse the interview data in their context as the author is aware of the differences in the profiles of interviewees as well as her own possible bias in interpreting them.

Second, the format of ASEM meetings is inter-regional. The region-to-region, rather than country-to-country, relations are a distinctive and new practice in international relations that require an understanding of its merits and limitations. This inter-regional pattern of interactions in international relations has arisen in the last two decades, so it is reasonable to investigate what can work or not work and what can be expected from such relations. In addition, the Asia-Europe inter-regional relationship through ASEM is also a complex setting because it neither replaces the pre-existing bilateral relations between individual Asian countries with EU nor replaces the previous ASEAN-EU long-lasting but strained relations. Moreover, as a region-to-region relationship, ASEM has, to some extent, forced East Asian countries into a group, namely the "Asian side" in the ASEM process. This is the first international forum that has created such circumstances for the Asian countries (Nabers 2003). Furthermore, ASEM membership excludes the United States, creating other significant meanings of ASEM from politico-strategic as well as economic and cultural perspectives. Therefore, an investigation into the longevity of ASEM from Asian perspectives can reveal opportunities as well as challenges to the relations. This will facilitate a more thorough assessment of why Southeast Asian countries have persisted in their engagement with ASEM.

Third, this study employs three working hypotheses to probe different dimensions of the engagement Southeast Asian countries have with ASEM. The first relates to the issue of nurturing the sense of a shared (East) Asian regional identity. The second relates to Europeans' critics of the Asians' approach to human rights in Myanmar and the calculation by the governments of ASEAN member countries about making the diplomatic negotiation an advantage. The third relates to ASEM's institution and the effect it has had on the willingness of East Asian countries to maintain their engagement with ASEM. A distinctive feature of the study is that different theoretical lens are brought to bear on each hypotheses: the constructivists' lens to the hypotheses on regional identity, the neo-realist lens to the hypotheses about Myanmar and foreign policy manoeuvring, and the neo-liberal lens to the hypotheses about the institutional design of ASEM. In employing these diverse analytical frameworks the intention is not to pursue some elusive notion of paradigmatic unity but simply to bring the most useful analytical apparatus to the particular issues at hand. It is a more comprehensive approach in presenting various aspects of the Southeast Asian perspectives about ASEM. Thus, the study represents a more holistic approach to examine a phenomenon in international relations.

Fourth, one part of this study addresses the use of ASEM inter-regionalism for foreign policy advancement through a case study. This case study of Myanmar's accession to ASEM reveals the power bargaining between Southeast Asian countries and EU members in the inter-regional institution of ASEM. The case study, based on a broad range of in-depth interviews combined with documents and news studies is used to examine the bargaining behind the differences in their political values; it does not treat the problem arising from Myanmar's accession as the focus but uses it as a case study to demonstrate the manoeuvring of ASEAN member countries to take advantage of the inter-regional framework of ASEM to obtain foreign policy pay-offs.

Finally, this book examines the perceptions of states and people from Southeast Asian countries regarding not only the government-to-government relations but also the people-to-people relations in an inter-regional institution such as ASEM. This investigation of the utility of ASEM for Asian states in the words of ASEM official participants as well as scholars and observers can reveal what functions and interests ASEM has served for the Southeast Asian participants and ASEAN member countries. The findings will not only help provide understanding as to how Southeast Asian state and non-state actors perceive such an international institution as accommodating their quest for intra- and inter-regional cooperation but will also shed light on why an apparently unimportant and heavily criticized institution might survive amidst the complexity of regional and global relations.

In short, this study investigates the role of an informal institution in Southeast Asian regional affairs and Asian relations with another region, the EU. It goes beyond the commonly known political reasons behind the aversion of the Asian countries to formal institutions (Kahler 2000; Hettne and Soderbaum 2002; Acharya and Johnston 2007; Khong and Nesadurai 2007) by elaborating the complexity of the cooperation in the Asian context and by incorporating broad-based insights from Southeast Asian people's points of view.

This research uses several key concepts whose definitions have little consensus and are debatable. For clarity and consistency, however, those key concepts need to be defined, using the most common meanings. The term "inter-regionalism" refers to region-to-region relations which in this study relate to a group of countries in East Asia vis-à-vis EU countries. East Asian countries consist of countries in Southeast and Northeast Asia. Southeast Asia comprises Indonesia, Malaysia, Singapore, Thailand, the Philippines, Brunei, Vietnam, Cambodia, Laos, and Myanmar; the ten countries are members of ASEAN. East Asian countries in this study refer to China, Japan, and South Korea. "Regionalism" refers to the design and implementation of a set of preferential policies among countries within the same geographical area in order to build harmonious relations in any or all aspects such as politic-security, economy, or socioculture. Regionalization is defined as "the growth of societal integration within a region and to the often undirected process of social and economic interaction" (Hurrell 1995). Thus, what differentiates regionalism from regionalization is the design; while the former is directed by governmental agreements the latter is officially undirected and grows more naturally among non-state actors. The term "institution" in this study refers to the concept of "international institution", defined as a set of agreed norms, rules, and principles that govern states' relations and depict expected behaviours of its member states. Institutionalization can be defined as the process of strengthening or building the institution through the development of its structure/organ as well as the legalization of its agreements. The term "civil society" refers to participants of ASEM forums that come from NGOs or other societal or cultural organizations.

In Chapter 1, the role of ASEM in Asian identity building is examined based on the recorded perceptions of involved persons from Southeast Asian countries. A constructivist framework, depicting that identities and regions are socially constructed through institutive processes (Smith 1997; Ruggie 1998a), is used to analyse the role of ASEM in the development of East Asian identities in the 1990s and 2000s. It also explores the meaning of ASEM forums for Southeast Asian participants. ASEM has been perceived to have facilitated the development of East Asian identity but this perception has only been communicated by those directly involved in the ASEM process. The importance of the cognitive process and the development of inter-subjective understanding among Asian participants at ASEM/ASEF forums are highlighted. Although frequent ASEM forums provide opportunities for intra-Asian socialization and the emergence of a regional consciousness among East Asian participants, they also provoke what Ruggie (1998a) describes as a "collective intentionality" among the Asian participants, which differentiates them from their European counterparts. The shared regional awareness among Asian participants in ASEM and ASEF forums has strengthened their intra-regional linkages, and this has been used by Southeast Asian countries to increase their engagement with Northeast Asian countries in regional framework beyond ASEM. Regional identity in Asia, however, is frequently questioned because there is no single fixed Asian identity. Thus, because of the different scopes of inter-government engagement among Asian countries, several layered identities have emerged among the Asian participants in the ASEM process. These layered identities reflect different levels of contacts and engagement involved the East Asian countries inside and outside ASEM.[8]

Chapter 2 assesses what ASEM has provided to key actors in Southeast Asia based on the interview data that perceived the success of ASEAN countries and China in supporting Myanmar's accession to ASEM as an Asian victory over the EU countries. These data are analysed through the framework inspired by the neo-realist concepts of traditional power games and the state's interest in international institutions. States may cooperate if they "realistically" see benefits in such a strategy to advance their interests (Jervis 1988); within the neo-realist framework, international institutions are "the object of strategic choice by states" (Simmons and Martin 1998, 2002). Myanmar's accession becomes the case study to investigate the building of Asia's common position in ASEM and the role of ASEAN and China in the ASEM process.

The case study on Myanmar's accession to ASEM is used for two reasons: it represents perhaps the most difficult political obstacle to ASEM that could have terminated the inter-regional relations; and the Myanmar case took place during the first ASEM enlargement which created the most critical point in ASEM's longevity, reducing the relations to, arguably, the lowest point. By taking the conflict between Asian and EU countries in this first ASEM enlargement as a case study, this chapter explores the most difficult phase of the relations and examines how the two regions sought a solution. Data from interviews, news, ASEAN documents and ASEM documents are used to shed some light on what happened behind closed doors and in the tough negotiations over ASEM's first enlargement in 2004. As the Myanmar case study reveals, ASEAN member countries and China took advantage of the ASEM enlargement in 2004 to gain political advantages in their relations with EU countries and with each other. ASEAN countries were, for the first time, able to negotiate a common position to advocate Myanmar's accession and to obtain China's support, leaving the EU countries with no other choice but to give in. China also took advantage of the Myanmar case by appeasing the ASEAN countries to strengthen its own regional relations and to send a strong political message to the EU countries. This chapter thus highlights the success of Asian countries in extracting foreign policy benefits from ASEM as an inter-regional institution, underlining the notion that multilateralism actually works for the realist.

In Chapter 3, the complexity of ASEM inter-regionalism, especially with its enlargements, and the role of the informality of the ASEM institution are examined. An institutionalist framework is applied to investigate ASEM's informal institutional arrangement that has seemingly been used to overcome the challenge of cooperation in inter-regional relations and to cope with ASEM growing membership. Data from interviews, documents and meeting observations are used to help explain the significance of adopting such informal arrangements to overcome the challenges that ASEM has been facing. ASEM's design, that is, inter-regional relations managed by an informal institution, influenced by the "ASEAN way", is preferred by Southeast Asian countries and apparently encourages them to remain in the ASEM process. This argument is based on two considerations. First, the informality of the ASEM institution, which is described by some scholars as a "soft institution" (Soesastro and Nuttall 1997; Dent 2001; Yeo 2003; Reiterer 2004), creates flexibility for ASEM, allowing the inter-regional forums to accommodate the diversity, varying interests and different capabilities of its growing number of partners. Second, ASEM's soft or informal institutional arrangement seems to reduce the cost of maintaining cooperation through region-to-region relations between the Asian and European states, while opening up opportunities for the two regions to develop different kinds of strategic relations. Therefore, for Southeast Asian countries, ASEM is a cheap form of diplomacy.

In the conclusion, the arguments shaped by the three working hypotheses are drawn together as a basis from which to answer the question of what ASEM has delivered to Southeast Asian countries. The usefulness of ASEM, as the channel of regional building and developing regional awareness, as a strategic forum to pursue foreign policy advantage, and as a less costly, informal linkage with regional countries and with the EU, has made ASEM a valuable forum from Southeast Asian perspectives. Terminating the ASEM process would be a risky action for states and leaders; maintaining ASEM is more useful than getting rid of it. The very fact that ASEM has been established also helps sustain it. Thus, for Asian leaders, there is seemingly nothing to lose by maintaining ASEM. ASEM has apparently delivered significant outcomes that suit Southeast Asian countries.

Notes

1. For the purpose of this book, "Asia" refers to Asian countries that participated in ASEM until before the seventh Summit in 2008 (Table 1).
2. For the purpose of this book, Europe refers to the EU countries that participate in ASEM (Table 1).
3. For consistency, the term European Union (EU) is used throughout the book despite the fact that the term was only officially used to replace the term European Commission (EC) on 1 December 2009 when the Treaty of Lisbon entered into force.
4. The ASEM process refers to a series of meetings, forums, initiatives, activities in politics, economics and social areas involving state and non-state actors organized for ASEM partners.

5. The complex relationship among ASEM partners is explained in Chapter 3.
6. ASEM uses the term "partners" for participating countries.
7. There are no data available on the leaders' attendance of ASEM Summits except for the first and the seventh Summits. But the absence of many EU heads of states and government from ASEM Summits is a telling point made by Asian countries' officials and scholars from Asian and European countries (Letta 2002; Pereira 2007; also interviewees S35; S20; D01; S10; D48; D50; I42; I45) to indicate the lack of serious commitment by EU countries in ASEM.
8. Consequently, the term "identity" in the first and second sections of Chapter 3 will be replaced with "identities" in the last section as it refers to these layered identities.

1

ASEM AND THE DEVELOPMENT OF AN ASIAN REGIONAL IDENTITY

The Asia-Europe Meeting (ASEM) has been associated with the development of a regional identity in Asia.[1] There are reasonable grounds for believing that the inter-regional characteristic of the ASEM process played a significant role in facilitating the identity construction among East Asian countries involved in ASEM (Lee and Park 2001; Liu and Régnier 2003; Gilson and Yeo 2004; Gilson 2002, 2005; Terada 2006). Until 2008, ASEM's Asian partners were confined to countries from East Asia. The regional relations in East Asia, which involves ten Association of Southeast Asian Nations (ASEAN) member countries, with Japan, China, and South Korea, generally known as ASEAN Plus Three (APT), have intensified since the end of the 1990s. Although regional integration has not been an immediate goal of APT, the intensification of the regional relations has encouraged the emergence of a "we" feeling among the APT. The development of regional identity building in Asia is a significant regional and global phenomenon because of its impact on shaping Asian regional affairs and the increasing Asian participation in global politics as well as global economics.

Linking ASEM with the process of constructing an East Asian identity is one of the salient views gleaned from the interview data of this thesis. The data also reveal ASEAN countries' "achievement" to incorporate the big states in the Northeast Asian countries in constructing the Asian side in ASEM and to transcend the "we-ness" in ASEM to other regional initiatives. What makes this thesis different from previous studies is the richness of the interview data that provides broad range insights into the cognitive processes of ASEM forums. The in-depth interviews with elites from Southeast Asian countries have enabled this research to identify not only the problems and concerns about the development of an Asian identity in the ASEM process, but also the hopes and aspirations for ASEM.

This chapter articulates the contribution of ASEM in the development of an Asian identity and how the "we" feeling among the East Asian countries benefits ASEAN countries inside and outside ASEM. It is based on the experience of those who have been involved in the ASEM process, and considers this development in the larger context of Asian regionalism. Having the insights of ASEM and Asia-Europe Foundation (ASEF) forums allows one to explore the cognitive dimension of the ASEM process and to analyse the relations between the growth of Asian identity and ASEM inter-regionalism. This understanding of the link between the development of Asian identity and ASEM, in turn, can contribute to answering the question of what ASEM has delivered to Southeast Asian countries and why ASEM has been maintained.

This chapter examines the opinions of ASEM participants and elites to find out how identity or identities among Asian countries have been shaped by the ASEM process. The common lens for this focus is the analytical framework of constructivism whose paradigm holds that identity is endogenous and, like for a region, identity is constructed through social process (Smith 1997; Ruggie 1998a; Gilson 2002, 2005; Reus-Smit 2009). Ruggie (1998a, p. 862) investigates the "inter-subjective bases of social action and order" to study the social construction of the identity and interest of international actors. As their theoretical framework develops, the constructivists contend that the social identities of political actors are influenced by both normative and ideational structures around them through "imagination, communication, and constraints" (Reus-Smit 2009, p. 222). This book treats the imagination, communication and constraints as a cognitive process (Gilson 2002) that may lead to either the development or failure of inter-subjective understanding among actors or creates what Gilson (2002, 2005) describes as "self" and "other". Before being actualized as the identity of "self" and "other", Gilson's concepts of inter-subjective understanding creates what Ruggie (1998a, p. 869) and Searle (1995, pp. 24–25) describe as a "collective intentionality" in which a collective consciousness is developed within individuals (Ruggie 1998a), but is shared by those who share their inter-subjective understanding.

This chapter also refers to constructivist institutional concepts from Ruggie (1998b) when analysing layered identities in Asia, treating Asian regionalism as various cognitive institutions embedded in the Asian consciousness when they are in different social arenas. Under this framework, ASEM is perceived as a social arena that allows the flow of information and ideas not only between Asian and European groups but also among Asian partners. So one actor from an Asian country may embrace an Asian identity when he or she attends an inter-regional forum in ASEM but he or she may refer to ASEAN and non-ASEAN identities in an intra-Asian meeting.

This study finds that ASEM is perceived to have facilitated the development of Asian identity especially among those who are directly involved in the ASEM process. Because frequent ASEM forums provide opportunities for intra-Asian socialization and the emergence of regional consciousness among Asian participants, they provoke what Ruggie (1998*a*) calls "collective intentionality" among Asian participants in order to differentiate themselves from their European counterparts. The idea of Asian identity has aroused questions of who are "in" and who are "out". This thesis reveals that Asian participants in the ASEM process have brought three layered identities. The layered identities reflect different levels of contacts and engagement among East Asian countries inside and outside ASEM which are actually within different social arenas.[2]

This chapter is organized into three main sections. This introductory section includes the framework of analysis that identifies the concepts through which the construction of regional identity is viewed. The chapter proceeds with the first section, presenting classified interviewees' opinions about ASEM and the development of regional identities among East Asian countries. The second section provides an analysis of channels and processes in the identity construction. It investigates linkages between the interviewees' opinions and the mechanism of the ASEM process. It also analyses how the process facilitates collective Asian experience and the cognitive process in identity building. The chapter ends with further analysis of the place of ASEAN in three levels of regional identities in Asia and how the layered identities were brought to ASEM.

OPINIONS FROM THE IN-DEPTH INTERVIEWS: INVOLVEMENT DOES MATTER

This section analyses Asian elites' opinions on ASEM and Asian identity building to demonstrate how East Asian people — be they journalists, scholars, non-government organization (NGO) activists, or government officials — perceive ASEM. Some of them link ASEM inter-regional forums with the development of Asian identity but some do not. Differences in opinions seem to relate to whether or not they were directly involved in the ASEM process or personally attended ASEM forums. It begins with a brief overview of existing research on the possible relationship between ASEM and Asian identity building before presenting and analysing the interview data.

This research is built on previous studies of relations between the ASEM process and construction of Asian identity. Lee and Park (2001) have argued that Asian countries established an Asian identity in the inter-regional forum as a defensive identity vis-à-vis their European Union (EU) counterparts. Similarly, Gilson and Yeo's article (2004) suggests that the Asian coordinating mechanism of the ASEM process has helped to create self-identification of "we" among Asian participants as their European counterparts acted as the "other". In addition, in her 2002 book, *Asia Meets Europe*, Gilson argues that ASEM provides more regular channels of communication and interaction not only between the Asian and European countries but also among Asians. Through those channels, it is argued, the Asian identity has been constructed and reconstructed (Gilson 2002). This section investigates who experienced this self-identification and felt an inclination to connect with regional fellows among the East Asian participants and how the social construction of the Asian identity took place.

The interviews for this research were carried out with an open mind and were intended to record the interviewees' instant images of ASEM. The notion that ASEM facilitates the development of regional identity among its Asian partners was not initially brought up in the interviews. However, a number of respondents associated ASEM with the development of regional awareness and Asian identity. They spoke of the relations with different tone, from mere suggestions to claims and strong arguments. Their responses are illustrated in Figure 1.1.

Figure 1.1 shows the percentage comparison of interviewees' opinions on the relations between ASEM and Asian identity building. As seen in Figure 1.1, ASEAN former officials and ASEF staff were the strongest advocates of a positive association between ASEM and regional identity building in Asia. Members of civil society and diplomats constituted mostly those who perceived that ASEM had helped create a sense of regional awareness as "Asia" and strengthened an Asian identity. In addition, whereas scholars were the most sceptical of the idea of the relations between ASEM and the development of Asian regional awareness, the business community did not mention it at all.[3]

Figure 1.1 reveals the gap in perception about ASEM's impact on Asian identity building between those who are used to being involved in regional affairs and those who have never or seldom dealt with them. A majority of ASEAN former staff, ASEF staff, together with a large minority of civil society and diplomats expressed the idea that ASEM seems to be linked with the

FIGURE 1.1
Interviewees' Opinions about Relations between
ASEM and Asian Identity

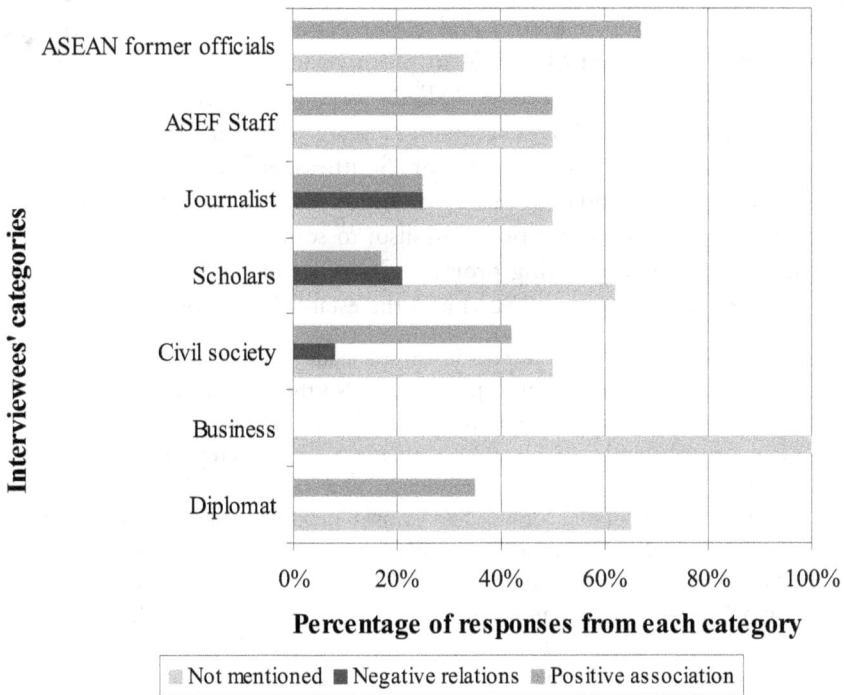

Not mentioned ▪ Negative relations ▪ Positive association

emergence and strengthening of a regional identity in Asia in the last decade. Those four categories are among interviewees who actually attended or have dealt with ASEM forums, so they are direct actors in the ASEM process. Their views reflect a strong impression of attachment to other Asian participants. Some of them acknowledged that their direct involvement in ASEM forums had influenced their cognitive process regarding who "we" — the Asian participants — were and who "they" — the European counterparts — were. Thus, interviewees' perceptions on this issue seem to be determined by their degree of individual involvement in regional activities and issues. Consequently, concepts such as cognitive process and collective experience in the process of identity building are needed to analyse ASEM's practical role in regard to Asian regional building. How an individual's involvement depicts his or her perception of the relations between ASEM and Asian regional building is elaborated in the following sections.

Former ASEAN high-ranking officials and ASEF staff expressed relatively strong linkages between ASEM and the development of a regional identity in Asia. It is understandable that they mostly support the idea because their work relates to the idea of regional community building and their intensive relations with regional leaders and elites. Naturally, they would see, and prefer to see, that ASEM is able to promote linkages among participants from Asian countries. Indeed, as ASEAN former top bureaucrats and ASEF managers, they are the main actors in creating what Ruggie (1998*b*) called the cognitive institution. The ideas of "Southeast Asian community", "East Asian community", and even "Asian community" have not only been lingering around people in their positions but also, to some extent have become the vision of their daily working projects. Examples of their statements below reveal the linkage between ASEM and the establishment of APT:

> Politically, APT is important because it has made ASEAN [countries] closer to Northeast Asian [countries], and [the] Northeast Asian countries talk to each other. From the economic point of view, APT is also crucial as the framework behind the Chiang Mai Initiative. ...Various regional forums in Asia are good to foster mutual confidence and to increase dialogue among countries; each of the forums has its own function and aims. *APT was facilitated by ASEM* but this link *should not be exaggerated*. Coordination of Asian common positions in pre ASEM meetings took place intra-ASEAN and intra-Northeast Asia; I am not sure if they [the Northeast Asian diplomats] met. There is no official Asian position. Even though the intra-regional coordinating meeting may discuss some issues, it is not formal at all; it is not binding like those in the EU. Coordination is a natural thing to do but it does not necessarily bind [them]. (S35)

> *ASEM relates to APT and EAS.* The two forums took advantage of the dialogue in the ASEM process. In the 2005 Toronto Conference on Climate Change, ASEM people had a sideline meeting during the conference; then, in 2006 Helsinki Climate Change Declaration which continued to the 2007 UNCCC, and the UN Convention on Cultural Diversity. Discussion among [people representing] ASEM [countries] can take place at other forums.... *ASEM takes credit for formation of APT and EAS even though indirectly.* (I45)

> Asian coordinating meeting [in the ASEM process] is useful to let other Asian fellows know the thoughts [or ideas of any Asian countries] on particular issues...so surprises at the ASEM meetings can be avoided (I46).
> (Emphasis by author)

The interviewees mostly refer to high-level meetings in the ASEM process such as summits and ministerial meetings (MMs) in which Asian leaders had opportunities to meet and talk to each other in informal settings. The fact that it was "only" talk among leaders and officials may seem an intangible outcome of months of preparation. Nevertheless, for those who work for the ASEAN Secretariat and the ASEM institution of ASEF there is a clear understanding that the opportunities for leaders and key persons to meet and talk are indispensable "meetings of minds" before other regional initiatives can proceed. As individuals involved directly in the ASEM process, the ASEF staff had been aware of other intra-Asian movements or other regional forums in Asia that directly or indirectly impacted on ASEM. Similarly, the ASEAN former top bureaucrats had observed the influences that regional forums such as ASEM intra-Asian coordinating meetings had brought to ASEAN, and vice versa. Further analysis of how the ideational structures of regional communities influence Asian individuals in the ASEM process is elaborated in the next section.

In addition, participants from civil society are among those who remarked upon strong correlations between the ASEM process and the emergence of regional awareness among Asian people. Personally attending ASEF workshops or symposiums, NGO activists provided useful insights into what happened in the inter-regional forums and how the forums connected them with their Asian fellows. They shared their perspectives that were derived from their personal experience of attending the forums. The first interviewee participated in the second Asia-Europe Young Political Leaders Symposium (AEYPLS) in Copenhagen in 2007; the second was in the first AEYPLS in Beijing in 2005.

> Asian participants were united when the EU started talking about politics… Southeast Asian and Northeast Asian participants interacted more often. (C25)

> Asians were more sensitive and quite unified when controversial issues [were] raised by the Europeans. We stood by our neighbours [when they were criticized for their human rights practices] but we believed things were changing. Asian participants held a special meeting to discuss how to deal with the European criticism. At this point, the Asians were unified in a common position to counter and refute European harsh criticism…[In the future] I want to see more unified Asia. (C38)

Whereas the above opinions reveal that external pressure from European participants at the forums encouraged a more solid voice of Asian participants, the driving stimulus to group among Asian participants can also come from within. A Malaysian activist who organized an environmental forum in cooperation with ASEF and an Indonesian participant in the first and second

AEYPLS organized by ASEF, directly linked their attachment to Asian fellows to cultural reasons. The two saw the unification of Asian participants at the forums as a natural process when shared historical experiences and similarities of their cultures are present.

> There were also cultural differences in interactions; the Europeans tended to behave openly whereas the Asians were more reserved and tended to group among Asians. (C24)

> We, Asian participants, prefer to mingle with other Asian people at the forums because I was more familiar with them. I felt [that I was] more like them [the Asian participants] than the European participants. (C12) (translated from Indonesian)

The above insights given by individuals who were directly involved indicate that non-state actors at ASEF forums were more likely to identify themselves with other Asians than to their European counterparts at ASEF forums. They thought they had a natural inclination to form partnerships with other Asians first before associating with European counterparts, affirming what Ruggie calls an "inter-subjective cultural affinity" (1998a, p. 883). This perception is shared mainly by elites from Southeast Asian countries which is discussed later in the "Asian Layered Identities in ASEM".

Moreover, some Asian diplomats acknowledge the strong linkages between the ASEM process and the development of regional awareness among people from East Asian countries probably because they are the main actors and are directly involved in and steer the ASEM process. Those who have been involved in the intergovernmental meetings — the first track — of the ASEM process also provide insights into the relations. They express their perspectives on the ASEM forums in a context of the emergence of a sense of shared identity among East Asian participants involved in the ASEM process:

> We do not come to ASEM with a common position, and not to coordinate a common position, but for a "meeting of minds" — for Myanmar and all other issues — just to see others' awareness and get an idea who is interested in ideas or proposals. It is because ASEM is not a negotiating forum — where we have to have a fixed position — between Asia and Europe, but only a forum to exchange views and how to do cooperative plans; *even some proposals need confidentiality and exchange info without making it too public.* (D30)

> Asian countries have never been in common positions so we have to attend the meeting to protect our interest. In Asia, our national identity comes first; we have never thought about ASEAN identity. A feeling of *Asianness*

comes when we are surrounded by external actors; I needed friends, not because I share the Asian fellows' perspective of the world. The feeling does not exist when we are among Asian fellows. We thought differently from each other. (D49)

EU did not pressure us to be a group but EU action pressed us to act together more. Asian countries in ASEM feel the indirect pressure but I am not sure how and to what extent Asian countries discuss it directly.... Asia is very diverse so it will be difficult to integrate. We feel comfortable with our own difference and not much pressure to be integrated yet. During the [second] AEYPLS, EU participants were a bit reserved when interacting with Asian participants, so did the Asians. Yet, interaction among Asian participants was smoother. (D50)

ASEM is not much heard except for people who dealt directly with it. But in 2005, ASEM Ministers of Foreign Affairs meeting was back-to-back with the annual meeting of the APT Foreign Ministers. *ASEM has given a sense of grouping.* EU inspires other regions including Asia to cooperate and to integrate. APT is the most developed, successful cooperation is among financial ministers who have annual meeting. With 10 year APT in 2007 there was a vision for EA community. (D51)
(Emphasis by author)

When ASEM was newly established, a high-level Asian official both acknowledged and hoped that ASEM would eventually help bring Asian countries together. This official stated that "a close relationship with Europe, which has developed a strong regional identity, will help define and encourage an Asian identity. The ASEM process is already helping Asia to define itself..." (Han, quoted in Gilson and Yeo 2004, p. 30). This statement may simply be perceived as wishful thinking if it had not come from former Korean foreign minister Han Sung-Joo at the Council of Asia-Europe Cooperation (CAEC) conference in 1997. His statement also reflects an active Korean participation in the ASEM process which has targeted not only the enhancement of relations with European countries but also with its Asian neighbours (Bersick 2002). Korea hosted the third ASEM Summit in 2000. In addition, in 2003, the Ministries of Foreign Affairs of Korea and China promoted and sponsored the establishments of the Network of East Asian Think-tanks (NEAT) which includes scholars from all Asian partners of ASEM (Kim 2006).

In contrast to the positive outlook on ASEM by Korean officials, Indonesian diplomats have perhaps been the most pessimistic government officials in ASEM. The main reason for their pessimism is the burden of the financial crisis that underplayed Indonesian diplomacy[4] (D02; D03; also Bersick 2002). Those who were interviewed did not see ASEM as a top priority for foreign policy-makers or as important as the Asia-Pacific Economic Cooperation (D01, D02, D03, D04, D06) but two of them pointed out that,

> Asian countries are solid enough in the Myanmar case to "fight" against EU especially due to EU policy towards the country. (D03)

> In the communication process, the sense of identity grew among Asian participants especially when encountering EU on issues of democracy. (D04)

The comments above indicate that the diplomats also acknowledge the positive impacts ASEM has had on regional awareness among Asian people growing out of EU's pressure on human rights practices in Asia.

Furthermore, the establishment of APT in 1997, which followed ASEM inauguration in 1996, has been perceived as evidence of the linkage between ASEM and the process of regional building among East Asian countries. The first ASEM Summit in 1996 was the first forum in which the ASEAN countries' leaders met the heads of the governments of Japan, China and South Korea together. The ASEM Bangkok Summit was also the first time leaders from the three largest Northeast Asian countries had convened. It was not an accident that the APT was established only one year after the initial ASEM summit. As a result of the ASEM process, more frequent meetings have occurred which have brought Asian leaders and high-ranking officials together to interact more intensely and to provide them with more channels of communication. Indeed, the most significant role in the ASEM process has been seen by some as being to force Asian leaders and officers to coordinate (S34; D04; S54; S67). In turn, the sense of shared regional identity — the Asian group in the ASEM process — is believed to facilitate the establishment of the APT (S35; D51). Their views are in line with previous studies by Higgot (2006), Terada (2006), Ruland (2005), Gilson and Yeo (2004), and Stubbs (2002), indicating a link between ASEM meetings and the APT.

The bridging factor that connects the ASEM process and the APT is put forward by a senior Thai diplomat who was personally involved in ASEM establishment and the preparation of the first ASEM Summit in Bangkok. Having taken part in many ASEAN meetings, the diplomat later dealt with his country's participation in the APT. He believes that ASEM not only contributed directly to the growth of regional consciousness among Asian leaders and officials but also inspired the tradition of policy coordinating among East Asian countries. This point is remarkable in his explanation below:

Asian consciousness has developed because of ASEM. The need for coordination was felt also by other Asian countries [outside the ASEAN], not only in political affairs but also in economic sectors so EU [countries] could not do "divide and rule". In July 1996 during a meeting in Phuket, Asian Ministers of Foreign Affairs set [the] tradition to discuss and coordinate foreign policies and economic affairs. This [tradition] becomes APT [later]. (D47)

Indeed, interviewee D47 asserted that it was the available channels and the sense of a shared region resulting from the ASEM process, manifested in APT, that instilled East Asian leaders with confidence and enabled them to formulate a regional response to the Asian financial crisis, namely the Chiang Mai initiative in 2000. Apart from becoming an initial movement towards a regional financial integration (MacIntyre, Pempel, and Ravenhill 2008) and a main important step in Asian regionalism (Corbett and Fitriani 2008), the Chiang Mai Initiative indicates a growing awareness among the East Asian countries of their shared economic interest and their common need for a stronger regional voice. The importance of the ASEM coordination mechanism during the financial crisis was pointed out by the Thai diplomat:

Like ASEM and ASEAN, the APT coordination takes place in three levels: SOM, MF, and summits. Summits create informal coordination meetings among Asians.... This [informal coordinating tradition] allowed the leaders coordinate easier when financial crisis happened. (D47)

While acknowledging that ASEM was the first forum in which East Asian countries became a regional entity, scholars like Nabers (2003) as well as Aggarwal and Koo (2005) disregard the intensified communication, that had been built up by East Asian officials in the ASEM process before the Asian financial crisis, in the Asian collective response to the crisis. However, D47 describes that Asian leaders were more confident to seek regional solutions to the crisis because they had met Asian regional partners at previous ASEM, APT, and ASEAN Plus One forums (D47). It would have been difficult for East Asian leaders and officials to solicit regional solutions to the crisis if they had not known each other. A previous statement by S35 (p. 20) to some extent endorses D47's opinion. The two perceived that ASEM channels similar to those of ASEAN and APT were used by Asian leaders to undertake informal coordination. As D47 indicated, the tradition for region-wide policy coordination was initiated at the Asian coordinating meetings of the ASEM process.

Finally, the positive association of ASEM with Asian identity building is mainly asserted by interviewees who have been directly involved in the ASEM process or have personally attended ASEM forums. Two prominent Asian journalists, familiar with ASEM, mentioned in their interviews that ASEM seemed to be related to the emergence of regional identity and networks in Asia, but their awareness of the intensity of correspondence within the inter-regional forum is quite different. J75 used to follow the ASEM process quite closely but never attended ASEM meeting, whereas J57 attended some ASEF events. The differences in their views are clear:

> Political leaders have used ASEM as a talk-shop.... APT has developed more East Asian identity which is good but East Asian countries should deepen the integration though multiple ways such as APT +3, APT + EU, etc. (J75)

> ASEF is good and has done a lot of activities and networking that was missed in other forums. Dialogues developed into networks. (J57)

Figure 1.1 shows that the lowest percentage of interviewees who link ASEM with Asian identity and regional building comprises scholars.[5] The scholars who relate the inter-regional forums and regional awareness are in fact those who attended ASEF forums or closely observe Asia-Europe relations. They not only acknowledge ASEM's role in facilitating communication among Asian leaders and elites but also place the communication in context as revealed by their views below:

> The utility of ASEM is to force Asian leaders and officials to coordinate. ASEM is another form of EAEC[6] without calling it EAEC. (S34)

> In terms of Asia-Europe relations, ASEM is asymmetrical forum. But ASEM creates a forum for Asian leader to meet. (S67)

> ASEM gives a platform for Asian region building because [the] ASEM process is merely informal [so] there is no need to have a strong common position. Agree for what you can agree and not agree for things you don't or can't agree... It is also a test case of whether Asia can or cannot be unified. (S53)

> ASEM is not only a unique forum for Asian-European leaders but also the first meeting among Asian leaders in modern history ... ASEM gives opportunity for leaders to meet more often. This [opportunity] can contribute to agenda building and training ground for Asian leaders to deal with global powers and an integrated region ... ASEM is also good because it facilitates people-to-people to meet ... Asian economic integration has been there. Market driven regionalism is obvious. Now how the governments address the need to facilitate and accelerate the integration. (S54)

A Thai academic who participated in an ASEF political forum for Asian and European youth asserted that an "Asian" identity emerges almost naturally among Asian participants when discussing political matters with European counterparts. While pointing out the pressures from European participants, he also related the grouping of Asian participants at the forum to historical and cultural factors. His view below actually emphasizes previous opinions from non-state actors.

> In the meeting, Asian participants talked easily with other Asians but they are reserved when talking with Europeans. We tend to think if Europeans approach us, they must want to get something from us. Asia-Europe cultural difference is too deep, hindering closer interaction. It must happen too in the first track meetings.... In the meeting, Asian participants talked first among themselves because it is "safer". It was easier to talk first with Asian fellows because there was less conflict among Asian nations. We are linked by some old culture, and among Asians we did not argue unlike Europeans. Due to historical experience in which Europeans were always seen as suppressors, if we have to talk with European, we feel reluctant... When European participants stated straight forward on human rights issues, it created resentment among Asian participants who then held separate meetings to discuss how to counter the Europeans. The Asians talked about Chinese human rights issues too among themselves but when talking with the European they talked differently. (S52)

Thus, almost all interviewees who perceived the positive relations between ASEM and the development of Asian identity are those who have been directly involved in the ASEM process, have participated in ASEM or ASEF forums, or have closely studied the relations between Asia and Europe. For those who did not have these experiences, their opinions are to the contrary, as will be seen subsequently.

Figure 1.1 indicates that scholars comprise the largest group of interviewees who do not think that ASEM relates to Asian identity building. Interviews with scholars such as S22, S33, and S55 showed they had reservations in relating the ASEM process with the development of Asian identity in particular and the emergence of Asian regionalism in general, as indicated by their following comments.

> APT is more important and more feasible to bring tangible results to Asian countries than ASEM. (S22)

> ASEAN has internally different interests while North East Asian countries have divergent interests so there is no common Asian policy. In Asia-EU relations, Asia has no common position. Various free trade agreements

(FTAs) in Asia reflect competition in Asia even though officials claimed they did not compete with each other. The debate is between national interests versus collective interest. (S33)

Asian leaders meet in ASEAN Summits and ASEAN+1. I do not think Asia has been unified because of ASEM. However, ASEM is the first meeting between APT and Northeast Asian leaders. I do not think Asia has reached the level of oneness. Asian participants in the ASEM consist of 3 levels: (1) ASEAN 5; (2) ASEAN 10; and (3) ASEAN 10+3. Asian people do not like institutionalization. (S55)

In fact, many pessimistic views on Asian regionalism exist due to the huge diversity of Asian people, in language, cultural background, political system, ideology and the level of economic development, as suggested in the interview data below. This view is shared by scholars, journalists and diplomats.

Many factors prevent a common position in East Asia. Asia is still very diverse both in ASEAN 10 and Northeast Asia 3. In Northeast Asia, leadership issue is crucial. Japan will never let China lead and vice versa. South Korea is too small to lead. However, Asian countries have realized they need regional forums to communicate and cooperate among the Asian countries. Regional cooperation is a problem in Southeast Asia since the countries compete with each other, for foreign investment and international trade. Southeast Asian countries also have to compete with China. (D02)

Asia is very diverse. Asian regionalism can only be accepted by Asian states if it can bring benefit. The process towards Asian regionalism is also a test to what extent rich countries in the region want to support other states and provide solidarity. (J11)

Asian countries do not have a common front in ASEM. For Laos, Cambodia, Myanmar and Vietnam, it is more important to talk with China and Japan than with the EU. So it is difficult for Asia to find common ground to come together as a group in the ASEM process. Defensively, Asia can stand together vis-à-vis the EU but where is our interest? In Asia, commonality in policy is difficult. Practical factors hamper Asia from uniting. (S22)

The main commonality among those individuals who rejected the relations between ASEM and Asian identity building is that they have never attended ASEM meetings or ASEF forums, with the exception of D02.[7] This fact may explain why they rejected the relations.

Identity affiliation, regional solidarity and regional consciousness are feelings that usually emerge when actors or agents intensively engage in particular social interactions. As regional consciousness and regional identity are socially constructed, their emergence and development require direct involvement of agents or actors. It would be difficult, if not impossible, for those who did not attend meetings or events to understand fully the cognitive processes occurring among participants at the forums. As outsiders, they could only observe the events from a distance; the socialization, among the insiders, in the forums would hardly influence their cognitive process. Those who do not attend the forums do not share the ideational structure that shapes the regional consciousness of ASEM or ASEF participants. The outsiders hardly build any inter-subjective understanding with other Asian fellows if they do not take part in the socialization. They miss the cognitive processes that help create the inter-subjective understandings among the interviewees personally involved in the ASEM process.

The linkage between the ASEM process and the development of Asian identity among East Asian participants is perceived not only by Asian interviewees but also by ASEF European staff who have closely observed the ASEM process. The ASEF staff argue that this positive association is one of ASEM's achievements, one of the positive impacts ASEM has brought to Asia. The arguments are apparent in their comments below:

> All ASEF activities are tools for regional integration as it is easier for Asian and Europe to understand who they are when encountering external actors. There were distance and ignorance among Asian but when they met EU, the Asian tended to get together easier... ASEM Asian coordination has established synergy and enforcement with APT and ARF. ASEM has been the driving force for Asian regionalization, whereas Asian countries meet only 2–3 times annually before ASEM Summits. It is a big leap forward compared to pre-1996 but it is not enough. (I42)

> ASEM is not only the most important channel for Asia-Europe relations but also a provider of closer linkages for intra-Asian countries such as in education hubs which is not only Asia-Europe education hub but also Asia-Asia hub...[At ASEF forums] Asian participants came to common understandings more easily in issues such as development and government — Asians were more assertive with establishment even though they supported civil society. (I43)

On one hand, it is necessary to consider that the ASEF staff, because of their duties, are not neutral in assessing ASEM as their arguments show so much credit to ASEM in Asian regionalization. On the other hand, the arguments can be perceived as the result of their close involvement in the ASEM process that they were able to obtain the cognitive understanding among involved actors and relate it with the identity building in Asia.

Nevertheless, ASEM or ASEF forums appear to act as social platforms among Asian participants whereby their regional identity is socially constructed. This process is investigated in the next section.

IMPORTANCE OF COMMUNICATION AND INTERACTIONS AMONG ASIANS IN ASEM

This section addresses the relationship between the development of an Asian identity and the ASEM process. The previous section found that direct involvement in ASEM or ASEF forums significantly influences Asian actors to identify themselves with Asian identity. Subsequently, it is necessary to investigate what happened in the forums to understand the process of identity construction among Asian participants in ASEM.

An understanding of structure, agents and scope of the ASEM process is needed to trace the relations between ASEM and Asian regionalism, in particular the emergence of regional identity or identities in Asia. There are two characteristics of the ASEM process that facilitate intra Asian communication and the development of Asian identity: region-to-region meetings (inter-regionalism) and multi-channels.

First, the main mechanism of the ASEM process is the state-level dialogue that takes place as region-to-region meetings. Unlike other international forums where interactions are conducted at state level, the inter-regional meetings assemble Asian countries as a group to meet the European group that consists of EU member states. The meetings take place as summits, Ministerial Meetings (MMs), Senior Officials Meetings (SOMs), and Working Group Meetings (WGMs). These intergovernmental forums make up the main organs in ASEM. ASEM itself was started, and according to interviewee S31 originally intended, as intergovernmental relations. The biannual summits are the highest level of decision-making in ASEM (Yeo 2003).

The structure and agenda of the inter-regional meetings are arranged by regional coordinators (Yeo 2003), namely, the Group of Coordinators, consisting of two EU coordinators and two Asian coordinators. The role of the EU coordinators is undertaken by the EU presidency and the European Commission. On the Asian side, the two coordinators comprise one representative of the ASEAN countries and one representative of the Northeast Asian countries. The European coordinators follow the EU presidential rotation whereas the Asian coordinators are changed every two years (MOFA Finland 2006, p. 77; also interviewee D48).[8] The coordinators deal with the technical management of the ASEM process. The Group of Coordinators is also in charge of setting meeting agendas and providing first drafts of outcomes.

According to Annex 2 of the Chairman's Statement of the fifth ASEM Summit (ASEM Infoboard 2006e), coordinators are to conduct intra-regional coordination before SOM as well as coordinate the follow-up and information dissemination. Despite its main principle of informality, the ASEM process has developed an institutional mechanism that follows a regional-based channel of coordination which allocates authority to present the group to particular actors. This mechanism is identified as a form of "soft institutionalism" among ASEAN analysts (Reiterer 2001, p. 18; CAEC 1997, p. 27). The intra-regional meetings that are held before inter-regional forums help the coordination at regional level, and thus encourage regionalization (Reiterer 2006).

The inter-regional mechanism can be conceptualized diagrammatically as in Figure 1.2.

On the Asian side, the position of coordinators is vital for inter and intra-regional coordination. At inter-regional meetings, they steer the agenda and represent the ASEM Asian partners vis-à-vis their European counterparts. At the intra-regional level, they are the ones who have to take initiatives and solicit ideas among regional states. The tasks of the Asian coordinators are to speak on behalf of the Asian partners in meetings of the Group of Coordinators and, inevitably, to stimulate prior consultation (CAEC 1997, p. 27). They are responsible not only for negotiation with the European side but for coordination among Asian countries (Soesastro and Nuttal 1997, pp. 82–85). Thus the tasks of both inter-regional representation and intra-regional coordination make the Asian coordinators vital integrating agents of Asian regionalism in the ASEM process.

Due to the collegial style of Asian diplomacy, the mechanisms of intra-Asian coordination are undertaken informally.[9] For example, short visits or telephone calls are common (D01). In the early years of ASEM, consultations were conducted through telegrams too (CAEC 1997). In the period preceding the meetings or in the evenings before meetings, Asian coordinators tend to share information and updates as well as coordinated agenda building (D48). The time frame for such coordination is flexible and may extend to the last minute before an inter-regional meeting.

Coordinators, however, are not the most crucial actors in steering the ASEM process: the foreign ministers are, through Foreign Minister Meetings (FMMs). Point 22 of the Asia-Europe Cooperation Framework, adopted at the third ASEM Summit in Seoul in 2000, stipulated that ministers of foreign affairs and senior officials are responsible for the overall coordination of the ASEM process (ASEM Infoboard 2006e). The FMMs also manage political dialogues and appoint officials to undertake coordinating tasks. The FMM is held every two years. The intra- and inter-regional coordinating mechanisms

FIGURE 1.2
Pre-summit Mechanism of the ASEM Process

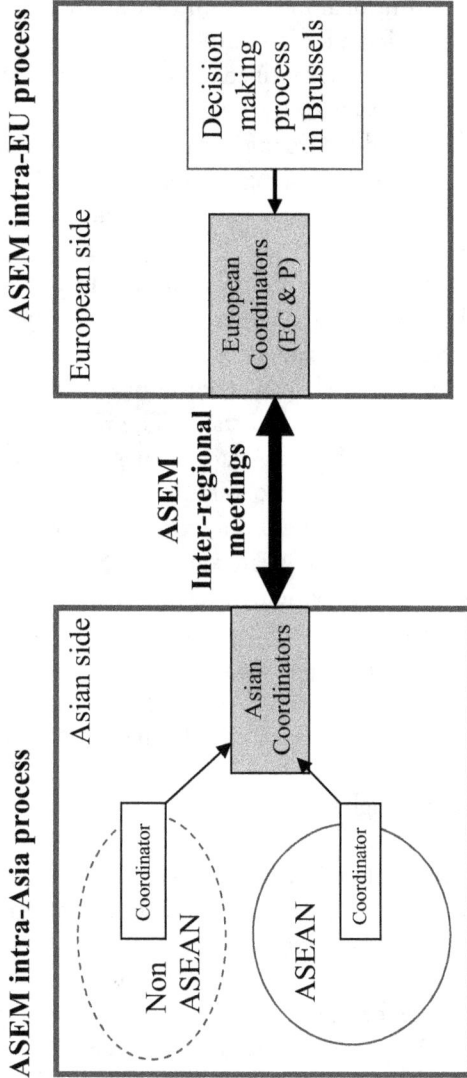

are mainly undertaken through SOMs (D01). The SOM is usually called twice a year and reports to the foreign ministers.

Apart from ministers and senior officers, in each partner country there is also an ASEM contact officer. This official is responsible for day-to-day communication among ASEM partners. Their tasks are "to facilitate a rapid and effective exchange of information among all ASEM partners and their relevant officials, and will provide a direct and informal channel of communication" (ASEM Infoboard 2006e, point 23). In most ASEAN countries, the ASEM contact officer positions are taken up by those who are in the European Division of the ministries of foreign affairs such as in Malaysia, Singapore and Thailand. In Indonesia, it has become part of the duties allocated to the Director of Multilateral Cooperation under the Directorate General of America and Europe, Ministry of Foreign Affairs. In Japan, the ASEM contact person is the Director of Economic Cooperation Division of the Ministry of Foreign Affairs.

The second important characteristic of the ASEM process is its scope which involves multi-actors, multi-levels and multi-fields. Despite the intergovernmental coordinating mechanism, the ASEM process treats all the participating states equally and allows all dialogues and cooperation to be undertaken multilaterally.[10] In terms of actors, the ASEM process has worked as the mechanism of three concerted tracks of formal and informal interactions between state officials, business communities, and civil societies. These three kinds of actors usually interact in three tracks consecutively: the first track is the meeting of state officials (the intergovernmental forums), the second track is the meeting of business communities,[11] and the third track is the meeting of civil society representatives such as NGO activists, artists, journalists, and students. The third track is also known as people-to-people (P-to-P) relations whereas the first track deals with government-to-government (G-to-G) relations. According to Soesastro and Nuttall (CAEC 1997, p. 77), the inter-regional meeting format is also used for the meetings between government and non-government participants. So ASEM includes both state and non-state actors and facilitates the meeting between those two types of actors. This means that various levels of communication and interaction occur within the track as well as across the tracks.

The ASEM process has also been developed to cover political, economic and cultural sectors that are known in ASEM as the three pillars. The three pillars consist of political dialogue, economic cooperation and cultural-social interaction (ASEM Infoboard 2006k). The three pillars embrace almost all sectors of cooperation, accommodating any interests that ASEM members may have. ASEM has also adopted the EU principle of "variable geometry" to allow flexibility in aligning cooperation and to deal with differences among ASEM countries. This means ASEM partners are not required to be involved in all sectors; they can choose to just participate in projects that they are interested in. At the seventh ASEM Summit in 2008, the principle of variable geometry became the basis from which ASEM leaders were able to launch issue-based leadership programmes.[12] Clearly, the multi-field nature of the ASEM process has significantly increased volume of communication and interactions among ASEM partners. Various activities in the three pillars extend and perhaps intensify channels of communication and interaction for not only Asians and Europeans but also among Asian participants.

One indispensable ASEM organ that contributes to the extension of communication and interaction channels is ASEF. This institution was established in 1997 to facilitate the third track of ASEM and to encourage activities in the cultural pillars. As a result of the first ASEM Summit, ASEM leaders endorsed the initiative to facilitate more P-to-P relations and to develop outreach activities to involve non-state actors. In the fourteen years since its establishment, ASEF has organized over 500 thematic-based projects that cover a variety of themes such as education and academic cooperation; health, environment, and sustainable development; arts development, artistic practices and cultural policy; human rights and governance; intercultural dialogue and international relations; media and society; and youth (ASEF website 2012). Up until mid-2008, ASEF activities had involved more than 14,000 participants (I42; I43). This figure reached 15,000 participants in mid-2012 (ASEF website 2012).

While fostering the involvement of civil society in inter-regional relations, ASEF activities also convene state officials, scholars, business peoples and NGO activists. They also generate recommendations from ASEF forums to be submitted to ASEM intergovernmental meetings (Participant observation, the second Asia-Europe Young Leaders Symposium (AEYLS), October 2007). ASEF thus contributes to the ASEM process by providing the forums for interactions between state and non-state actors and by conveying the voice of non-state actors for officials' consideration. This linkage is absent in the Asia-Europe People Forum (AEPF). Therefore, ASEF forums provide a linkage between the third track and the first track. The accommodation of non-state actors' participation in regional inter-governmental meetings is actually in line with ASEAN's current policy (D07).

ASEF's role is acknowledged by certain ASEM leaders. The Senior Minister of the Republic of Singapore, Goh Chok Tong, wrote the following on the occasion of the tenth ASEF anniversary in 2007:

The leaders pledged to build a bridge of friendship between Asia and Europe. For the bridge to endure, it has to rest on the strong foundation of political trust, economic collaboration and close interaction between the peoples of the two regions. Several ideas were discussed to achieve this. I proposed the establishment of ASEF. The foundation would promote people-to-people, intellectual and cultural exchanges. It would be funded by the members and ASEF would belong to ASEM. This idea was welcomed by the other leaders. They backed their support with voluntary financial contributions. This enabled ASEF to be set up within a year of its conception. Ten years on, ASEF has matured into a vibrant and proactive institution. It has implemented many exciting initiatives and projects. By complementing inter-governmental process and aligning its activities with the formal ASEM process, ASEF serves as a vital partner for ASEM (ASEF 2007).

As the main promoter of the establishment of ASEF, Singapore is also perhaps the largest contributor to ASEF. Goh's statements remind ASEM leaders of ASEF's usefulness and emphasize the important place of ASEF in the ASEM process.

Although ASEF has accomplished a great deal, it seems not to have been appreciated to the extent it deserves; because ASEF mainly deals with non-state actors, what has been done by ASEF is frequently overlooked. Complaints about this situation were especially emphasized by ASEF staff (I42; I43; I45). The neglect may derive from an existing perception that overstates the role of government officials, the states, over the people, the non-state actors, in international and inter-regional relations as well as in regional building.

Non-state actors are significant agents in international, inter-regional, and intra-regional relations. In fact, ASEF activities have stimulated the development of an Asian regional identity among their participants, the non-state actors. The results of interviews with civil societies, quoted on pp. 21–22, indicate that ASEF activities contribute to the development of regional awareness among Asian non-state actors. In addition, the ASEF Cultural Director in 2003–2006 said that, "unlike countries, people are very eager to learn. At P-to-P level, ASEM and ASEF are very worthy [institutions]…" (D49). Although she acknowledged there was less segregation between Asian and European participants in ASEF cultural activities,[13] she pointed out that participants from different regions tended to select different types of activities. For example, Asian participants seemed to have different preferences from their European companions in the way they perceived the arts. The Asian participants shared a commonality that treasured traditional dances and other ancient cultural products, whereas the Europeans tended to prefer creativity and innovation that produced modern dances or other postmodernistic artistic presentations. While ASEF contributes significantly to the ASEM process by providing meeting opportunities for Asia and Europe, it has helped Asian people to interact with other Asian fellows too.

Thus, the ASEM process has opened up more channels of communication and interaction among Asian state and non-state actors in various sectors. The role of ASEF is important in providing more channels of communication and interaction for different actors, helping mitigate gaps not only between state officials and non-state actors but also among civil societies in Asia. The available meeting opportunities generate wider contacts among Asian peoples than they have had before. Some of the contacts initiated at the ASEM or ASEF forums may be carried forward either by diplomats and leaders involved in G-to-G meetings or by other participants in P-to-P forums. This occurred among journalists as indicated from the comment by a Thai journalist, "[Our] dialogues developed into networks" (J57). The following part investigates how the dialogues turn into networks.

COGNITIVE PROCESSES AND A COLLECTIVE INTENTIONALITY AMONG ASIAN PARTICIPANTS IN THE ASEM PROCESS

After assessing meeting mechanisms that, by design, have provided more channels of communication and interaction, this part investigates the cognitive processes taking place at those meetings to analyse the process of identity building among the Asian side of ASEM. The analysis relies on the framework of constructivist thoughts that holds the proposition that state's interests are endogenous (Ruggie 1998*b*; Gilson 2002; Reus-Smit 2009), meaning that interests are created, shaped, and reshaped through social process; they are not given, fixed or unchangeable. This constructivist view is demonstrated in the ASEM process not only in the interactions between Asians and Europeans but also among the Asians. A diplomat from one of the Asian countries reflected that:

> At the ASEM meetings, we first come with our state's interest. But in the meeting, our interest is crossed and adjusted to other countries' interest too. (D30)

D30's reflection indicates that the process of shaping and reshaping a state's interests happens in the state officials' interaction with actors from other countries. The reflection verifies the constructivists' proposition on the endogenous nature of a state's interest. The construction of a state's interests is in line with the development of its identities as the latter informs the former (Reus-Smit 2009).

The growth of shared regional awareness and construction of collective intentionality among Asian leaders and elites is facilitated by increased intra-regional communication and interaction. Improved communication and interaction among East Asian leaders and other participants at ASEM and ASEF forums has helped mitigate tensions in the region and encouraged the development of a sense of Asian identity. This is why interviewees D30 and S20 said that ASEM meetings are actually meetings of minds and hearts. The ASEM meetings provide opportunities for elites in the region to talk about their fear, and considerations. Liu and Régnier (2003) also noticed that improved communication — in which ASEM contributes — has seemingly drawn Asian countries together.

> It does not however imply that regional countries may merge into a new body, although it has become apparent that, as a consequence of intensive interactions among regional countries in East Asia, there has indeed been a developing sense of a loosely knit community. The main function of regional cooperation in this context has been to promote mutual understanding and mutual trust, so that regional consensus may be reached and regional tension is largely reduced (Liu and Régnier 2003, p. xvii).

At ASEM and ASEF forums, Asian participants meet both their Asian fellows and European counterparts. The first cognitive process that takes place in those forums is determining the concept of self — who am I being in this forum — which is the identity a participant carries into the forum. The cognition of an individual's existence and identity is informed by ideational and material structures surrounding ASEM. The cognitive process, in turn, facilitates the Asian participants to find ground for what is described as a "collective intentionality" (Searle 1995, pp. 24–25; Ruggie 1998a, p. 869; Ruggie 1998b, p. 20) as an Asian group.

In ASEM forums, Asian participants experienced two stages of the cognitive process: first, by determining their concept of self as part of the Asian group and, second, by comparing their Asian positions with the positions of their European counterparts. For Asian participants at the ASEM meetings, the ideational and normative structures that inform their identity were to be a part of the Asian group and to contribute positively to the Asia-European partnership (Fitriani 2011). The cognitive process that takes place in the forums helped the Asian participants to become more familiar with the perceptions, concerns, and intentions of other Asian fellows. They might have known or met their Asian fellows before, or could assume their intentions, which make them even closer and more familiar with each other.

At the same time Asian participants also compared and contrasted their interests with their European counterparts. This second process is actually an identity construction, which takes place interactively among the constitutive units. This stage of identifying the differences of "other" is significant in constructing their "Asian" identity. A constructivist scholar acknowledges that "On the premise that every identity implies a difference, constructivist scholars have also explored the role of 'the other' — denigrated, feared, or emulated — in the mutual constitution of identities…" (Ruggie 1998*b*, p. 24). The cognitive process during the communication and interaction with the European participants helps the Asian participants to identify the similarities or differences of their concerns and interests from those of the European group. This idea was raised by S52 and D48 in their statements previously. The cognitive process brought about awareness among the Asian people that they were different from the European people and that they shared more similarity with other Asians. Subsequently, they began to feel more comfortable with the Asians than with the Europeans. The in-depth interviews reveal that the Asian participants felt more secure to talk and interact with other Asian participants than with the Europeans because they thought that they were more familiar and could understand their Asian fellows better (C24; C25; D50).

The feeling of closeness and commonality among participants from Southeast Asian countries has possibly existed previously because of ASEAN. Some literature supports the idea of connecting identity building in Asia with ASEAN (Acharya 2004, 2009; Pablo-Baviera 2007; Beeson 2007). Through the interviews, this research found that ASEAN meetings are intensive in terms of frequency and deeply cognitive in term of process. An Indonesian senior diplomat who has dealt with political issues and ASEAN revealed that the intergovernmental meetings among ASEAN countries, including ministerial, SOM or lower levels, and non-state actors' meetings could amount to a total of more than 600 meetings annually (D07, personal correspondence 20 August 2009). In addition, a former staff of the ASEAN Secretariat, now a scholar, indicated ASEAN as a source of closeness and acquaintance when he said that ASEAN forums are essentially a meetings of minds in which ASEAN states' officials exchange information and their perceptions or positions (S20). He explained that the meeting of minds enabled ASEAN countries to understand the positions or behaviours of other ASEAN countries even though they might not necessarily agree (S20). As a result, the Southeast Asian participants felt closer to ASEAN fellows than to Northeast Asian people. But in the ASEM process, participants from ASEAN countries felt closer to the Chinese, Japanese, and Koreans than to the Europeans (PC12).[14]

This closeness and acquaintance among the Asians allows, among elites, the emergence and development of shared regional identity as "the Asians" in the ASEM process.

How interactions take place in ASEM or ASEF forums also influences the shaping and reshaping of regional identities among the Asian participants. This research used the participant observation method to watch the interactions during the ASEM third track at the 2007 AEYPLS in Copenhagen and at the 2008 Asia-Europe Youth Network for Sustainable Development (AEYNSD) Steering Committee Meeting in Kuala Lumpur. This revealed, despite some individuals mingling more widely, a tendency towards grouping with their fellows among the European participants as well as among the Asian participants. As indicated by C24 and S52 in their statements previously, Asian participants appeared more reserved. Perhaps, this was because of their unfamiliarity with European customs. "They were 'fearful' of making mistakes [in interactions] because they do not know the European people. They tend to talk with other Asian participants because they are more confident that they know their Asian fellows" (C38). Some Asian participants also revealed that they thought the Europeans were rather distant, and the fact that they grouped among themselves became a barrier to the Asians' approaching them (C12; C13; D50).

Due to the distant atmosphere that seemed to pervade the ASEM or ASEF forums, polarization took place into Asian groups and into European groups. Most Asian participants of ASEF forums experienced the Asia-Europe polarization.[15] Similar polarization also took place at ASEM intergovernmental meetings, the first track. This issue was echoed by I45, I46, D48 and D50.[16] It seems that "ice breaking activities" did not significantly remove the cultural and geographical distances between people from the two regions.

This Asia-Europe polarization subsequently informs cognitive processes in the identity development among the Asian participants because the "other" and the "us" were quite obvious. This phenomenon was observed by an NGO activist who participated in two ASEF environmental forums:

> The 2007 Asia-Europe Youth Network on Sustainable Development (AEYNSD) in Mindoro and the 2008 Steering Committee meeting in Kuala Lumpur showed that the European behaved like to give whereas the Asian behaved like to receive. They tended to group and very few mingled. (C24)

In the presence of the "other", which was distant and identified as a "Western" group, the Asian participants were conditioned to affiliate themselves as the Eastern group with other Asian fellows. The tendency to group themselves with

Asian fellows is not only because of their collective experience of polarization at the forums but also because they felt they were closer and more acquainted with other Asians. This process also allowed the Asian participants to experience the feeling of collectiveness among them.

The result of the cognitive process during the ASEM and ASEF forums is the emergence of what constructivists call "inter-subjective understanding" among the Asians. It means the understanding among Asian participants that derives from their interactive sharing of consciousness, hopes, concerns, and fears. While not necessarily finding common interests among each other, the Asians establish common understandings among themselves through communication and interactions in the ASEM process, in addition to other regional meetings like ASEAN, ASEAN Plus One, and APT. This inter-subjective state takes place not as a hard objective such as formal and legal agreements but more as an understanding of each other's concerns and interests, and as an acknowledgement of their reciprocal tasks towards each other. This inter-subjective understanding is actually a form of trust between them. A former ASEAN high-ranking official endorses this notion in an interview, as he reveals that:

> ASEAN agreement is not necessarily a common position; it is only a common understanding… ASEAN common understanding exists when Southeast Asian states came [to meetings] at individual basis. It was not written [as a legal document] but might be presented by any [ASEAN] states [to the meeting counterpart]. (S20)

Interviewee S20's remark provides insights into ASEAN, into ASEAN influence on the ASEM process, and into important factors shaping Asian identity building. It sheds light not only on ASEAN behaviour for not performing as one regional organization in accordance with EU experience of regionalism, but also on identifying ASEAN influence on ASEM. It is clear from S20's words and other statements from ASEAN countries' diplomats in interviews (such as D06, D07, D47, and D51) that Southeast Asian countries have brought the ASEAN's diplomatic styles into the ASEM process. In this sense, a Japanese scholar is right in endorsing ASEM as an outreach of ASEAN (S71). The ASEAN diplomatic style of pursuing common understandings seems to influence the Asian group in ASEM as they adopt what Ruggie called "collective intentionality" (1998a, p. 862) shaping their Asian identity through inter-subjective understanding.

In the ASEM first track, where the inter-regional mechanism is prominent, the main role of the Asian coordinators is actually to build a common understanding among the Asian states through sharing relevant information, updating new developments in the agenda and issues preceding the meetings and communicating different positions or interest among Asian countries. Interviews with Indonesian and Malaysian diplomats revealed that through the regional coordinating process, communication between the Asians was intensified. The communication was undertaken either by top leaders like ministers and heads of governments or states, or relevant officials, using a variety of channels such as MMs, SOMs, WGMs, and other coordinating mechanism as described earlier. These intensified communication channels helped the Asian countries to explain and discuss their policies, concerns and hopes based on their countries' characteristics (D06; D07; S20; D30; S35; D47; D48).

In the ASEM third track, development of a common understanding among Asian participants was being facilitated on a personal level. Asian participants in ASEM forums seemed to prefer to establish communication and interactions with Asian fellows first before they talked to their European counterparts (C13; C24; C25; C39; S52).

Political issues play a seemingly significant role in raising a sense of grouping among the Asians in the ASEM process, which in turn construct Asian regional identity. Asian participants established inter-subjective understandings among themselves relatively more easily when they were countered by European criticism of human rights or democracy. This phenomenon showed itself clearly at the Asia-Europe forums for young political leaders organized by ASEF in Beijing and in Copenhagen. Some participants of the forums asserted the role of ASEF activities in connecting the non-state actors in Asia.

> My participations at the AEYPLS1 in 2005 and 2007 allowed me to meet and make contact with other Asian young politicians… Unfortunately, we did not do these [kinds of] activities much among Asian countries. The human rights issues created tension in Beijing when EU participants — mainly Youth Socialist Party — raised the issue to the Chair of External Affairs of the China Communist Party. This created polarization: Asian versus European participants; encouraging the Asian to hold a special meeting to discuss how to encounter the European. Malaysian and Singaporean delegations were the vocal actors with the Thai as the drafter, whereas the Japanese, Chinese and the Korean were passive followers. (C12)

> I like this ASEF activity because it made us meet our Asian fellows too. We should have more opportunities to connect young people in ASEAN and Asia. We can start cooperation on less sensitive, common interests like environment. I want to see a more unified Asia. (C38)

We should have more forums for youth to meet either with the EU or with other Asian fellows so we can grow the understanding towards each other. At the peaceful time, this event is important. We also need this forum so Asian young leaders do not grow in Western values. (C25)

I do not hear much about ASEM but ASEF has been able to bridge Asia-Europe people-to-people relations. From my participation in 2004 to 2008, there has been more participation, more commitment and more interaction among Asian and European participants. Asian participants were quieter; only Malaysian, the Philippines and Singaporean were more vocal. But there was much separation between Asian and European participants. (C39)

These interviewees are individuals from civil society who participated in either the first or the second, or both, AEYPLS.

At ASEM intergovernmental meetings, the first track, segregation between Asia and Europe on political issues was also experienced by involved officials. One said that in the communication process, the sense of identity grew among Asian participants especially when countering EU participants on issues of democracy (D04). Others reveal that ASEM has given Asian actors a sense of grouping because of different political values between Asia and Europe (D01; D03; S20; D51); "Asian consciousness has developed because of ASEM" (D47). To borrow the words of a Thai diplomat, "EU did not pressure us to be a group but EU action pressed us to act together more." (D50)

In sum, Asian people's cognition of their political practices and their collective experience in encountering European criticism influence their behaviour towards EU countries in the ASEM process. For them, European criticism shows that the EU countries and their people do not share the "inter-subjective understanding" that the Asian people have among themselves.

Cooperation between Asia and Europe cannot flourish if there is no inter-subjective understanding because this means there is a lack of trust. The ASEM process is steered by the first track, mainly by meetings among foreign ministries, that takes the overall coordination of ASEM. This indicates that the political dialogue, the first pillar in ASEM's inter-regional relations, has become the main guide and control in the agenda setting and decision making mechanisms of the ASEM. The focal role played by the Ministers of Foreign Affairs (MFAs) also shows that the economic cooperation (the second pillar in ASEM) and the socio-cultural interaction (the third pillar) have not been and will not operate outside agreed political frameworks. It also reflects that common positions taken by Asian countries are set parallel with their foreign policies. So, any common positions, be they in political, economic or socio-cultural fields, among the Asian countries in the intra-regional coordinating will only occur when they are politically approved or have manageable political consequences.

Past relations with both Asian and European fellows have also helped to shape an Asian identity in the ASEM process. Although the past relationship between Asia and Europe is much more complex and rich than during colonial period, it is the exploitative nature of European colonialism that has become a remarkable legacy of the past relations between the two regions (Kwa 1998). Almost all Asian countries in ASEM are former colonies of a European state; most of them escaped from colonialism only a little more than a half century ago. The Chinese and Vietnamese indeed perceived their countries as still fighting against the colonial powers until the 1970s. While East Asian countries still have a bitter and painful relationship regarding their colonial history inter-regionally, especially in regard to Japan,[17] in the ASEM process the social interactions between the two regions cannot escape from the notion of former colonial powers vis-à-vis former colonized states. In addition, the relations between the two regions have also been studied mainly in terms of power relations in which the European countries, in addition to the United States, are perceived as major powers. Thus, the majority of studies of the two regions frame their relations in hegemonic terms, placing Europe as a dominant power in global political, economic, and cultural affairs (Ravi, Goh, and Rutten 2004). Post colonial studies have challenged this view (Ling 2002; Darby 2004; Jabri 2007).

Nevertheless, in contemporary international relations, the colonial memory has often been referenced among the countries that are categorized as the "third word", "under-developed countries", or the "South" in dealing with pressure from the more powerful, developed states in global political and economic affairs. The formerly colonized countries in Asia usually perceive themselves as the victims of the Western colonization whose legacy has marginalized their positions in the post-colonial global affairs (Ling 2002; Rose 2005; Wirth 2009). Perceptions of the past have also played a significant role in the ASEM process; Wirth (2009, p. 477) argues that the "interpretations of the past are crucial in defining a nation's role and place in international society".

Therefore colonial memory cannot just be neglected in ASEM or ASEF forums. A Malaysian anthropologist has pointed out that "Colonialism creates psychic unity" (S21). To be able to sit face-to-face with the leaders of former colonial countries, at ASEM or ASEF forums that are governed by principles of equality and mutual interest, obviously gives the Asian participants a strong sense of sovereignty. It also brings awareness that their unity with other Asian partners, or alliance with other Asian countries, is essential to counter the Europeans. One of the interviewees reveals that:

> In the meeting, Asian participants talked easily with other Asians but *they have reserved when talked with Europeans. We tend to think if Europeans approach us, they must want to get something from us.* Asia-Europe cultural difference is too deep, hindering closer interaction. It must happen too in first track meetings.... In the meeting, Asian participants talked first among them because it is *"safer". It was easier to talk first with Asian fellows* because there was less conflict among Asian nations. We linked by some old culture, and among Asians *we did not argue, unlike Europeans. Due to historical experience in which Europeans was always seen as suppressors, if we have to talk with European, we feel reluctant...When European participants said straight* forward on human rights issues, it created resentment among Asian participants who then held separate meeting to discuss how to encounter the Europeans. The Asian talk about Chinese human rights issues too among themselves but *when talking with the European they talk differently.* (S52) (emphasis by author)

A general sentiment expressed in several interviews is that bitter historical experiences with Europeans strongly influenced the Asian participants to act together in an ASEF workshop for Asian and European young political leaders (C12; C38; S52). The history of economic exploitation during the colonial period and the perception that the exploitation has continued through the capitalist system appear to be confirmed by what is perceived as the economic and materialistic motives of the European involvement in the ASEM process. In addition, the behaviours and diplomatic style of the European participants that tend to be "pushy" and "preaching", especially in the political issue, have been perceived by the Asians as the European efforts to maintain the pattern of colonial hierarchy that underplayed the Asians as subordinates.

The shared awareness of the past regarding European colonialism seems to contribute in uniting the Asian participants in the ASEM process. This is in line with Rose's (2005) argument that shared understandings of the past and common history are a major influence in unity. Yet, the shared understanding in regard to colonialism seems to exclude participants from Japan and perhaps Singapore.[18] In situations when the Japanese and Singaporeans aligned themselves with the Asian group, other factors appear to play the unifying role such as the strategic calculation in the Myanmar case (Chapter 2), or solidarity factor for the first AEYPLS.

In short, ASEM and ASEF forums have become channels of communication and interaction among Asian leaders and elites. The forums facilitate social interaction that may lead to common understanding and, occasionally, to shared collective experiences. The common understanding and the collective experience then in turn become collective intentions for development of Asian identities. However, Asian identity has not yet become a single collective intention. The next section explores the concept of layered identities among Asian states.

ASEM AND ASIAN REGIONALISM

The previous section analysed the construction of Asian identities through cognitive processes among Asian participants in the ASEM process. ASEAN leaders and key persons use ASEM and ASEF as social forums in which they communicate and interact. Through those channels their common understanding and shared collective experiences grow into collective intentions that indicate the development of Asian identities.

Nevertheless, linking ASEM with the development of identity building in Asia has generally provoked questions because the very idea of Asian identity has also been debated: "who are Asian?", "Who are inside and who are outside 'Asian'?". In international relations, there has not been a general, widely accepted, agreement on the boundaries of "Asia", although some countries may assert that they are members of East Asian, Northeast Asian, Southeast Asian, and South Asian grouping due to their geographical location. Asian regionalism, according to scope and participating countries, has been invented, as this space is socially constructed, in that people invent it (Ruggie 1998a). Accordingly, there have been different scopes of engagement in Asia with different memberships. Consequently, the concept of "Asian identity" cannot be homogeneous.

The in-depth interviews conducted during this study revealed that Asian participants had brought different layers of identities into the ASEM process. These layered identities among Asian participants in ASEM reflect their different levels of engagement and communication with their regional partners. The layered identities also indicate the institutionalization of their preferred identities given the social forums they encounter, identified as "cognitive institution" by Ruggie (1998b). The preferred identity may be identical with the most highly intensified communication because of the shared inter-subjective understanding and acquaintance that has been built through the communication. Thus, the layered identities of Asian participants in the ASEM process are shaped by the development of Asian regionalism indicated by the increase of regional initiatives in East Asia.

The task of this section is to identify and describe the source of Asian layered identities in ASEM and how such a complex set of identities may influence the behaviours of the Asian group in the ASEM process. This section consists of two sub-sections. The first part explores ASEM's place in the context of Asian regionalism to understand the source of identities that Asian participants bring into the ASEM process. The second sub-section identifies the layered identities Asian state and non-state actors have brought in to the ASEM process.

In the last two decades, global and regional circumstances such as regional integration in Europe and Northern America, and the Asian financial crisis have driven East Asian countries to seek their own regional frameworks. The literature has examined the emergence of regional initiatives in East Asia and its impacts on regional and global affairs (Palmujoki 2001; Beeson 2007; Curley and Thomas 2007; *Journal of East Asian Studies* 2007; Acharya 2009). Some of the studies see ASEM as the part of the movement towards Asian regionalism (Liu and Régnier 2003; Beeson 2007; Curley and Thomas 2007). Even before the Asian financial crisis, which strengthened the East Asian identity, some scholars acknowledged that ASEM had encouraged East Asian countries to perform as a regional entity; as argued by Maull, Segal and Wanandi (1998, p. 171), "[I]t was not until the ASEM process got underway in 1996 that East Asians began caucusing on a regular basis on matters of high policy".

A number of this study's interviewees also acknowledged that Asian regional building has been developing and that regional awareness plays a significant role in the regionalizing process. Comments from some interviewees also indicate the emergence of Asian regionalism even though they did not directly correspond the trend with ASEM.

> Asian people do not like institutionalization. [A] Formal institution does not work for us but we do need institution to enforce agreements. Asian [countries] do not like institutions since it will take [their] sovereignty and we have historically bitter experience. Asian regionalism is not soon or immediate. Current movement of … Asian regionalism is good but [I] hope it continues…The second easiest path is culture. We understand each other more easily. There must be objectives for people to integrate. Trade can be a good, tangible objective while politics is not tangible for common people. (S55)

> Asian integration in [the] economic sector is more probable whereas political integration is still far away because countries still compete. Rather than external pressure like [the] EU, internal drive is more significant to encourage Asians to integrate. With or without EU, Asian countries need to cooperate. EU integrated to prevent conflicts among themselves, political motivation with economic instrument, whereas the Asian people want to integrate to achieve a better economic stage, an economic motivation. (D04)

Compared with Europeans, Asian [countries] are very slow in reconciliation. Yet Asia feels pressure to reconcile and to smoothen regional building. (I41)

These 12 years of ASEM has been learning process for Asia. They are now more aware of political discourses. This [phenomenon] generates expectation among epistemic community. But the main reason for Asia to get together is economic [motivation] after the financial crisis. The Asian identity is not there yet. We are in the process. (S31)

A comment from a senior Malaysian diplomat summarizes the regionalizing process in Asian: "Asia is not ready to be a region yet but the process is underway." (D16)

Some European scholars have observed the emergence of Asian states as a regional group as they reflected on their own experience in the EU in the excerpts from interviews below,

Asian region building has been flourishing in 1990s–2000s. But it is less institutional building and no regional architecture — many institutions but overlap and do many things but not thoroughly. Problems are in leaders' decisions and plans to deliver… APT should be the driving force for Asian regionalism. East Asia Summit should be the second track. [Having] so many regional initiatives creates trust issue and security problems. (S32)

Asia is diverse and it does not have [any] institution to guide and define Asian common interests. EU is not in the position to tell Asian [people] to integrate and what to do. Asian integration will happen when Asian [people] want it. Let the Asians choose the path and the phase… As in other parts of world, integration in Asia is unavoidable. If you do not do it, [the] market will do it for you. (S36)

Asian psychology is not to copy the EU but it wants to see and learn lesson from the EU. Currently Asian wants to move to financial integration but it won't happen before basic integration, such as customs union, takes place. There are a lot of political issues in Asia, lacking of trust and there are still many conflicts. (S19)

While reflecting on the specific characteristics of the Asian regionalizing path, the comments above highlight certain problems connected with Asian regionalism. Given the diversity of Asia and history of conflicts in the region, these problems derive from a low level of trust among Asian countries, as mentioned by S19 above. Thus, any measures which contribute to trust building may contribute to the development of Asian regionalism. Institutions and mechanisms that may trigger the development of regional consciousness and shared identity, such as the ASEM inter-regionalism, play a significant role in trust building.

As in other regions, Asian regionalism will take a long time in its shaping process. The phase in which Asian state and non-state actors can build trust has been slow, reflecting natural boundaries such as oceans and geographical distances between states that limit interaction and socialization. As a region is a social construction that is shaped by actors' cognitive processes through social interaction, the more intense the interaction, the greater the possibility there is for people to become acquainted and build trust. In this context, meeting opportunities, especially among Asian leaders and people in ASEM, help increase the interactions. Indeed, the interactions may create what S20 called earlier a "meeting of minds and hearts".

ASEAN has been used as a "meeting of minds and hearts" among Southeast Asian elites, but it took several decades for the ASEAN countries to nurture trust among themselves. The main obstacle for ASEAN to create a more developed regional institution was not only ASEAN internal problems and limitations (Acharya and Johnston 2007; Emmerson 2009; Acharya 2009; Stubbs 2009) but also the involvement of external powers in the region (Palmujoki 2001; Acharya 2004; Murphy and Welsh 2008). However, given the change in the global and regional environment after the end of the Cold War, ASEAN seems to need and want to embrace other big countries in Asia to strengthen its rationale and relevance. The ASEAN intention seems to be in line with China's move to approach its southern neighbours (Shambaugh 2004; Kuik 2005; Percival 2007). As a result, Asian countries took various steps that had a regional dimension in the 1990s. Previous studies suggest that Asian regionalism has emerged in varying forms (Dieter and Higgott 2003; Katzenstein and Shiraishi 2006; ADB 2008). ASEAN countries' involvement in the ASEM process has become one of those regionalization movements. Table 1.1 illustrates selected regional groupings in Asia promoted by ASEAN.

ASEAN is the key agent in Asian regionalism. Table 1.1 shows that ASEAN is certainly the oldest if not the most established regional group in Asia. Although it has been criticized for its ineffectiveness, ASEAN has been praised as the longest survivor of regional institutions outside Europe. Out of ASEAN, ideas were developing to create broader boundaries by including some preferred countries and excluding others. One of the important proposals was launched by former Malaysian Prime Minister Mahathir Mohamad in 1989 on the East Asian Economic Group (EAEG) with a membership to that similar of APT. But this proposal failed due to its strong anti-Western spirit and internal disagreement in ASEAN (D04; D06; S09; D17). In a twist on that proposal, EAEG has actually been established under the name APT.

TABLE 1.1
Country Membership of Regional Institutions
Promoted by ASEAN Countries

No	Country's name	ASEAN	ASEAN Plus Three (APT)	ASEAN Regional Forum (ARF)	Asia-Europe Meeting (ASEM)	East Asia Summit
1.	Indonesia	1967	1997	1994	1996	2005
2.	Malaysia	1967	1997	1994	1996	2005
3.	The Philippines	1967	1997	1994	1996	2005
4.	Thailand	1967	1997	1994	1996	2005
5.	Singapore	1967	1997	1994	1996	2005
6.	Brunei	1984	1997	1994	1996	2005
7.	Vietnam	1995	1997	1995	1996	2005
8.	Myanmar	1997	1997	1996	2004	2005
9.	Laos	1997	1997	1997	2004	2005
10.	Cambodia	1999	1997	1999	2004	2005
11.	Japan		1997	1994	1996	2005
12.	China		1997	1994	1996	2005
13.	Korea		1997	1994	1996	2005

Thus, ASEAN has played an important role in the development of East Asian regionalism (Beeson 2007; Curley and Thomas 2007; Pablo-Baviera 2007). Many, if not all, regional institutions established in East Asia since 1990s are extensions of ASEAN or are forums in which ASEAN is the driving force such as APT, ASEAN Plus One, ASEAN Regional Forum (ARF), and East Asia Summit (EAS) (Liu and Régnier 2003; Pablo-Baviera 2007; Emmerson 2009). In each of those institutions, ASEAN engages with different states, creating various scopes of engagement.

The inclusion and exclusion of states in the ASEAN-sponsored grouping in fact reflects the preference of alliance from ASEAN countries' point of view. As ASEAN countries cannot always come to an agreement on who they would like to invite to their club (S09; S10; J11; S20; S22; S34; D51), the membership of ASEAN-sponsored groupings can vary as reflected in ARF and EAS membership. In addition to internal disagreement over their preferred allies, ASEAN countries also have had to face changing regional and global environments since the end of the Cold War. This means new problems and new opportunities are arising for ASEAN and the Asian countries.

Problems and opportunities, together with fear and optimism, towards regionalization have created a dynamics in Asian regionalism. This is where the context of ASEM's initiation by one of the ASEAN countries, Singapore, can be better understood. ASEM inter-regional mechanism can be seen as a part of the dynamic factors. The dynamic process of regional building in Asia has been acknowledged by those who have observed the ASEM process as well as the Asian affairs in Malaysia, Thailand, and Japan. The comments from interviewees below also show the relations of ASEM with other regional movements in East Asia, especially with the ASEAN-sponsored grouping elaborated in Table 1.1.

> *ASEM gives platform for Asian region building because ASEM process is merely informal.* Asian integration discussion has changed from not relevant for some countries to highly relevant, e.g., Japan now thinks it is important to improve relations with ASEAN and China and others than only having a special tie with the United States. Asian integration is driven by economy. The condition for integration is now stronger because of high level of trading. (S53)

> APT is as an entity in the ASEM. *Decision [by Asian countries as a whole] was taken when at meeting others [the EU countries in the ASEM] set conditionality.* Asian [countries] are supposed to collaborate. (D17)

> [A] common position in inter-regional forum is difficult. Indeed, among ASEAN common positions are not always 100% agreed. A common position requires negotiation and compromise. [Asia's] common position in ASEM is more as *a strategic initiative* — which is fine. (S23)

> Common positions develop through time as they — the Asians met, as issues were discussed overlapped in several forums. *Various and frequent forums enable the Asian to be familiar with the issues.* So ASEAN+1 and APT are processes to develop common positions... At ASEAN meetings, there is always agenda to prepare for APT, ASEM, ASEAN+1. (D16)

> Data show that if we move forward with regionalism, we may have a less legalistic but structured regional body to allow economic activities without [a] legal frame. [It does] not necessarily follow [the] EU model. We learn but we pick what we think works here. Unlike EU, in Asia ideological and politically dangerous spots still exist. We also have territorial disputes that are more crucial than those in [the] EU. (D60)
> (Emphasis by author)

While the Asian interviewees above express mostly positive views of Asian regionalism, nevertheless, there were some pessimistic views too. These views were mainly expressed by Japanese scholars who seemed to have less enthusiasm for Asian regional building. During the interviews, a strong impression was given that the Japanese prioritize their special relations with the United States over other bilateral and regional relations, as shown below:

The boom for East Asian Integration is already over. The chance of East Asian community to be born is very small, considering the difference of opinions between Japan and China whose economic networks with ASEAN are competitive. Northeast Asian countries share common goals in building East Asian community but they differ on scope and method of negotiation. (S64)

Asian regionalism is [a] fake as members do not like binding rules. As long as sovereignty still plays highest law, binding regional organizations will not appear in East Asia. For time being, APT is useful. Due to competitive nature of [the countries in] Northeast Asia, movement to regional integration is still a long way even though market forces have pushed so powerfully. It does not matter whether there is or not region building in East Asia as long as neighbouring countries do not fight each other. Pushing [factors] to [establish] regional organizations are market forces and less leverage in global forums. What hinder regional organizations in Asia are Northeast Asian political problems and domestic politics that do not like binding rules... ASEM is ineffective due to Japan-China problem. It is much more useful for smaller powers. For big countries, ASEM is not a high states' forum so investment in ASEM is low. (S66)

ASEM is another example where ASEAN is a hub; ASEM is an outreach of ASEAN. Asian regionalization is far more complex, driven by market. East Asian will make the most important market. China is definitely not leading Asian regionalization... Regionalism in Asia is network style, functional style; membership is various depending on the function. ASEAN always serves as the hub but leadership can be any other countries. In Asia, regional building can follow when regionalization takes shape. Regionalization is always more important than regionalism. (S71)

Despite some pessimism, however, Asian regionalism has been developing and the role of ASEM in the regionalizing process cannot be overlooked given its role in providing regular meeting opportunities for Asian leaders and for stimulating the cognitive processes towards regional awareness among its Asian participants.

The link between ASEM and Asian regionalism is embodied in APT. ASEM leaders themselves acknowledge the development of APT and indicate their support for East Asian regional groupings. This acknowledgement indirectly indicates self-acknowledgement of the thirteen Asian countries in ASEM. Their pledge can be seen in point 5 of Chairman's Statement of the third ASEM Summit in Seoul in 2000:

5. Leaders ... also acknowledged that great progress had been made in East Asian cooperation at the ASEAN+3 Summit held in Manila in November

1999, where ASEAN countries, China, Japan and the Republic of Korea affirmed the importance of meeting on a regular basis and adopted the Joint Statement on East Asia Cooperation. In this connection, they welcomed the progress made at the inaugural ASEAN+3 Foreign Ministers' Meeting held in Bangkok in July 2000. They further welcomed the progress made at the ASEAN+3 Finance Ministers' Meeting held in Chiang Mai in May 2000 and the ASEAN+3 Economic Ministers' Meeting also held in Chiang Mai in October 2000, as further strengthening East Asian financial and economic cooperation. (ASEM Infoboard 2006d)

Interviewee S22's statement previously suggested that APT is more important and more promising for Asian cooperation than ASEM. However, it is questionable that APT could have been established without ASEM. As elaborated earlier, the interviewee D47 described that the first ASEM Summit in 1996 and the meetings afterwards started what has become a tradition of coordinating policy and response among East Asian leaders and officials. In line with the constructivist framework used in this chapter, one may argue that inter-subjective understandings and collective intentionality among East Asian state and non-state actors would not have been established without social construction taking place at various coordinating meetings including those initiated in ASEM. This argument is in line with Schmit (2001), Ofken (2001), and Reiterer (2002a, 2006), who write that the ASEM process is an exercise area or a learning process for East Asian regionalism.

Given the importance of the authoritative decision-making body in any institution, what makes Asian regionalism seem "unready" is perhaps the absence of a supranational "political" institution in Asia. Unlike the EU that has several organs of regional decision making, Asian countries reject any notion that is considered as eroding their sovereignties (Kahler 2000; Acharya and Johnston 2007; Khong and Nesadurai 2007) and taking away their decision-making power. The political will for regional integration is not yet present. Thus, in Asia, economic integration is more appealing than political integration. Indeed, economic regionalization has long taken place (S65; see also Katzenstein and Shiraishi 2006). This phenomenon is observed by interviewees D04, S31 and S55 as reflected in their comments previously that in Asia, economic integration is more likely to take place than political integration. Similarly, the ADB *Annual Report* (2008) and Corbett and Fitriani (2008) also present the increasingly integrated trends of Asian economies.

Through its intra-Asian coordinating mechanism, ASEM has contributed a very important element to Asian regionalism. As elaborated previously, the tradition of policy coordination among Southeast Asian and Northeast Asian countries was initially seen in ASEM. This tradition has been carried forward in APT (Ruland 2005; Terada 2006; Higgot 2006; Pempel 2008) and later in EAS. With a number of common interests in the economic sector confirmed in the chairman's statements of the summits (ASEM Infoboard 2006*b*, 2006*c*, 2006*d*), ASEM partner countries especially those from Asia seem to use the policy coordination mechanism to manage the economic cooperation and economic regionalization in the region. The efforts to build regional frameworks in the economic sector are quite remarkable, especially since the Asian financial crisis (S63; S67; S74; also MacIntyre, Pempel, and Revenhill 2008).

Thus, Asian regionalism has been evolving and taking shape in various forms. This section has revealed the linkages between the increased contacts and interactions among East Asian people involved in ASEM and in regionalism in Asia. The linkages between ASEM and Asian regionalism are more obvious for government officials who were involved in the first track of the ASEM process. The sense of emerging regional awareness and shared identity has also been felt by non-state actors who have participated in the ASEF P-to-P forums. Different levels of contact and interaction, however, can create different identities as shown in the next section.

ASIAN LAYERED IDENTITIES IN ASEM

In a Jakarta seminar in 2005 discussing ten years of ASEM, one participant threw out a question that was not answered until the end of the forum: "Whose interests are carried by an Indonesian representative when she or he attends an ASEM meeting? Indonesia's? ASEAN's? or Asians'?" Data from the interviews help to answer this question.

The previous section revealed some of the linkages between the increased contacts and interactions among East Asian elites involved in ASEM and regionalism in Asia. The contacts and interactions, however, are not equal among Asian participants. This fact, combines with the premise that the ideas of a region and its boundaries are socially constructed (Ruggie 1998*b*; Hettne and Soderbaum 2002; Gilson 2002; Fawcett 2004) resulting in a varying scope of "region" in Asia and consequently creating different layered identities.

The "Asian" is the regional identity with which Asian participants affiliate themselves in the region-to-region relations of the ASEM process. This is the cognitive level of identity that the Asians seem to develop through the cognitive process in ASEM, as discussed earlier.

The result of research shows that the Asian participants of the ASEM process carry with them different levels of identities. These layers of identities reflect their preferred affiliated regional institutions at their cognitive level. Layered identities appear in such a way that in front of their European counterparts, Asian participants are inclined to group as "Asia". In forums where their European counterparts are absent, however, Asians are divided into ASEAN and non-ASEAN. There again, among themselves, people from ASEAN countries tend to stand with their own national identities. Insights from the interviews reveal these phenomena.

> Asian regionalism has been built in several sub-groups as Asia has no clear boundary. (S56)

> In Asia, our national identity comes first; we have never thought about Asian identity. Feelings of Asianness came when we are surrounded by external actors; I needed friends, not because I share the Asian fellows' perspective of the world. The feeling does not exist when we are among Asian fellows. We thought differently from each other. (D49)

Indeed, different identities at ASEM forums have created scepticism about the unity of Asian states in the ASEM process. Two interviewees' comments below reveal this scepticism.

> Defensively, Asia can stand together vis-à-vis the EU but where is our interest? In Asia, commonality in policy is difficult. Practical factors hamper Asia uniting. (S22)

> There is no Asian regionalism as such. What appears is localized regionalism in Asia. Asian unity is localized such as South Asia, Southeast Asian, Northeast Asian. (S21)

Looking beyond the scepticism, however, one can find that there are at least three layered identities carried by Asian participants from Southeast Asian countries when they attend ASEM forums. The first is his or her national identity, the second is the ASEAN identity, and the last is the Asian identity. Participants from Northeast Asian countries, probably, bring with them only two layered identities: his or her national identity and Asian identity. Depending on the circumstances and who the "others" are at the forums, an Asian participant presents different identities.

The layered identities are acknowledged by comments from Asian and European diplomats, as below:

> ASEM includes many participating countries from very far locations so sometimes it is different for member countries to have interaction as often as intra ASEAN or EU. (D62)

> In attending ASEM meetings, Asian countries did not come as APT but as individual countries. The ASEAN minus X spirit is taken to the Asian group in the ASEM process: [an] Asian does not necessarily come with [a] common position but [a] common understanding. (S20)

> At the beginning of ASEF forums, Asian participants tended to stay close to each other to avoid being alone or with Europeans. Later they could mingle with Europeans. But when [they] got tired, they tended to group with their national colleagues. (I44)

The layered identities reflected what Ruggie (1998*b*) describes as institutions at cognitive level. These different levels of identities among Asian participants in the ASEM process derive from different cognitive institutions that the Asian's participants identify with. Therefore the layered identities are similar to concentric circles, indicating different degrees of state affiliation in Asian regionalism. For example, the layered identities for an Indonesian in the ASEM process can be illustrated as in Figure 1.3.

The layered identities of Asian elites develop in line with the frequency of their communication and interactions. The more frequent their interactions and the more channels of communication they have, the stronger the identity can be developed. This is because the cognitive process takes place between

FIGURE 1.3
An Indonesian's Layered Identities in the ASEM Process

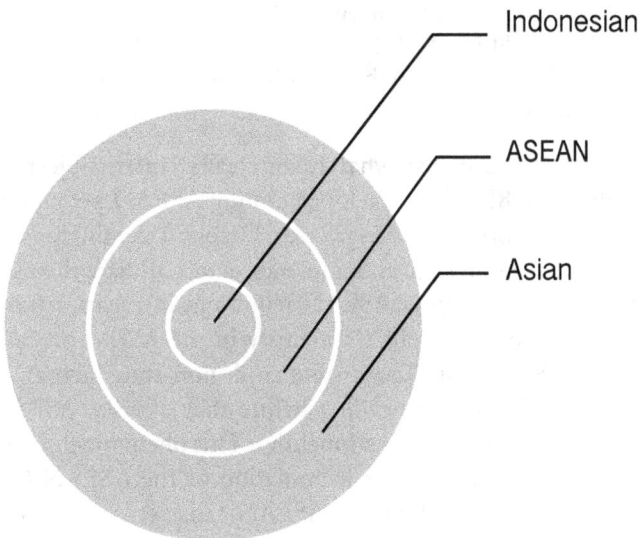

and among interacting and communicating actors. An Indonesian diplomat who dealt with ASEAN affairs and took part in the development of ASEAN Charters noted that the meeting intensity among officers from ASEAN countries is very high. They could have approximately 600 meetings per year which is much more than meeting frequency for APT (D07, translated from Indonesian, personal correspondence of 21 August 2009). He also revealed that while ASEAN foreign ministers meet at least seven times annually, APT ministerial meetings only take place once a year. The intensive meetings among ASEAN officers and leaders are intended to create a better mechanism for the ASEAN Community 2015. ASEAN Secretary General Surin Pitsuwan once wrote about his perceptions of the indications of a growing sense of ASEAN community. He expects the citizens of ASEAN countries to embrace double identities, constituting their national identity and that of ASEAN (Pitsuwan 2009).

In addition, the identity affiliation can also be shaped by closeness and acquaintance, either in cultures or historical experiences. Southeast Asian states and state actors bring their "ASEAN identity" to the ASEM process as shown by the statement from Thai and Indonesian diplomats below.

> Among ASEAN, opinion is usually easier to be united since they feel close to each other. We meet them frequently and often we have to work or talk with the same persons. (S48)

> To have common positions, ASEAN countries' relations with the dialogue partners are coordinated by ASEAN, not bilateral, such as for issues like migrant workers. ASEAN relations with the dialogue partners are undertaken at SOM, DG meetings, Ministerial meetings, and summits. For efficiency, the meeting is held in ASEAN countries, back to back with the ASEAN meetings. ASEAN collegiality has been built pretty strongly especially to counter external actors. (D06)

The comments indicate that what Ruggie calls "inter-subjective cultural affinity" (1998a, p. 883) has developed among ASEAN peoples more than between them and Northeast Asian peoples. Despite a seemingly weak ASEAN identity, Southeast Asian state and non-state actors affiliate themselves — to a different degree — to other ASEAN fellows in international forums.

The appearance of an ASEAN identity in the ASEM process suggests that, for their Southeast Asian state and non-state actors, collective intentionality as ASEAN comes first before that of Asia. ASEAN is their cognitive institution after their nationalities. This phenomenon is confirmed by S07 who was involved in the formulation of the ASEAN Charter. All ASEAN documents, including the ASEAN Charter, imply that ASEAN relations with other partners, including the APT and EAS, are aimed at strengthening the ASEAN community (D07, translated from Indonesian, personal correspondence of 23 August 2009). In addition, D16's remark (see p. 47) indicates that ASEAN has become like a clearing house to prepare interactions with dialogue partner countries. Over time as they meet, diplomats from ASEAN countries develop better understandings towards each other. They may not hold the same position on a particular issue but each of the parties understands why other countries take different positions. This is the stage referred by S20 as "common understanding" among ASEAN countries.

The cognitive process grows out of the intense communication, frequent interaction, closeness and acquaintance, allowing trust to emerge and strengthen. This cognitive process in turn informs affiliation when other actors are present. For example, an Indonesian acts as Indonesian among other fellows from ASEAN countries. But an Indonesian, and participants from other countries in Southeast Asia, acts as ASEAN in the presence of participants from Japan, Korea and China because Indonesians interact more closely and frequently with ASEAN fellows. Moreover, the layers are as in a concentric circle, the bigger the ring or the bigger the outer layer, and the weaker the identity. Table 1.1 shows regional groupings in Asia and the year of members' accession. The involvement of certain countries in particular groups and their accession years can indicate that countries' degree of acquaintance and interaction. For example, state and non-state actors from the ASEAN 5[19] would usually share identity affiliation to ASEAN more strongly than those of Vietnam or Myanmar (S10; C12; S20; S69). Nevertheless, ASEAN countries in general would tend to identify themselves more towards ASEAN than with APT, let alone EAS. This phenomenon can also be gleaned from interviewees' comments, as follow:

> At ASEF Intellectual Exchange forums, Southeast Asian participants were more unified because they had come along quite far whereas Northeast Asian participants are less close to each other. In ASEF University network, intra-SEA network is also bigger than intra NEA network. (I45)

> Relations among Asian participants were closer. We had a sense of belonging, feeling close and more confident because we knew their culture. Yet, this feeling was stronger towards Southeast Asian participants than Northeast Asian ones. (C25)

> The first priority for Asia is regional security. Southeast–Northeast Asia cooperation is pragmatic approach, converging national and regional interests. (D15)

Nevertheless, as Gilson (2002) indicates, that identity is shaped and reshaped in the interaction, the ASEM process and regional dynamics do not allow the layered identities to assume fixed or permanent shapes. Because identity building is a process, the layered identities are also built in through processes. So, among the ASEAN countries, too, difference can emerge between "the founding countries" and the "others", as suggested by S55 below:

> I do not think Asians have reached the level of oneness. Asian participants in the ASEM consist of 3 levels: the first is ASEAN 5; the second is ASEAN 10; and the third is ASEAN 10+3. (S55)

Indeed, in the absence of external actors, competition for regional leadership may emerge among the ASEAN "founding states". One can see the tension between Indonesia and Malaysia regarding the regional path as indicated in the interviews with two diplomats from those countries.

> APT and EAS should go on simultaneously because geopolitically it will put Indonesia in the middle and the two would create [a] balance in the region. Malaysia would prefer APT and wants to establish APT headquarters in Kuala Lumpur. Indonesia developed the East Asia Summit (EAS) concept. But the first focus is ASEAN community. (D06)

> There is competition on leadership and initiatives among Asian countries, not only between Japan and China. For Malaysia, APT is priority. It should not be equally placed with EAS. ASEAN and APT are main vehicles for regional building. (D17)

The "competitive" approach between Indonesia and Malaysia in "inventing" the border of Asian regionalism indicates their different preferences for their own cognitive institution beyond ASEAN. Malaysian officers and elites tend to maintain Mahathir's legacy of East Asian Economic Caucus, creating boundaries to APT whereas Indonesia and Japan — for their own reasons — would like to create a bigger boundary to include Australia and India.

ASEM AND ASIAN IDENTITIES

The in-depth interview data reveal that a number of elites in Southeast Asian countries acknowledge ASEM's role in facilitating the emergence and development of the "we" feeling among Asians. The social arenas that were provided by the ASEM and ASEF forums have become important channels of communication and interaction among officials as well as representatives of civil society, business community, journalists and scholars from East Asian countries. The forums facilitate social interaction which seems to lead to the development of common understanding and, occasionally, to shared collective experiences. The common understanding and the collective experience, in turn, become the collective intentionality for being "we" that may lead to the development of Asian identities.

This chapter finds that the rise of regional identity has been experienced and communicated mostly by the officials and non-official actors who have been directly involved in the ASEM process or have personally attended ASEM forums. In the forums, the cognitive processes among Asian participants occurred in two ways: by determining their concept of self as part of the Asian group and by comparing their Asian positions with those of their European counterparts. The communication and the socialization in the ASEM and ASEF forums inform perceptions, concerns and intentions of other Asian fellows, making them even closer and more familiar with each other and creating inter-subjective understanding. At the same time, Asian participants also compare and contrast their interests with their European counterparts. This second process is actually an identity construction through contrasting and differentiating themselves (the Asian group) from the "other" (the European group).

The cognitive process during the communication and interaction with the European participants helps the Asian participants to identify the similarities or differences between their concerns and interests and those of the European group (interviews with C24, C25, D50, S52 and D48). The socialization in the ASEM process also brought about awareness among the Asian people that they were different from the European people and that they shared more similarity with other Asians. Subsequently, they felt more comfortable among the Asians than among the Europeans. This is also an explanation of why the linkage between ASEM and the development of Asian identity has been communicated mostly by those who have been involved directly in the ASEM or ASEF forums. Those who do not attend the forums have not experienced those cognitive processes.

The development of a shared regional awareness and an inter-subjective understanding among Asian participants in the ASEM and ASEF forums is shaped by three factors present during their interactions with the European counterparts. Those three factors are the polarization of Asians versus Europeans, political issues, and the growing self-esteem among Asian participants in relation to their former colonial powers from Europe. The interview data reveal that the Asian people's cognition of their political practices and their collective experience in countering European criticism influence their behaviours towards EU countries in the ASEM process. For the Asian participants, the European criticism implies that the EU countries and people do not share the "inter-subjective understanding" that the Asian people have among themselves.

This chapter has also revealed the linkages between the increased contacts and interactions among East Asian people involved in the ASEM and regionalism in Asia. Asian regionalism has been evolving in various forms but the tradition of policy coordination among Southeast Asian and Northeast Asian countries was initiated in ASEM. This argument is supported by interview data (S35; I45; D47) as well as some studies in the literature (Ruland 2005; Terada 2006; Higgot 2006; Pempel 2008). In his interview, a Thai senior diplomat who had been involved in the organization of the first ASEM meeting in 1996 revealed that,

> In July 1996 during a meeting in Phuket, Asian Ministers of Foreign Affairs set [the] tradition to discuss and coordinate foreign policies and economic affairs. This [tradition] becomes APT [later]' and "Asian leaders were more confident to seek regional solutions to the crisis because they had met Asian regional partners at previous ASEM, APT and ASEAN plus 1 forums". (CD47)

The tradition of meetings among the ASEAN countries with Japan, China and Korea was started in the ASEM process. The linkage that ASEAN countries' establish with the Northeast Asian states creates opportunities for the Southeast Asians' role in regional affairs. Although the linkages between ASEM and Asian regionalism are more obvious among officials who are involved in the first track of the ASEM process, the sense of emerging regional awareness and the "we-ness" has also been felt by non-official actors who have participated in the ASEF P-to-P forums.

ASEM, thus, has contributed an important element to Asian regionalism through its intra-Asian coordinating mechanism. This is also an arena in which Southeast Asian countries establish a more structured regional framework with Japan, China, and Korea. The coordinating tradition has been carried forward in APT and other regional initiatives in East Asia. Southeast Asian countries have used the tradition of a policy coordination mechanism initiated in the ASEM process to engage the three big countries in the Northeast Asia to deal, in a more concerted way, with the economic challenges, social problems, and political dynamics in the region. Then, more concerted regional movements may take place beyond ASEM such as the establishment of Chiang Mai Initiatives in 2000, support for Myanmar accession to ASEM in 2004, and the establishment of EAS.

In addition, Southeast Asian participants have developed different layers of identities when being involved in the ASEM process and other fora beyond

ASEAN. The layered identities have emerged as a result of different frequencies of communication and varying intensities of inter-action among different groups of countries in East Asia. In ASEM inter-regional forums when they have encountered their European counterparts, the Asian participants involved in the cognitive process have built a collective intentionality to identify themselves as "Asian". In the forums when the EU counterparts were absent such as in intra-Asian coordinating meetings or in intra-ASEAN coordinating meetings (Figure 1.2), however, the Asian participants tended to "break down" their identities to ASEAN versus the Northeast Asian or ASEAN 5 versus "ASEAN new members", respectively.

In short, the analysis of in-depth interview data in this chapter suggests that ASEM plays a significant role in facilitating and forming the cognitive process of identity building among East Asian participants. In the words of a Thai diplomat, "Asian consciousness has developed because of ASEM" (D47). The shared regional awareness with China, Korea, and, to some extent, Japan has increased ASEAN profile and created opportunities for the Southeast Asian countries to enhance their relations with the Northeast Asian countries beyond ASEM.

The next chapter will focus on an advantage that Southeast Asian countries can acquire from their improved relations with the Northeast Asian countries like China. In such circumstance, another benefit that ASEM has delivered to Southeast Asian countries is the foreign policy advantage.

Notes

1. Despite the fact that until 2006 only thirteen Asian countries — all located in East and Southeast Asia — became ASEM partners, who called themselves the Asian group in the ASEM process. Consequently, the term "Asian identity", referring to the identity of this group, is used in this chapter. Debates over the claim of the "Asian identity" by those thirteen countries are not discussed in this research.
2. Consequently, the term "identity" in this chapter will be replaced with "identities" in the last section as it refers to these layered identities.
3. Interviewees from the representatives of business associations did not mention the linkage at all, perhaps because they tend to focus on competition and did not like the notion of sharing. One of the Malay business leaders in Malaysia said that "In terms of business, everyone is a competitor for Malaysia..." (B29).
4. At least until 2008, when the interviews were conducted with the Indonesian diplomats. See epilogue for some thoughts on ASEM in post-2008.
5. However, in absolute numbers, the number of scholars who said the positive

relations is equal to the number of representatives of civil society who said the positive relations, which is 5.

6. East Asian Economic Caucus, which is an economic cooperation made up of ASEAN countries with Japan, China and South Korea. This idea was suggested by former Malaysian Prime Minister Dr Mahathir Mohamad in 1989.

7. The former Indonesian senior diplomat is phenomenal in this regard. Despite his close involvement with ASEF, he hardly acknowledged the relations between ASEM and regional identity building in Asia. One reason for this could be related to his previous diplomatic posts outside Asia.

8. This collective coordination of both the Asian and European sides revolves around the summits, through a two-year cycle.

9. Some diplomats from ASEAN counties mentioned that they had built long friendships with diplomats from other ASEAN countries due to their frequent meetings and interactions not only when dealing with ASEAN projects but also when being posted in non-ASEAN countries (D04; D07; D15; D16; D49; D50).

10. The role of the regional coordinators is more to organize than to dictate. The nature of relationships between coordinators and other regional countries is more egalitarian than hierarchical (I45; D48).

11. Sometimes the second track is also referred to scholars or epistemic community of ASEM.

12. The issue-based leadership consists of programmes that involve a number of co-sponsoring countries willing to drive projects and initiatives in a certain policy area. Without prejudice to the role of Coordinators, countries can take the lead in sectors and on issues in which they have a particular interest and expertise (ASEM Infoboard 2008).

13. She thought it was because of the nature of culture itself that tended to be borderless (D49, Interview 2008).

14. The different levels of closeness among Asian participants in the ASEM process are examined as layered identities in Asia in the next section.

15. There were some anomalies, however, which are usually found among Japanese or Singaporean participants. The interviews with C12, C13, D50, and S80 confirmed the observation that sometimes people from these two Asian countries identify themselves as part of a "Western" rather than "Eastern" group.

16. A challenge is to find out whether this polarization also occurred among the leaders during the summits.

17. The Southeast Asian countries still perceived Japan's political and security participation in their region with more suspicion than its economic relations (Tilman 1987; Singh 2002); Japan–China relations and Japan–Korea relations are still problematic (Hundt and Bleiker 2007; Hughes 2008; Wirth 2009; Yahuda 2009).

18. A number of interviewees told with disdain that ASEM's participants from Japan and Singapore often perceived themselves as closer to the European group

than the Asian one (C12; D50; S80; see also footnote 16). This view is in line with the participant observations taken for this study. In addition, Japan does not seem to harness the ASEM process to enhance its relations with its Asian neighbours, an opportunity that was "recommended" in earlier period of ASEM establishment (Gilson 1999). Most of Japanese interviewees (D61; S64; S68; S71; S72; J75; C77; C78) also gave the impressions that underplay ASEM.

19. The founding states of ASEAN: Indonesia, Malaysia, Philippines, Singapore, and Thailand.

2

ASEM AND SOUTHEAST ASIAN COUNTRIES' FOREIGN POLICY
Case Study: The Issue of Myanmar in the 2004 ASEM Enlargement

This chapter argues that, contrary to some criticism of its role, ASEM has actually been quite useful in enhancing foreign policy advantage, at least for some Asian countries, and especially for the ASEAN countries and China. This chapter presents empirical data that show the way in which ASEAN countries and China have been able to make use of ASEM to advance their foreign policy goals. To undertake this task, this chapter uses the case of Myanmar's accession to ASEM in 2004. The case study of Myanmar was chosen for two reasons. First, the disagreement between the Asian countries and the EU countries over Myanmar's membership of ASEM created the most critical point in ASEM's history, degrading the relations between the Asians and the Europeans to their lowest point. Yet both sides managed to agree to a compromise solution to the crisis. Second, human rights is the most difficult and sensitive political issue between Asian and European states. It reflects not only the most serious difference between the two regions but also the biggest obstacle to harmonious inter-regional relations.

ASEM has been maintained because it fulfils certain interests of ASEAN and China. As the Myanmar case study will reveal, ASEAN member countries and China were able to take advantage of the ASEM enlargement in 2004, at least in this instance, to gain political advantage in their relations with the EU countries. The argument is built on the results of the interviews about the common Asian position in supporting Myanmar's accession to ASEM in

2004. The in-depth interview data as well as documentary and news studies are analysed by using the framework of traditional power games among states to pursue interests through international institutions.

This chapter investigates the advancement of foreign policy by states, a focus that has been traditionally observed by realism. Realists perceive international relations as an arena wherein states, or other international actors, pursue their interests. Even though realism treats cooperation with cynicism, one of neo-realist premises holds that states may cooperate if they "realistically" see benefits in such a strategy to advance their interests (Jervis 1988). Within this framework, international institutions are not treated as arenas of cooperation but as places in which states can exercise power (Evans and Wilson 1992; Simmons and Martin 1998, 2002). The neo-realist framework is employed to help answer the research question on the reasons for ASEM's longevity because it provides the most relevant analytical tool to examine foreign policy advantages pursued by states through international institutions to explain that joining and maintaining ASEM may be a strategic choice for East Asian countries. This chapter therefore treats ASEM as the arena where Asian and European countries exercise their power and pursue their interests through contested foreign policies.

Because ASEM appears to be their strategic choice, East Asian countries in ASEM have maintained ASEM's existence. For ASEAN countries, ASEM could provide an opportunity to enhance their regional role and to take more regional initiatives. For China, ASEM seems not only another vehicle by which to counter U.S. unilateralism as well as strengthen relations with its Asian neighbours and EU countries but also an arena in which to deal with the political hurdles of its foreign policy deriving from its democratization and human rights problems.

This chapter aims to explore the extent to which ASEAN countries and China manoeuvred in the case of the first ASEM enlargement to pursue their own foreign policy advantages. It proceeds in two main sections. The first describes the process of Myanmar's accession to ASEM in 2004 and addresses ASEAN countries' manoeuvring to support Myanmar's accession during the ASEM enlargement. The second section identifies the foreign policy advantages that China might obtain from the accession of Myanmar to ASEM in 2004 before analysing China's interests and its role in ASEM.

ASEM AS AN OPPORTUNITY TO ENHANCE ASEAN COLLECTIVE DIPLOMACY PROMINENCE

The enlargement of ASEM was envisioned from the inauguration of the forum in 1996. In the Chairman's Statement of the first ASEM Summit, point 18, it is written that, "ASEM process needed to be open and evolutionary" (ASEM Infoboard 2006*b*). In addition the Chairman's Statement of the second ASEM, point 3, states that, the "ASEM process should be open and evolutionary process; enlargement should be conducted on the basis of consensus by the heads of state and government" (ASEM Infoboard 2006*h*). Yet the challenge of the enlargement process almost suspended ASEM, and the consensual approval of new partners between the Asian and European countries proved to be difficult. ASEM faced these challenges in its first enlargement in 2004 because of power bargaining between the two regional groups which eventually became an interesting case study through which to examine how the partner countries use of ASEM's inter-regionalism to augment and support their foreign policies.

ASEAN countries continue to participate in the ASEM process probably because they have gained certain foreign policy advantages from this inter-regional forum. This section implies that the ASEM process has helped boost ASEAN's confidence and its role in Asian diplomacy. Leifer and Djiwandono (1998) observe that in the early 1990s the broad Asian regional meeting of ASEM, involving Japan, China, and Korea, served as a strategic forum to break the deadlock of the institutional linkage between ASEAN and EU countries. This research suggests that ASEM has done more for the Southeast Asian countries than just safeguard their relations with the EU. ASEM seems to have not only given ASEAN member countries opportunities to play more significant roles among East Asia countries but also to take a more assertive position towards their European counterparts when dealing with a politically sensitive issue.

This section investigates the political advantages that ASEAN countries gained from the Myanmar case. The first section elaborates the Myanmar case in the ASEM enlargement process. The second section analyses Myanmar's human rights problems in Asia-EU relations and the ASEM process that enables ASEAN to take a leading role on the Asian side of ASEM. The former focuses more on the tensions over Myanmar's accession in the ASEM process whereas the latter places the Myanmar case in the broader context of ASEAN-EU and Asia-EU tensions over human rights. Although repetition seems unavoidable, it reflects the parallel tensions created by the Myanmar human rights problems in the ASEM process and in ASEAN-EU relations.

The process of Myanmar's accession to ASEM is an important case not only to observe the challenge in the ASEM's enlargement but also to study the role of ASEAN in Asia-Europe relations. The EU concern about human rights violations in Myanmar has been dominating the political dialogue in the ASEM process. Historically, Myanmar's human rights problem was a key obstacle in EU relations with ASEAN (Yawnghwe 2004; Petersson 2006; Li and Zheng 2009). The problem has been hindering ASEAN-EU relations since the Myanmar military government, known as the State Law and Order Restoration Council (SLORC), now renamed State Peace and Development Council (SPDC), denied the victory of the opposition party of the National League for Democracy (NLD) at the general election in 1990 and imprisoned its leader Aung San Suu Kyi in 1993. This suppression of the democratization movement has provoked immense international criticism of SLORC/SPDC, not only by EU and the United States but also some Asian leaders. The Asian countries, however, reject the intervention of Western countries, including the EU, in their political affairs and urge that their approach, "the ASEAN way" that has become "a distinctive diplomatic and security culture of the Southeast Asian countries" (Haacke 2003, p. 58), is more applicable to the Myanmar case. The ASEAN countries insist that other countries should approach the military regime by establishing collegial dialogues and cooperation rather than through boycotts and condemnation.

The different approaches towards human rights and democratization problems in Myanmar have sharpened the differences in values and heightened the political debate between Asian and EU countries. The practice of human rights is the toughest issue in the relations between Asian and Europe countries, and has been a critical point in their political relations (Palmujoki 1997; Petersson 2006; Wiessala 2007). In ASEM, the human rights issue has been perceived as a "weak point" too (Fouquet 2002; Nguyen, Nguyen and Duong 2004; Wiessala 2007); it has been made more complicated with the involvement of civil society (Gilson 2002, pp. 161–65). ASEM documents such as the Chairman's Statement of the first Summit, especially point 7[1] and the Chairman's Statement of the third Summit, point 5[2] and 8,[3] have been criticized as having an ambivalent nature regarding human right issues. Indeed, the Myanmar case was the issue that almost created a deadlock in the inter-government track of the ASEM process, especially preceding the fifth Summit in Hanoi in 2004.

In the early 2000s, the EU made its position clear in regard to ASEM enlargement. The European countries unilaterally determined that while ASEM had to accept the EU's new member countries, which were under the accession process, the inter-regional forum could not automatically accept ASEAN's new member countries. In the European Commission's policy entitled "Europe and Asia: A Strategic Framework for Enhanced Partnerships" issued in 2001 (EC 2001), it is stated that:

The value of the ASEM process will be further enhanced through a broader participation. The Commission would welcome an enlargement of Asian participation in ASEM to include key representatives of the Sub-Continent, as well as Australia and New Zealand (just as the EU's participation in ASEM should in due course *be enlarged in line with the enlargement of the Union itself*). (EC 2001, p. 25) (emphasis by author)

In addition, in their specific policy for the Southeast Asian countries issued in 2003, "A new partnership with South East Asia", the EU states,

The EU and ASEM partners, in particular those of South East Asia, will have to meet the challenge of their respective enlargement in time for the 2004 Hanoi Summit. In this regard it is encouraging to note that the members of ASEAN have recently and publicly expressed their support to the resuming of the national reconciliation process in Burma/Myanmar. Both sides will strive to avoid letting the question of the participation of Burma/Myanmar endanger the ASEM process itself. (EC 2003, p. 13)

Preceding the fifth ASEM summit, however, ASEAN countries took advantage of the momentum of EU enlargement to push forward Myanmar's accession. When the EU insisted that ASEM enlargement include ten new EU countries, Southeast Asian countries in ASEM also urged that three newly accessed ASEAN countries — including Myanmar — be made ASEM partners as well. Some interviewees revealed this circumstance as below,

Myanmar issues started when the country acceded to ASEAN in 1997. The EU refused to automatically accept Myanmar as ASEM partner due to its human right problems. ASEAN did not like EU refusal but did not insist on Myanmar membership. When EU insisted its ten new members to be automatically accepted as ASEM partners in 2004, ASEAN used the momentum to push forward their support for Myanmar membership in ASEM. (S09)

ASEAN used the momentum of the EU enlargement to push Myanmar admission to ASEM. (I14)

It is ASEAN movement that pushed membership of Myanmar during 1997–2000 till 2004. General rule is: it is better to have Myanmar in than out so we can tell them. (S53)

By this point, the Myanmar issue had not only developed into an irritant in Asia-EU relations but also become the dominant political agenda, overshadowing other important cooperative proposals.

The tension between Asian and European countries arose during the period from 2003 to 2004 when the two regional groups in the ASEM process negotiated their position on Myanmar's accession to the inter-regional forum. EU's criticism of human rights violations in Myanmar had been articulated rigorously through economic sanctions, beginning in 1996, and political isolation. When ASEAN opened membership to Myanmar in 1997, the EU was disappointed and some EU-based human rights groups criticized ASEAN. In addition Myanmar accession to ASEAN also led to the suspension of political dialogue between ASEAN and the EU. The Myanmar problem added to the already problematic political areas between the ASEAN and the EU which included democratic problems and human rights abuses in Singapore, Cambodia, Laos, Indonesia, Thailand and Malaysia. One result of the political tension between the Asian and European states on Myanmar's accession to ASEM was the cancellation of two ASEM economic ministerial meetings several months before the fifth ASEM Summit in Hanoi on 8–9 October 2004 by the European countries. The ASEM financial and economic ministers meetings were planned to set a path for a closer economic partnership between Asia and Europe that would be presented at the Summit. Ironically, this economic cooperation was halted by a political disagreement.

The tension started when the European partners sponsored by the United Kingdom insisted that human rights problems in Myanmar, exemplified by the detention of NDL activists and their leader Aung San Suu Kyi by the SPDC Regime in May 2003, were put on the agenda for the fifth Foreign Ministers' Meeting (FMM) on 23–24 July 2003 in Bali, Indonesia. The talk on Myanmar in this forum led to disagreement between the European and Asian countries on the ASEM enlargement at the 2004 Summit. The European countries asserted that Myanmar had to meet certain political criteria before this country could be accepted as an ASEM partner, whereas the Asian countries argued that if ten EU member countries were to be accepted automatically as ASEM partners, then so should new ASEAN members which consisted of Laos, Cambodia, and Myanmar (*Asia Times*, 25 July 2003; Bersick 2004; Friberg 2004). The Southeast Asian countries did not press hard for ASEM to include Myanmar earlier, not only because not all ASEAN members welcomed Myanmar membership to ASEM but also the ASEAN way of dealing with difficult issues is to avoid conflict and to move in directions through which unanimity can be reached. Their diplomatic style is "reserved", avoiding potential refusal by fellow members as well as external partners. In addition, the ASEAN and Asian countries had low confidence due to the Asian financial crisis.

In May 2004, when the EU widening process with new ten member countries from Central and Eastern Europe was being finalized, the ASEM European partners indicated that those new members would automatically become European partners in the ASEM process. Since Myanmar, Laos and Cambodia had been admitted to ASEAN in 1997 and 1998, they took this opportunity to log their applications to be ASEM partners too. Their applications were supported by the Asian countries, especially some ASEAN countries, namely Malaysia (D15; see also Friberg 2004; *Taipei Times*, 23 June 2004) and Indonesia (D01; D06). Whereas the European countries used the Myanmar application to express their concern over the human rights situation in the country, the ASEAN countries made use of the accession of the ten EU new members to guard the inclusion of its new members. ASEAN took advantage of the new EU member accession to the ASEM as a golden opportunity to push Europe to accept Myanmar.

The opposing Asian and European positions on this enlargement process increased political tension between the two regional groups. Senior officials from Asian countries developed their common position in early March 2004 in Hanoi before meeting their counterparts in Kildare, Ireland, in April 2004. Indeed, the negotiations between senior officials from the Asian countries and EU countries also took place in an unusual place for an ASEM meeting, in Washington, DC, on 24 April 2004 (Appendix II). However, the Washington meeting was conducted only among key actors in the Myanmar case.

While normally holding different positions regarding support for Myanmar, ASEAN countries managed to form a relatively common position in Myanmar's accession to ASEM in 2004. The informal ASEAN foreign ministers meeting in early March 2004 reconfirmed the ASEAN position that all members of ASEAN must be able to participate at the Hanoi Summit. "We did agree ... that no political conditions be attached on their admission to ASEM", said Indonesian Foreign Minister Hassan Wirajuda (Rowse 2004). A report in the European media mentions that Indonesia would blame EU if the ASEM process collapsed over the Myanmar issue (*EU Business*, 28 June 2004). Despite Cambodia's previous request for EU support, Cambodian Prime Minister (PM) Hun Sen also mentioned that Cambodia would not join ASEM unless the two other new ASEAN members — Laos and Myanmar — were accepted at the same time (Boyd 2004; *Vietnam News*, 9 August 2004; *Xinhua*, 7 July 2004). Myanmar PM General Khin Nyunt met Vietnamese PM Phan Van Khai in August to talk about Myanmar's participation at the October ASEM Summit. The meeting was also attended by Hanoi-based ambassadors and diplomats from ASEAN members to show ASEAN solidarity (*Vietnam News*, 9 August 2004).

The ASEAN countries' common position in supporting Myanmar's accession into ASEM was derived from the ASEAN position on Myanmar in general. Several key ASEAN diplomats mentioned in interviews that:

Asian countries are solid enough in Myanmar case to "fight" against EU especially due to EU policy towards the country. (D03)

The common position is external actor has to treat ASEAN as 10 and APT as 13; excluding Myanmar is not accepted.... Decision on Myanmar is made in consensus. ASEAN does not want to be divided because of Myanmar. (D17)

In ASEM meeting 2006 in Tokyo, Asian took a common position on Myanmar when EU raised the issues. Only a few EU countries are vocal on Myanmar, usually the United Kingdom and Netherlands, but they do have common position. So ASEAN [countries] too want to come with common position but there is always problem in practice. ASEAN will maintain collective position and will not break up due to Myanmar. Due to difference in interests, thirteen Asian states usually produce compromise position on Myanmar. There has been qualitative change on ASEAN approach to Myanmar. (D16)

Relatively, there is no significant disagreement among the Asian countries; all suggested that the European understand the Asian way when considering human right issues in Asian countries. (S10) (translated from Indonesian)

The basic principle of non-interference is respected. ASEAN does not want to be dictated by external power. ASEAN regional cohesion to protect the non-interference principle is strong because it is suitable with our values and culture. (S20)

At non-government level, some Asian countries have stronger position against Myanmar Junta but at government level, Asia seems have "common positions". (S23)

Yes, there are ASEAN common positions on Myanmar. Every year ASEM MFA heard briefing from Myanmar MF. Then the FMM made Joint Communiqué in which points on Myanmar are included. The Joint Communiqué reflects ASEAN common position on Myanmar. (S35)

EU-ASEAN differences in political values mentioned by S20 and S21 are not the only reasons behind ASEAN common position to support Myanmar's accession to ASEM. As countries located in the area surrounding Myanmar, the Southeast Asian countries understand well the negative geopolitical implications of condemning and isolating Myanmar. Some scholars expressed this point,

As for human rights and democracy problems in Myanmar, ASEAN cooperation has maintained prudently due to geopolitics, i.e. India versus China and the risk of Myanmar disintegration. These concerns are not shared by EU and the United States, at least not at the same degree of the ASEAN countries. (S10)

Malaysia's vision is for Myanmar to be safe and be a democracy. We need to understand their problem; They do want to be a democracy but they also have dilemma. Other Asian diplomat shared Malaysian vision on Myanmar. (D15)

ASEAN current concern does not only derive from bad treatment to Myanmar people by the Junta but also by Myanmar's engagement with China. ASEAN concern because Myanmar opens the door for China and India to get into Southeast Asia. It diminishes ASEAN's effort to engage China and India strategically in Asia. (S33)

The concern for geopolitical implications of Myanmar's disintegration and its involvement in India–China competition has become one of the driving forces behind the push from ASEAN countries to approach the military junta. ASEAN countries have pursued several initiatives including the flexible or constructive engagement policies and high-level visits to the country. ASEAN countries' strategy to deal with Myanmar is revealed by several senior diplomats:

Inside ASEAN pressed Myanmar but it maintained support to the country at international forums. ASEAN common position is to oppose UN resolution on Myanmar — in 1990s — due to the principle of non-interference. ASEAN position was seconded by China. (D18)

ASEAN common policy on Myanmar is (1) to Myanmar, ASEAN put internal pressure; and (2) to EU, ASEAN [countries] explain the circumstance. (D06)

The Asian talked about and to Myanmar "behind the door". (S19)

For Asia, engaging Myanmar is better than boycotting the country. "Face-saving" in Asian diplomacy is also important. There was difference of opinion in ASEAN when accepting Myanmar as a member but the need to have ASEAN 10 was bigger. (S22)

ASEAN won't take harsh step towards Myanmar; internally, ASEAN does have a problem with Myanmar but ASEAN is aware of pressure from the West. ASEAN usually took face-saving solution for Myanmar... To be consistent with the ASEAN way and to help Myanmar, like Vietnam-Cambodia case, ASEAN has also tried to discuss solution with Myanmar. But they were mostly done outside of ASEAN framework — by individual ASEAN countries like Indonesia, Malaysia, and Thailand — in order to protect ASEAN reputation in case of failure. (S20)

Thus, ASEAN countries which had barely achieved a common position on Myanmar (Haacke 2006) were able to solicit support from all ASEAN members to promote Myanmar's accession to ASEM. To borrow the words of a senior Indonesian diplomat, "[The] ASEAN collegiality has been built pretty strongly especially to encounter external actors" (D06).

In addition to their success in internal negotiations to promote Myanmar's participation in the ASEM process, ASEAN countries took the lead in the formulation and the defence of the "Asian" position to support Myanmar's accession to ASEM. They managed to obtain support from the Northeast Asian countries in ASEM. The ASEAN countries' position to secure Myanmar's participation in ASEM was supported by China (S01; S18; see also Bersick 2004) and to some extent by Japan (Togo 2004). A former ASEAN Secretary General revealed that:

> When EU insisted to include their new members in the ASEM process, Asian countries in ASEM also insisted that all ASEAN members be included. I believe Northeast Asian countries supported this ASEAN position but I do not know how intense their support was. Because it was an ASEAN matter, the Northeast Asian countries left it to ASEAN to decide. (S35)

On Japan's behaviour, a Thai diplomat commented:

> Japan has [an] interest in Myanmar and [is] close to both ASEAN and EU so this country would not say anything on Myanmar at the ASEM forums. (D48)

However, a Japanese diplomat revealed further insights,

> EU uses ASEM to press ASEAN on Myanmar. Japan is somewhere in the middle [between ASEAN and EU] but human rights is Japan's basic value and no compromise on it. Japan's position is close to ASEAN and hope ASEAN is more active. Unlike EU, Japan also did bilateral pressure on Myanmar through engage policy and maintaining small humanitarian aid. (D61)

The region-to-region meeting format of ASEM appeared to benefit ASEAN's effort to push forward Myanmar's accession and to gain the support of key ASEM partners in Northeast Asia. This is the application of what Gilson (2007) describes as "strategic regionalism". The ASEAN countries joined with China to put pressure on the EU countries regarding Myanmar's participation in ASEM. With support from the Northeast Asian countries, ASEAN was more determined to force the EU members to accept Myanmar to ASEM. Asian countries would block the admission of EU's new members to the

ASEM if the EU would not accept Myanmar (D01; D06; also *Taipei Times*, 23 June 2004).

From the European perspective, the EU put forward conditions for Myanmar's accession to ASEM in addition to previous economic sanctions, travel bans, and the freezing of financial assets as stated in the European Parliament's resolutions on Burma, in particular those of 11 April 2002, 13 March 2003, 5 June 2003 and 4 September 2003, and the Council Common Position 2003/297/CFSP of 28 April 2003 (*IIAS* 2004). The EU's conditions for Myanmar's participation were the release of Aung San Suu Kyi from her house confinement, free participation of the NLD at the National Convention, and a more concrete timeframe for Myanmar democratization (Rowse 2004; Burma Campaign UK 2004; *BBC*, 13 July 2004). As a result, both Asian and European officers and diplomats were concerned that this tension would result in the cancelling of ASEM's fifth Summit in Hanoi (Asia-Europe-network 2004; Friberg 2004; *Guardian*, 27 August 2004), which might eventually shatter the ASEM process (Haacke 2003; Yawnghwe 2004).

Until the beginning of 2004, the problem of Myanmar's admittance was still unable to be resolved by the Asian and European countries and it became a serious hindrance to the ASEM process. This political disagreement haunted the sixth FMM on 17–18 April 2004 in Kildare, Ireland, as time was elapsing towards the fifth summit. The foreign ministers addressed the issue of the enlargement of ASEM and specifically mentioned the Myanmar case through the Chairman's Statement, but it was clear that political dialogue between the two camps was unable to reach a consensus. This difficult situation was heightened by the uncooperative attitude of the Myanmar military regime that stalled the second round of the Bangkok Process in April 2004 and held the National Constitution Convention without NLD participation in May 2004.[4] The climax of this tension was reached when the European countries cancelled the ASEM Financial Ministers' Meeting, scheduled for 6 July 2004 in Brussels, and the ASEM Economic Ministers' Meeting, scheduled for 16–17 September 2004 in Rotterdam. Asian countries, particularly Indonesia, Malaysia and Thailand, were outraged at the cancellation which was not a result of proper consultation with ASEAN (*Taipei Times*, 23 June 2004; Vichitsorasatra 2004). Following the deadlock, the ASEM SOM Meeting in Tokyo on 8–9 July 2004 was not able to bring the Asian and EU countries to a common position on the Myanmar issue either (Boyd 2004).

Nevertheless, the Europeans strove to bridge the gap between the Asians' and the Europeans' positions by approaching ASEAN countries. Britain's Deputy Foreign Minister, Mike O'Brien, met Vietnam's Deputy Prime Minister Vu Khoan in March 2004. EU foreign policy chief Javier Solana and

Commissioner Chris Patten lobbied strongly with ASEAN ministers to narrow the EU-ASEAN differences during the ASEAN Post Ministerial Meeting and ASEAN Regional Forum (ARF) in Jakarta at the end of June (*World News*, 2 July 2004). The Dutch Government, holding the EU presidential chair, appointed a senior diplomat and former Dutch foreign minister and EU Commissioner of External Relations, Hans van den Broek, as a special envoy to Hanoi, Bangkok, Beijing, and Tokyo to negotiate with the Asian countries (*BBC*, 13 July 2004; *China View*, 26 August 2004; *Daily Times*, 1 September 2004). In addition, Dutch Foreign Minister Bernard Bot visited Indonesia in August 2004 and the Secretary of State for Foreign Affairs of France, Renaud Muselier, flew to Singapore in September 2004 (Boyd 2004) to negotiate with the Southeast Asian countries.

ASEAN's assertive position in backing up Myanmar's accession to ASEM successfully placed the European countries in a dilemma between their relations with Asian countries versus their human rights values. Under pressure not only to save the ASEM Summit but also EU relations with the Asian countries, the European Council met informally on 3 September 2004 in Maastricht, the Netherlands (*AFP* 2004). The United Kingdom took the strongest stance against Myanmar's admission whereas France and Germany called for a compromise (*Daily Telegraph*, 21 July 2004; MacAskill and Gentleman 2004). Determined to save the ASEM process but not send the wrong message to the Myanmar military regime, the Council decided to accept Burma's entry into ASEM during the ASEM Summit in Hanoi as long as it was represented by a lower level officer (rather than a head of state) (Westerfield 2004). This decision was followed by the European Parliament decision to call on ASEAN to exercise more influence on the SPDC regime (European Parliament 2004)

The ASEM Summit took place as scheduled on 8–9 October 2004 in Hanoi, attended by thirty-nine partners: twenty-five EU and thirteen Asian leaders, as well as EU president Romano Prodi. As part of the compromise, Myanmar was represented by Foreign Minister Major General Nyan Win. Both Asian and European sides avoided an open discussion of Myanmar issues and directed the agenda more towards economic and cultural relations (*Bangkok Post*, 6 September 2004). To the disappointment of many Europeans, Myanmar was admitted to ASEM in the Hanoi Summit. But this was a victory for ASEAN; the EU gave in (S08).

In regard to this circumstance, one may perceive the Myanmar case not as a power game between the Asian and the European countries but as a learning process in which the EU countries were willing to learn and respect the perspectives of their counterparts, in this case the East Asian states. In a conversation regarding the relations between Asian and European countries, an Austrian senior diplomat who used to live in Asian countries revealed that:

> EU has been developing an understanding on the Myanmar case. Unlike the United States, we would like to put pressure on the military regime but at the same time we do not want to sanction them and become harsh to them; it does not work. We would prefer to cooperate with them and help their way to democracy. This is the European value (A01, personal communication, 2005)

In the interviews for this study, European interviewees such as B26, B27, S36, I42, and S32 shared A01's view.

Nevertheless, by supporting Myanmar's accession to ASEM, ASEAN countries took advantage of the region-to-region framework to respond to the European criticism of human rights practices. In this case, the EU refusal to Myanmar united ASEAN and made the Asian countries stand up for Myanmar even more strongly. In addition, the Myanmar case allows ASEAN countries to take the lead on the Asian side of ASEM as their position is supported by China, Japan and Korea.

ASEAN COUNTRIES' GROWING CONFIDENCE IN THE ASEM PROCESS

The previous section described the tension between the Asian and European groups in the ASEM process during the first ASEM enlargement over the Myanmar issue. This section analyses the place of Myanmar's human rights problems in ASEAN-EU relations and shows how ASEM's inter-regionalism has enabled ASEAN to take a leading role on the Asian side in regard to support for Myanmar's accession to ASEM.

In the last few decades, the EU has risen up as a global actor regarding human rights issues. While still striving to apply consistent practices of human rights norms, especially in relations to immigrants from Africa and Islamic countries, EU countries have emphasized that human rights are at the centre of "the European Common values" (Palmujoki 1997; Bretherton and Vogler 2006) and has actively promoted the values as universal (Schmit 2001; Bretherton and Vogler 2006). In addition, the European concept of human rights has recently expanded to human security and this value has been projected to other countries as it is imbedded in the European Security and Defence Policy (Kaldor, Martin and Selchow 2007). As a result, EU countries apply the strongest external pressure on the SLORC/SPDC. Although human rights and Free Burma activists have criticized the EU for its inconsistent policy towards Myanmar (Burma Campaign UK 2004; Yawnghwe 2004; Wiessala 2007), the EU still maintains economic sanctions, including aid, to Myanmar companies, and a ban on visas for military officials.

Due to the EU's ambition to create an image as the global promoter of human rights, the European countries have criticized Asian countries, including those who are perceived as supporters or protectors of abusive countries in the region. Human rights issues in Myanmar have been raised by EU countries when they encounter people from Asian countries in various forums, as revealed by interviewees below:

> In ASEM meetings, pressure from EU on Myanmar issues was very strong. (S73)

> EU talked about Myanmar everywhere, including in bilateral meeting (with Thailand) as if there are no other more important things. (D50)

> ASEAN and Asian states have to encounter Myanmar issues whenever they have meeting with external power. (D16)

> The Myanmar issue has especially been raised by EU to press Asia. (D01)

> In ASEM process, Asia and Europe have agreed many things and not much to disagree and be suspicious. The difference is on the speed of how to do things. ASEM forum is to exchange opinion and understand the difference. Asian countries discussed a lot on Myanmar issue and explained it to the EU. Currently we also want Myanmar to explain its circumstances. But Myanmar is not the only issue but it is certainly where strong voices were heard. (D30)

> EU pressure may present indirectly when ASEAN diplomats were invited at the Myanmar debates at European Parliament. EU uses soft power to influence the Asian. (D04)

Consequently, EU criticisms of Asian human rights practice have become psychological pressures for Asian officials and elites in their relations with European fellows.

Nevertheless, Asian human rights practices have been improving. From the early 2000s, one cannot make the generalization that all Asian countries have neglected human rights standards. Southeast Asian countries have adopted a human rights clause in their ASEAN Charter despite their internal disagreement and have launched the regional human rights commission body in the fifteenth ASEAN Summit in Thailand in 2009. Indeed, SPDC's responses to ASEAN approaches and pressure from Western countries on ASEAN to put more pressure on Myanmar have lately changed ASEAN countries' policies towards this country. This movement is revealed by some interviewees:

> The non-interference in ASEAN has been calibrated due to changing global context. Joint communiqué on Myanmar is not perceived as interference anymore... ASEAN will keep engaging Myanmar. There is always ASEAN joint communiqué on Myanmar but at the same time ASEAN encourages Myanmar to go further with democratization. (D07)

> At the beginning, ASEAN had been conservative to reject EU's intervention to Myanmar's human right issue. However ... EU's pressure on human rights issues on ASEAN is currently in line with domestic changes within the ASEAN countries and human rights initiative at regional level ... Internally Asian position was relatively solid to support Myanmar. However, among scholars there was an understanding that the EU pressure on Myanmar and Asia on the human rights should be seen as a lesson learned by Asia that regional and global relations were intertwined with domestic problems ... EU's pressure on human rights issue in ASEAN was in fact in line with domestic change within the ASEAN countries and HR initiative at regional level. (S10) (translated from Indonesian)

> In the Myanmar case, the Asians maintain non-interference at g-to-g level. At p-to-p level however, Asian diplomats and people have intervened a lot in Myanmar. (S23)

> There has been a shift in ASEAN's policy on Myanmar. Domestic change has changed ASEAN's policy on Myanmar too. (S32)

> ASEAN's common position on Myanmar has shifted from that in 1990s. Despite rhetoric principle of non-interference, ASEAN has challenged the principle: through the engagement policy, Ibrahim's and Mahathir's visits, Thai's constructive engagement, etc. (S33)

The change in ASEAN policy towards Myanmar resulted from the ASEAN countries' frustration with the military junta and a growing common perception that the country has become a problem for ASEAN.

The human rights issue in Myanmar had actually been problematic both internally and externally for ASEAN countries since the country was admitted to the regional organization in 1997. Internally, despite their formal statements, ASEAN had not had a coherent, single policy on Myanmar due to the different degrees of attachment each country had with the military regime. Externally, Myanmar also put ASEAN in a difficult situation in international forums. ASEAN was warned by the European Union and the United States to put more pressure on Myanmar. Many Asian diplomats expressed their disappointment that the Myanmar issue was brought to almost every international forum especially by their European counterparts as if no other issues were more important (D04; D17; D48; D50).

Nevertheless, ASEAN used the ASEM enlargement issue to press the EU harder on this politically sensitive point. In the past, ASEAN-EU relations were drawn by political issues, and as a result the two sub-regional organizations failed to move forward into more successful economic and cultural relations. Clinging to the ASEAN principle of non-interference, ASEAN warned those Western countries not to intervene in domestic issues (I42; also Palmujoki 1997). In the ASEM enlargement conflict, while adopting a changed policy towards Myanmar,[5] ASEAN countries determined to send a message to the European countries that they had their own approach to deal with Myanmar and that the Europeans could not dictate their human rights practices. In addition, ASEAN had its own considerations regarding the human rights and democracy problems in Myanmar that were not concerned with the EU and other Western countries. For example, the ASEAN approach has been maintained prudently due to geopolitics, India versus China, and the risk of Myanmar's disintegration (S10; D15; D18). Through its strong position in support of Myanmar's admission to ASEM, Asian countries insisted that the European countries acknowledge the "Asian way" in dealing with political issues of its member countries.

While ASEAN and Asian support for Myanmar admission was somehow predictable for the EU, the European countries apparently did not expect that the Asian countries were willing to back up Myanmar at the expense of the ASEM process. In spite of the frequent absence of European leaders at the ASEM summits, the EU side was very active in approaching the Asian countries to break the deadlock (*BBC*, 13 July 2004; *China View*, 26 August 2004; *Daily Times*, 1 September 2004). This behaviour can be understood since EU's economic interest in Asia was paramount. Asian countries were the EU's second largest trading partner at the end of the 1990s and became the biggest trading partner in 2008 (EC 2007, 2009*b*). After their success in overcoming the Asian financial crisis, the Asian economies have become stronger. In the strategy document issued by the European Commission (EC) in July 2003 entitled *A new partnership with Southeast Asia*, it was mentioned that "the EU has stronger common interests — economic, political and security — with South-East Asia than ever before" (EC 2003).

Previously, economic interest had also been the basis for European relations with ASEAN, but what was different in the ASEM enlargement case was the fact that China, the giant economic attraction and perhaps the most "attractive" Asian state for the Europeans, was on the Asian side (as will be described later in this chapter). It was clear that the Europeans could afford not to compromise their political values at the ASEAN-EU forum, thus creating a substantial hurdle blocking progress of the forum, but they could not act similarly in ASEM due to the China factor. Compared with Japan and South Korea, China was much closer to Myanmar (S32; I42; S53; S70) and this regional power was very supportive to the ASEAN's position in the enlargement dispute (D01; S09; S10: S33; D47; S66). With the support of large Asian countries, ASEAN was confident that it could counter the EU political pressure on the Myanmar issues. ASEAN countries successfully pressed European officials to agree that sanctions were not a solution to the Myanmar problem; to engage Myanmar with international society would help the regime to understand common practices in democratic societies and the international society's expectations. The compromise solution to the Myanmar accession problem, in which European counterparts asked ASEAN and China to approach and encourage Myanmar to obey international law on human rights (Wiessala 2007; Li and Zheng 2009), indicates that the EU regarded that ASEAN countries had similar political influence on Myanmar as China. This was the leverage expected by ASEAN as it led the Asian position on the issue. The Southeast Asian countries were content because they knew that the Northeast Asian countries, especially China, would back up ASEAN's position regarding Myanmar's accession to ASEM.

ASEAN's confidence increased, parallel with the development of a regional movement in Asia. ASEAN is in the driver's seat of the ASEAN Plus Three (APT) and this fosters closer relations with each of the Northeast Asian countries. The establishment of APT since 1997 has given ASEAN special relations with Japan, China and Korea within a broad framework, including the East Asia Cooperation, declared in 1999, or in particular fields such as the financial agreement manifested in the Chiang Mai initiatives. Beside the APT format, ASEAN Plus One has also been developed. In 2003, China was amended to the Treaty of Amity and Cooperation (TAC) and signed the China–ASEAN Free Trade Agreement (CAFTA) (Ba 2003; Saw, Sheng and Chin 2005). China was a more active partner in this movement and had employed a comprehensive strategy to increase relations with the Southeast Asian countries for economic as well as political reasons (Percival 2007; Ravenhill and Yang 2009). Consequently, China's move encouraged Japan to revise its policy on bilateral trade agreements and to negotiate on the Japan–ASEAN FTA. Korea followed a similar path to that of Japan and China (Chalermpalanupap 2009).

Another development was the transition of ASEAN to a more institutionalized sub-regional institution. At the 2003 summit, ASEAN leaders launched a sub-regional vision for the ASEAN community that would comprise a security community, economic community and socio-cultural community, as well as affirm external policies that would make ASEAN a vital player in the international community, able to advance ASEAN's common interests (ASEAN 2009*b*). Later, after the Myanmar case in ASEM, ASEAN countries have continued to strengthen the ASEAN's institution. According to several ASEAN diplomats interviewed for this study, in the last decade ASEAN has developed into a more reliable regional institution and the Southeast Asian countries now place ASEAN as the first priority in foreign policy (D06; D07; D16; D17; D47; D48). The commitment of Southeast Asian countries to strengthen ASEAN is evident in their efforts, not only to undertake institutional reform (Chalermpalanupap 2009) but also to establish the ASEAN Charter in 2007 (Hernandez 2007; ASEAN 2009*c*) which includes a provision on ASEAN human rights commission; an indication of the emergence of supranational dimension in the political field. In the past, although ASEAN was unable to establish a deep economic integration (Simanjuntak 2004), ASEAN's vision seemed to be driven mainly by economic interests to achieve the ASEAN Free Trade Area in 2015. The ASEAN Charter reflects ASEAN leaders' determination to move ASEAN towards being a security community, indicating the changing nature of Southeast Asian regionalism (Hernandez 2007; Caballero-Anthony 2009). One of interviewees who participated deeply in the formulation of the Charter acknowledged that:

> Indonesia proposed ASEAN Security Community because it would be impossible to integrate further without political and security cooperation. (D07)

He also revealed the logic behind the ASEAN institutional development:

> The growth and rivalry of China-India encourage ASEAN to strengthen itself, to take driving force and to hold central role in Asia.... There is no specific institutionalization of ASEAN's role in the driving seat of EAS and ARF, yet the decision can only be decided when ASEAN countries agree. (D07)

The institutional development suggests ASEAN has been evolving to adjust to changes in the domestic level of its member countries and in regional and global environments. "Old ASEAN", characterized by a loose institutionalization and governed by the principle of non-interference, could not be relied on to help its member countries to counter post-Cold War security problems and the Asian financial crisis. ASEAN has been challenged to find its relevance and to reconsider an institutional development and norms revision, otherwise it will become obsolete. Since the enlargement to ASEAN 10 in 1999, the regional institution has taken prudent but progressive measures to build a community economically, politically and socially. The sub-regional institution managed to conclude a difficult negotiation for the Charter (D03; D16) and now is involving civil society (D07). It has diluted the principle of non-interference, too. In the case of the ASEM enlargement, while ASEAN assertively backed Myanmar's accession against the European countries' rejection, it also lobbied the military junta to release Aung San Suu Kyi and undertake democratic reform (D01; D07; D47). To borrow the words of an ASEAN scholar, "On Myanmar case, ASEAN maintains the non-interference at g-to-g [sic] level; at p-to-p [sic] level, however, ASEAN diplomats and people have intervened a lot on Myanmar" (S23). Therefore, we can assume that the actors (agent) and the institution (structure) of ASEAN have evolved in an interactive process to adjust to the current circumstances. This is the process that is expected of a regional institution like ASEAN.

Another factor that has helped increase ASEAN confidence is the uneasy relations between Japan and China. The two countries have a bitter historical experience that has been carried into their contemporary political relations even though their economic relations have been enhanced.[6] The strong economic relations between the two countries and the common interests to maintain regional stability, however, do not prevent people of the two countries from distrusting each other. Competitive feelings and antipathy could be felt when interviewing Japanese and Chinese scholars. With the rise of a regional grouping in East Asia, a quest for regional leadership inevitably must consider these two countries but neither is accepted to lead either by the other party or by the Southeast Asian countries (D02; S22; S33; S35; S65; S66; S68; S81). This circumstance gives ASEAN room to manoeuvre as indicated by some interviewees:

> Japan and China compete to approach ASEAN. Japan only rushed to establish FTA with ASEAN after China did it. Currently the political climate in East Asia is better as Japan-China relations are getting better. It is a big relief for ASEAN. ASEAN plays China-Japan card, trying to have equal distance with the two, and taking in India to balance them. (S56)

> Of the ten ASEAN dialogue partners, Japan, China and Korea are the closest. [Due to Japan-China competition] ASEAN is in the driving seat of APT. Individually, none of ASEAN country can do it but together under ASEAN they have tried to do their best. (D06) (Translated from Indonesian)

> Japan-China relations are [a] dilemma for ASEAN. If the two are in conflict, ASEAN has to "lead"; yet if the two are peaceful, ASEAN will be "dictated". (S22)

Asia [countries] versus China is not a bandwagon but soft balance. The more Japan-China competes, the more important ASEAN. (S71)

As a consequence, Japan and China appear to let ASEAN lead initiatives. A Japanese diplomat mentioned that, "It is a right decision for ASEAN to include Myanmar: to engage Myanmar and to keep ASEAN access to Myanmar" (D62). However, some people questioned that ASEAN was really in the driving seat in East Asia (S22; S68; S71). Despite questions about its institutional capacity, the competing relations between Japan and China make ASEAN a hub if not a leading player in East Asian politics and diplomacy.

The regional dynamics have also given ASEAN confidence to be more assertive in its external relations, including with European partners in the ASEM process. In the Myanmar accession case, ASEAN countries were able to negotiate, more or less, a common position not only among themselves but also with the three Northeast Asian countries. Whereas ASEAN diplomacy was segmented in the Cambodian conflict settlement in 1992–93 (Leifer 1999), in the Myanmar case the sub-regional institution managed a collective diplomatic voice to back up Myanmar's accession to ASEM. As a senior Malaysian diplomat says, "ASEAN will maintain collective positions and will not break up due to Myanmar…" (D16). When challenged by criticism that ASEAN countries are too diverse to come up with common positions (S09; S33; S53), a former ASEAN high-ranking official revealed that even when they did not share common positions, ASEAN leaders and officials had a substantial common understanding of each other's positions (S20).

Therefore, it is possible to argue that ASEAN countries are not only more confident but have also taken a leading role in Asian position-taking in the ASEM process. The ASEAN countries were more confident to take advantage of the ASEM enlargement process to press their political position even further regarding Myanmar's human rights practices to the EU. The participation of the Northeast Asian countries, particularly China, on the Asian side of ASEM added substantial weight to the Asian countries' bargaining position vis-à-vis their European counterparts in the ASEM process. The next section will analyse China's interest in ASEM and its role in ASEM's longevity.

COLLABORATION BETWEEN SOUTHEAST ASIAN COUNTRIES AND CHINA IN THE MYANMAR CASE

China has played a significant role in the ASEM process. This Asian regional power has not only actively supported ASEM activities but has also added significant weight to the Asian side of ASEM. China's support of ASEAN countries' efforts to promote Myanmar's accession to ASEM significantly enhanced ASEAN bargaining position with EU countries. However, the support China has given to ASEAN and its active participation in ASEM appears to be a strategy to pursue its own foreign policy advantage.

ASEM is one of China's vehicles to pursue certain interests at both global and regional levels. The inter-regional institution has helped China gain certain advantages in foreign policy towards the United States, EU countries and its Asian neighbours. Being the first and the only forum in which China interacts with other Asian countries and the EU without a U.S. presence, ASEM is a strategic choice for China. In the Myanmar accession case, ASEM provided a platform for China to align itself to ASEAN and create a pressure group towards the EU. China has built political coalitions with other Asian countries not only to support Myanmar's accession but also to support their refusal against EU intervention in political and human rights practices in Asia.

Participating and maintaining ASEM is a strategic choice for China. Simmons and Martin (1998; 2002) perceive that joining an international institution is a strategic choice for a state. In line with this perception, this section assesses China's support for Myanmar's accession to ASEM and analyses China's participation in ASEM. It argues that China has probably helped sustain ASEM's longevity because this inter-regional institution seems to have provided a useful platform for China to enhance its relations with Asian countries and, in coalition with ASEAN countries, to deal with EU political pressures.

Unlike the Myanmar problem in the ASEAN-EU relationship that had no place for China's role, Myanmar's accession to the ASEM inter-regional scheme allowed China to legitimately play its diplomatic role in pursuing its strategic interests (which will be elaborated later). By supporting ASEAN's common position, urging EU countries to accept Myanmar into ASEM, China not only enhanced its political alignment to ASEAN countries but also showed Myanmar's military junta that the China factor, rather than India, is crucial to help Myanmar counter the EU's refusal.

The Myanmar case in the ASEM enlargement process was also an appropriate arena in which Beijing could settle its long battle against EU criticism over the authoritarian regime and human rights problems in China. By aligning with ASEAN countries to support Myanmar's admission, China was actually engaging in an indirect battle with the EU (and other Western countries) to refuse external intervention in its human rights practice and democratization.

In the Myanmar case, China used the ASEM enlargement process not only to strengthen its relations with ASEAN countries and to maintain its leverage on Myanmar but also to force the EU to leave the resolution of democratizations and human rights practices in Asia in the hands of Asian countries. This behaviour is consistent with Kuik's argument (2005, p. 102), "Beijing now views multilateral institutions as a useful diplomatic platform that can be utilized to advance its own foreign policy objective".

The relations between ASEAN and China and Myanmar reflect the geopolitics of East Asia. The China factor is essential in the success of ASEAN's support of Myanmar's accession to ASEM in 2004. As elaborated in the previous section, ASEAN inter-regional relations with China developed in 1990s. This was the period when Myanmar, together with Vietnam, Laos and Cambodia were in the process of becoming ASEAN members. Despite criticisms from Western countries, including some European countries in ASEM, ASEAN accepted Myanmar's admission into the sub-regional group in 1997. As stated previously by two interviewees (S22; S34), Myanmar's accession to ASEAN had actually been rejected by some ASEAN countries but ASEAN countries' interest in incorporating all ten Southeast Asian countries was stronger. Interviewee S34 mentioned that ASEAN was in a rush to become ASEAN 10 on its thirtieth anniversary in 1998. ASEAN's rationale for incorporating all the Indochina countries, including Myanmar, however was its concern with Myanmar-China relations that had developed since 1980s. It was feared among the Southeast Asian countries that China's military and economic influence on Myanmar would instigate regional problems (McCarthy 2008). ASEAN's strategy to embrace Myanmar is in line with the logic of cooperation in international relations, as mentioned by S53, "...It is better to have Myanmar in than out so we can tell them ...". From the perspective of the Myanmar military regime, the country's membership of ASEAN was expected to give more external legitimacy, to help counter Western countries' pressure, and to mitigate Myanmar's economic dependence on China (Haacke 2006; McCarthy 2008).

Even though ASEAN managed to subsume Myanmar's democratization and human rights problems under other regional issues, these problems later became a key agenda item in ASEAN affairs. Indeed, ASEAN countries found themselves under pressure from Western countries to help solve Myanmar's political problems. Despite their relative success in maintaining the non-intervention policy towards Myanmar at the beginning, ASEAN countries took a persuasive approach, "the ASEAN way", to Myanmar's military regime through engagement policies, enhanced interaction, and several high-level visits to Yangon. However, ASEAN had to undertake double tasks: externally to defend, or at least to explain, Myanmar's dilemma to the Western countries whereas internally it encouraged the military regime to comply with international standards of human rights practices.

Efforts by ASEAN countries to help solve Myanmar's political problems have had little success due to the various interests of ASEAN countries. As elaborated in the previous section, various and contending interests among Southeast Asian countries in Myanmar have resulted in the failure of each individual country's approaches and the lack of a consistent, concerted ASEAN approach. In addition, ASEAN's failure is also derived from the fact that ASEAN and other Asian countries have also experienced democratization and human rights problems. Several interviewees commented that:

> To make a stronger pressure on Myanmar is difficult as some Asian countries, such as China, Malaysia, Singapore, have human right problems too in their countries. (S09)

> Myanmar issue has been highlighted because it is not politically expensive. China and India have similar issues but they are not condemned.... West easily criticizes ASEAN for Myanmar issue but not dare to criticize China and India. (S32)

> There are many hypocrites in Asia. Some Asian countries have more political prisoners than Myanmar. Myanmar is not the worst country but it is certainly very bad now. (I42)

Another main obstacle to ASEAN's attempts to deal with Myanmar's political problems is Myanmar relations with China and China–India competition over Myanmar. ASEAN leaders understand that ASEAN would not be able to force Myanmar into any solution because of those two factors (S22; see also Manea 2008). Myanmar's military regime has understood their country's strategic position as well (S09; S10; S33). ASEAN was simply unable to balance China's influence on Myanmar.

Myanmar interests in China are enormous, ranging from the economic to political and military spheres. The relations had developed since the two shared anti-Soviet and anti-Vietnam policies in 1979 but was enhanced after 1989 when Myanmar suffered various sanctions from the international community. A Myanmar expert in Japan revealed that:

> Myanmar's largest trading partner is China through [the] inland border. Main export is natural resources. Last year Myanmar-China signed a contract for inland oil pipeline from Indian Ocean to inland China. Except for airplanes which they bought from Russia, all other Myanmar military equipment are from China. (S70)

For China, the relations with Myanmar before the involvement of India were apparently not a big matter. China's trade with Myanmar is far lower than with other ASEAN countries (Ba 2003; Percival 2007). Despite China's frequent support for Myanmar in international forums, its political and military relations with Myanmar were modest (Haacke 2006; Percival 2007; Li and Zheng 2009). In the 1990s, China also prudently undertook its regional policies, concerned that high-profile relations with Myanmar would provoke resentment from Southeast Asian countries (Percival 2007).

Nevertheless, ASEAN's leverage on Myanmar has been escalating since the end of the 1990s because of India's interest in Myanmar. Because of its economic interest, especially its need for a supply of natural gas, India has made a historical shift in its foreign policy towards Myanmar and has been approaching the military regime since the end of the 1990s (Lall 2006). In addition, India appears to have a strategic interest in Myanmar as well (James 2004; Lall 2006). This circumstance has created strategic, political and economic opportunities for the military regime to play off two growing Asian powers, India and China, against each other (Ba 2003; Percival 2007; McCarthy 2008). Several interviewees commented that:

> Myanmar has ignored EU and Western pressure because the Junta was aware of their strategic importance for China and Russia. We might be a small country. But if a big country needs small countries, they would protect us. (D04)

> ASEAN increasingly realizes that flexible engagement and other approaches to Myanmar have failed. The answer for Myanmar problem can only be found in Beijing and New Delhi. (S32)

> ASEAN policy on Myanmar and EU's policy on Myanmar have both failed, indicated by worsening circumstances in Myanmar. Constructive engagement is not effective and sanction is not smart. The most important actors are China and India. As long as the two do not want to put pressure on Myanmar, prospect for Myanmar betterment is low. (I42)

> Japan coordinates its Myanmar policy with ASEAN and ASEAN should be in driving seat. However, it needs to approach China and India to solve the Myanmar issue. (J75)

> ASEAN realizes that flexible engagement and other approaches to Myanmar have failed. The answer for Myanmar problem can only be found in Beijing and New Delhi. Some Asian countries especially Singapore and China have close relations with Myanmar so the problem is complicated. China once promise me to talk quietly with Myanmar Junta but little have been done perhaps due to traditional position of China for non-interference, its commercial interest in Myanmar and its strategic calculation against India. India has interest in Myanmar also because there is a dissident group in the south near Myanmar border. (D18)

> China and India have also strategic relations with Myanmar and they are Myanmar's immediate neighbours. (B29)

As a result, Myanmar's military junta seems to be beyond ASEAN's reach. Indeed, the military regime seems to engage in economic and strategic affairs at the cost of ASEAN.[7] This circumstance has created concern for ASEAN: the military regime has not only brought problems and embarrassment in international forums but also precluded ASEAN strategy from taming Myanmar by incorporating the country into the association. In addition, Myanmar seems to have "invited" China–India strategic competition into the Southeast Asia region without the consent of the other countries in the area. Two Singaporean scholars revealed that:

> ASEAN's current concern does not only derive from bad treatment to Myanmar people by the Junta but also by Myanmar's engagement with China. ASEAN concern because Myanmar opens the door for China and India to get into SEA. It diminishes ASEAN's effort to engage China and India strategically in Asia. (S33)

> There was no vision that Myanmar would become proxy between China and India that complicates ASEAN position. (S34)

Nevertheless, ASEAN and China share disappointment over Myanmar. Whereas China apparently understands ASEAN's dismay over the behaviour of the Myanmar military regime, China has also its own concern due to the growing relations between Myanmar and India. To the surprise of China and other countries, China's leverage over the Myanmar military regime is increasingly limited (Li and Zheng 2009). Despite Myanmar's immense dependence on China, the Asian superpower is actually unable to intervene in Myanmar's domestic affairs (S18; see also Li and Zheng 2009). India's approach to Myanmar seems to be used by Myanmar to reduce its dependence on China, which in turn erodes China's leverage on the country.

China–Myanmar's uneasy relations because of the Indian factor arose at the same time as China–ASEAN relations were growing rapidly in the process of creating the framework of cooperation for CAFTA. One may observe China's changing and accommodating behaviour towards ASEAN in this period (Xiao 2009). Economically, China provided ASEAN with "gifts" even before CAFTA was achieved, such as a quick tariff reduction on the trade in goods (Ba 2003; Saw, Sheng and Chin 2005; see also Sohn 2008). Politically, China appeared to adjust its regional policy in line with that of ASEAN countries, especially the policies towards Myanmar. In 2004, both ASEAN countries and China diluted their non-intervention principle through publicly urging the Myanmar military regime to restore its democratic processes in a foreign ministerial meeting in Jakarta.[8]

China's support for ASEAN's proposal to include Myanmar in the ASEM process adds to ASEAN bargaining towards the EU. By gaining China's support, ASEAN sent a message to the European countries that ASEAN countries have a special relations with China and they are in one camp vis-à-vis the Europeans in this case. For the EU countries, China is an important actor not to be ignored. With its high economic profile, especially because of its lucrative market and rapid industrialization, and global political influence, China has become a very important country in the world such that the European countries would not like to create antagonism. Letting ASEAN and China to create a prolonged assertive pressure for EU to accept Myanmar in ASEM would create unnecessary political and diplomatic blunders that the European countries do not expect since they have heavy economic interests in those countries.

China's support for ASEAN's aim to include Myanmar in ASEM is part of China's strategy in playing the role of an ally of the Southeast Asian countries. After Suu Kyi's detention in 2003, ASEAN countries were not only under international pressure to persuade Myanmar to solve its domestic political problems (Yawnghwe 2004; Petersson 2006; Manea 2008) but were also anxious that Myanmar would turn into a battle ground of competition among big powers (China, India, and Russia) (S10; S22; see also McCarthy 2008). The pressure from Western countries on the Southeast Asian countries heightened in 2004 because Myanmar's turn to take the ASEAN chairmanship was due in 2006. In this context, ASEAN's support for Myanmar's accession into ASEM may also be seen as an ASEAN effort to appease Myanmar. China might have understood the ASEAN anxiety and might have observed that ASEAN's common position, to force the EU to accept Myanmar's admission, would not succeed without China's support. Thus, China's support for ASEAN over Myanmar's accession to ASEM was both demanded by ASEAN and wanted by China.

China has been participating actively in ASEM especially since the Asian financial crisis. China has been involved in various ASEM initiatives[9] and hosted the seventh ASEM Summit in Beijing on 23–24 October 2008. The high-profile Summit, attended by forty-three Asian and European leaders, reflected not only China's support for ASEM but also China as the magnet in the ASEM process.

The involvement of China in ASEM has attracted not only EU but also Asian countries to stay in the inter-regional meeting. Some interviewees reveal that:

ASEM is in difficult environment as ASEAN prioritizes more on ASEAN-EU as well as bilateral relations with EU whereas EU places more attentions on China and India. (D03)

EU is now more interested in China and India than in any other Asian countries. Thus, ASEM exists currently in a very difficult international environment both in global and regional levels. ASEM is a dialogue forum whose meaning is not significant; bilateral relations with EU or any European countries are much more important, stronger, and beneficial. ASEM is only meetings, not even summits or partnership. The Europeans have also tendency to "tell". Indonesia is not a target for their investments but China is. (D02)

Some EU officials did not attend ASEM meeting because their policy had been made in Brussels and their interest were protected. If they did attend, it is because they have something to do with the host. In Beijing Summit, EU must come full team. It is not to reflect ASEM is important but that China is important. (D49)

EU was much more interested in China than any other EA countries. (S63)

Indeed, certain Asian scholars who attended the ASEM workshop in Tokyo in 2005 believed that the EU countries had used ASEM to approach China (S10). But China's active role in ASEM is not without foundation.

It is undeniable that China's support and participation in ASEM are driven from the country's interests. China's interests in ASEM appear to come from several considerations. Strategically, ASEM is used to balance the U.S. influence globally and regionally (S09; also Shambaugh 2004; Li 2009). The inter-regional institution is in line with China's effort to pursue multilateralism (Kuik 2005). In addition, ASEM provides an indispensable forum that assists China to develop closer relations with EU countries and its Asian neighbours (S10; S22; S53; also Zhao 1999).

In the 1990s, China had risen as a strong economic power and sought political power regionally and globally. The reformation programme which brought China's economy to a competitive level in Asia and allowed the country to achieve high economic growth, gave the country confidence to take part in global and regional relations. China joined the Asia-Pacific Economic Cooperation (APEC) in 1991 (MOFA PRC 2000) and started participating in ARF in 1997 (Foot 1998). At global and regional levels, however, China's rising influence was hampered by American unilateralism after the Cold War (He 2008). In response to American unilateralism, China has been in favour of multilateralism in which global politics is not dominated by the superpower but dispersed into a multi-polar system (Chinese Premier Wen Jiabao, quoted from *FEER*, 6 May 2004, p. 30 in Bersick 2004).

Participating in ASEM is China's strategic choice for two reasons: to strengthen multilateralism in world politics and to exclude the United States. ASEM is one of the only forums in which China is able to pursue its multilateral strategy because the inter-regional institution places China with other world powers in Europe and Asia. Preceding its participation in ASEM, China had joined ARF and APEC, but both forums were dominated by the United States. ASEM does not include the United States. In the presence of other Asian and European countries, ASEM creates a multilateral institution supported by multi-polar actors; it is an alternative world scheme (Dent 2004). This multilateral nature of ASEM gives China more room not only to manoeuvre to counter the U.S. unilateralism (Bersick 2004) but also to strengthen the multilateral world system (Dent 2004). It is an effort to dilute power from the superpower's domination.

Indeed, the exclusion of the United States from ASEM has raised the strategic value of the inter-regional institution in the eyes of the Chinese. Bersick (2002; 2004) quoted China's perception of the strategic importance of ASEM from the country's high-ranking officials at the central Committee of the Communist Party and the Ministry of Foreign Office. He describes,

> They stress the importance of the process as a mechanism which allows for inter-regional cooperation with the Europeans without the participation of the United States. This is why the Chinese government is interested in the politico-strategic dimension of the process. The increasing interest of Beijing in ASEM coincides with the more prominent role being played by the PR China in the overall process. (Bersick 2002)

This view on ASEM's strategic importance is a shift from China's "traditional" approach to international institutions. Kent (2002) writes about China's concern over the impact of international institutions on its sovereignty, which becomes the base for its strategy to solve interstate conflicts through bilateral mechanisms rather than through international institutions. China appears to be more confident to participate in ASEM perhaps because of its economic power and its growing political leverage, regionally and globally. Given this, China would have the possibility of using ASEM to pursue its strategic interest, not as a minor participant that could be dominated by major players within the institution.

Another importance of ASEM for China is the fact that ASEM has facilitated China to establish more links with the EU. China's relations with the EU are not always smooth, either politically or economically, although the two parties established a diplomatic relation in 1975. The difficult relations date back to their bitter interactions during European colonialism over China, prolonged by the Cold War in which China was treated as a dangerous and aggressive communist country. China has used the colonial and Cold War experience to project images to the world that it was the victim of great powers' manipulation (Shambaugh 2004). This circumstance was worsened by EU criticism of China's human rights practices (Zhang 1998) especially after the 1989 Tiananmen incident[10] and the support by some EU countries of the Dalai Lama. But EU countries were also interested in China's high economic growth. On the one hand, they were worried about the economic dimension of China threat, but on the other hand, they did not want to be left out of possible benefits resulting from good relations with the rising China.[11] China also realized that its economic development requires a European market to maintain its high growth and to integrate into the world economy.[12] Moreover, China would need to develop stronger relations with EU countries if the Asian power pursued multilateralism in world politics (S80).

Participating in ASEM since 1996 has given China more channels through which to link with the EU, starting in the economic field then expanding to politics and social spheres as reflected in the ASEM pillars. Nevertheless, China's rationale for the importance of relations with the EU lies in its needs for European technology (Bersick 2004). China-EU contacts in the early ASEM process seemed to have given the two actors confidence to enhance their relations. Two years after the first ASEM Summit in Bangkok, the EC published a document, "Building a Comprehensive Partnership with China", followed by the first China-EU Summit in 2 April 1998 (EU 2009a) which took place just a day before the second ASEM Summit in London. In December 1998, the China-EU Agreement on scientific and technological cooperation was signed (EU 2009a). The EU supported China's accession into the World Trade Organization through the EU-China bilateral agreement on 19 May 2000. The China-EU relations was praised by one of Chinese interviewees as the relations indicated that China (then) was part of what she called "advanced countries" as revealed below,

> China is a big country and we can deal with world's advanced countries with dignity. We are very proud that our economic development has brought us to the same level of those Western countries. China has worked hard to achieve this success. (S81)

ASEM has also helped China to develop closer relations with its regional neighbours both in Southeast and Northeast Asia. It has seemed more natural for China to enhance its regional relations and to build political leverage after gaining its status as an Asian economic power. In addition, China needed to establish better relations with regional countries to maintain its economic development and high growth due to its dependence on capital, market and natural resources, especially energy, from countries in the region (S65; see also Percival 2007). Moreover, since the end of the Cold War, China has been convinced that ASEAN is not an instrument of the United States that would harm China's interest (McCarthy 2008). But China's strategy in dealing with regional relations is not provocative; it tends to position itself as a partner rather than a competitor or aggressor to the neighbouring states (Shambaugh 2004; Percival 2007; Xiao 2009). Thus, when ASEAN countries proposed the founding of ASEM in the mid-1990s, China saw it as an opportunity to align itself with regional countries as well.

China's inter-governmental relations with Southeast Asian countries have widened after the regional countries became involved in the ASEM process. Despite the suspicions of some ASEAN countries (Ba 2003; Tang 2009), China appears to be undertaking prudent foreign policies that are not provoking any resentment from its neighbours due to its economic strength and growing political and military power. Four months after China participated in the first ASEM Summit, ASEAN accepted China, with full status, as an ASEAN partner in July 1996 within the framework of ASEAN Plus One. The trust building that China and ASEAN countries had nurtured through the ASEM process, ASEAN Plus One and, later the APT resulted in further rapprochement of the two parties. To establish the CAFTA, the Framework Agreement on Comprehensive Economic Cooperation was signed in November 2002 (ASEAN 2002), followed by China's accession to the ASEAN TAC on 8 October 2003 (ASEAN 2003*b*; Ba 2003). The FTA between China and six founding ASEAN countries is scheduled to start in 2010, and the newer ASEAN countries may join in 2015. China-ASEAN relations have continued to grow through APT since 1997 and EAS since 2005. In the ASEM process, China's adaptive behaviour towards its Asian partners is quite remarkable (D48; D50; D57). ASEM enables China to project itself as a supportive and accommodative regional power.

Thus, the ASEM intra-Asian group has provided the opportunity for China to strengthen regional relations with its neighbours in Southeast and Northeast Asia, both economically and politically.

THE PURSUIT OF ASEAN COUNTRIES' FOREIGN POLICY ADVANTAGES THROUGH ASEM

This chapter has argued that one of the reasons of ASEM's longevity is that ASEM has been used at least on some occasions by its Asian partners as a vehicle to pursue selected advantage of their own foreign policies. The case study of Myanmar in the ASEM enlargement in the early 2000s suggests that ASEAN countries and China have taken political advantages of the enlargement. This chapter suggests that, despite its neglected position in regional affairs, ASEM appears to have delivered strategic advantages for ASEAN countries and China. ASEAN countries treat ASEM not only as an additional forum to address issues that cannot be settled in other forums but also as an opportunity to play a stronger role in regional decision making by taking leadership in the Asian common position to support Myanmar's accession to ASEM.

While creating some pressure on ASEAN's institutional development, the ASEM process has allowed the sub-regional institution to be more assertive vis-à-vis European countries. The case study of Myanmar's accession reveals that ASEAN had the confidence to engage in a politically tense issue with the EU. The views of the Asians in supporting Myanmar's accession to ASEM are represented by two of the interviewees, who stated:

> The common position is [the] external actor has to treat ASEAN as 10 and APT as 13; excluding Myanmar is not accepted.... Decision on Myanmar is made in consensus. (D17)

> Inside, ASEAN pressed Myanmar but it maintained support of the country at international forums ... ASEAN position was seconded by China. (D18)

The success in sponsoring Myanmar's participation in the ASEM process was a victory of ASEAN's diplomacy towards the EU countries (S08; also Dosch 2007).

In this particular case, ASEAN managed not only to take a common diplomatic position to back up Myanmar's accession but also to secure the support of the Northeast Asian countries, especially China. The manoeuvres of the ASEAN countries in the Myanmar issue during the ASEM first enlargement process seems to have allowed the Asian countries to take a more assertive stance towards their European counterparts when dealing with politically sensitive issues. In the ASEM process, ASEAN seems to be playing the role of a regional hub, thus enhancing its leverage regionally and in relation to the EU.

Previously, ASEAN countries had felt irritated by the closed Myanmar–China relations that disadvantaged ASEAN's strategic bargaining with China. But the Myanmar issue in ASEM created some opportunities for China to appease the Southeast Asian countries, while at the same time reassuring Myanmar of strong back up. A number of interviewees revealed that China was very supportive of ASEAN's position in the enlargement dispute (D01;

S09; S10; S33; D47; D66). China's support for Myanmar's accession to ASEM also appears to have been an indirect battle for China to counter the EU's criticism over the practices of human rights and democratization in China. By aligning with ASEAN countries to support Myanmar's admission, China sent a strong message to the EU (and other Western countries) that it rejected external intervention in its human rights practices and democratization process.

While its involvement in the ASEM process has added to the Asian countries' bargaining power in ASEM, China has taken advantage of its involvement in the process. The inter-regional institution has enabled China not only to strengthen its relations with Southeast Asian countries and to enhance its relations with European partners but also, as shown in the Myanmar case, to secure strategic ties with Myanmar and to counter some political hurdles in its foreign policy. It may be true that China's economic strength was the EU's political weak point in countering the Asian position on Myanmar's accession but the Asian success in circumventing the EU's political blockage was built up through the inter-regional framework of ASEM. Myanmar's admission to ASEM appears to have brought significant political achievement for the Asian countries.

Whereas ASEAN countries used China to enhance its political bargaining vis-à-vis the EU, China also took advantage of this case to gain political and economic advantage by establishing a pressure group with ASEAN countries while enhancing its regional relations with the Southeast Asian countries. In addition, China seems to have achieved a political impasse with the EU countries on democratization and human rights issues. China has also appeared to be the magnet of ASEM that attracts Asian and European countries to stay in ASEM. Despite China's interest in using ASEM for its own foreign policy advantages, its commitments and participation in the ASEM process have contributed to ASEM's longevity. The adoption of "Vision and action: Towards a win-win solution" as the theme of the ASEM Summit in Beijing 2008 clearly shows that China has an interest in supporting ASEM and in transferring the mere "talk-shop" into action in a way that it can also benefit from it.

In short, ASEM has provided Southeast Asian countries with certain foreign policy advantages. ASEM has survived because ASEAN countries have perceived it as a forum worth maintaining for the advancement of their traditional interest in foreign policies. Therefore, sustaining the ASEM process is a rational strategic choice for the Southeast Asian countries in ASEAN.

The next chapter will analyse the relations between the informality of ASEM's institution and Southeast Asian perspectives.

Notes

1. II. Fostering Political Dialogue: 7. The Meeting reaffirmed its strong commitment to the United Nations Charter, the Universal Declaration on Human Rights, to the 1986 Declaration on the Right to Development, the 1992 Rio Declaration on Environment and Development, the 1993 Declaration of Vienna and Programme of Action of the World Conference on Human Rights, the 1994 Cairo Programme of Action of the International Conference on Population and Development, the 1995 Copenhagen Declaration on Social Development and Programme of Action, and to the 1995 Beijing declaration and Platform of Action for the Fourth World Conference on Women. (ASEM Infoboard 2006*b*)

2. 5. Leaders welcomed the admission of Cambodia as a new member of ASEAN at the Special ASEAN Foreign Ministers' Meeting in Hanoi in April 1999 ("ASEAN 10") and noted ASEAN's achievement of their goal of embracing all ten countries in Southeast Asia. (ASEM Infoboard 2006*d*)

3. 8. Leaders committed themselves to promote and protect all human rights, including the right to development, and fundamental freedoms, bearing in mind their universal, indivisible and interdependent character as expressed at the World Conference on Human Rights in Vienna. (ASEM Infoboard 2006*d*)

4. The Bangkok Process is an international forum to help narrow the gap between EU's expectations and Myanmar's human rights practices, hosted by the Government of Thailand. One of the seven points presented by the Myanmar Prime Minister was to organize a reconciliation forum, the National Constitution Convention, that would include all components of Myanmar political stakeholders.

5. ASEAN foreign ministers made joint statements to encourage democratization in Myanmar and the release of their political activists was a powerful political statement emerging from their annual meetings in Phnom Penh in June 2003 (ASEAN 2003*a*) and in Jakarta in June 2004 (ASEAN 2004). The statements showed the emergence of a new path for the ASEAN way, breaking a tradition of non-interference in its member's domestic affairs.

6. Using the power transition theory, Sakuwa (2009) found that, despite China's economic growth and military modernization, Japan-China relationship "has been pacified" by economic and strategic calculations of the two states which reflect their compatible interests to maintain economic growth and peaceful region.

7. Later, after forfeiting its position as ASEAN chairman in 2006, Myanmar appeared to drift away from ASEAN, isolating itself except to China and India (see McCarthy 2008).

8. Later in 2005 China seemed to be helping ASEAN to discourage Myanmar from taking ASEAN chairmanship the year after (Percival 2007).

9. Such as anti-terrorism, culture and civilization, and agricultural cooperation (Bersick 2004), as well as issue-based leadership such as pandemic control, transportation, development of SMEs (ASEM Infoboard 2008).

10. Due to China's treatment of demonstrators in Tiananmen, the EU froze diplomatic relations with China and enforced some embargos, including an arms embargo (EC External Relations 2009).

11. This was one of the reasons for EU to launch "New Asian Policy" in 1994 and "A long-term policy for China-Europe relations" (EU website). EU's unease about the US-East Asia economic ambition through APEC was described by Dent as "…its [EU] anxieties over the prospect of potential geoeconomic marginalization in a transpacific-dominated world economy." (Dent 2004, p. 215).

12. In the 1990s, China was preparing to enter the world economy through its application to the World Trade Organization (WTO).

3

SOUTHEAST ASIANS AND THE INFORMALITY OF THE ASEM INSTITUTION

The ASEM institution reveals some characteristics of the relations between ASEM and Southeast Asian countries. ASEM has emerged as an inter-regional meeting forum espousing the principles of equality and informality, and is non-binding. These characteristics are very likely influenced by ASEAN member countries in ASEM. The informal characteristic has been highlighted in ASEM documents since the early period and seems to be sustained throughout ASEM discourse. The informality not only reflects the need of ASEM partners to avoid legal and formal institutions but also mirrors one of ASEM's purposes, to bridge the differences among ASEM partners and accommodate their varying interests. A number of interviewees raised the issue of the informality of the ASEM institution during in-depth interviews conducted for this study, and two participants' observations in ASEF workshops revealed the merits of these informal interactions among the participants. The data indicate that the informality can help ASEM to accommodate the diversity of its partners and to circumvent the complexity of the inter-regional relations, whereas a formal institution may decompose such inter-regional relations. The purpose of this chapter is to illuminate the influence of ASEAN in the ASEM institution and the contribution of the informality and non-binding characteristic to ASEM's longevity.

This chapter argues that the ASEM institution has been built in accordance with the needs of the Southeast Asian countries, that is, inter-regional relations managed by an informality and non-binding principle. Those characteristics mirror the influence of ASEAN countries on the ASEM institution. Indeed, ASEM seems to tolerate the Southeast Asian countries to bring in their "ASEAN way", which means consensus-based, informal decision-making, and non-binding. These circumstances, however, have helped to maintain ASEM's longevity in two ways. First, the accommodation of the ASEAN institutional style into the ASEM institution encourages the Southeast Asian countries to accept and support ASEM. Second, the informality of ASEM institution creates flexibility while the non-binding principle seems to reduce the cost of maintaining cooperation while opening up opportunities for the ASEM partners to develop different kinds of strategic relations.

The data from in-depth interviews regarding ASEM's institution are analysed within the institutionalist framework. One of the institutional approaches, which does not denigrate states' interests in cooperation, is useful in guiding the analysis in this chapter. In the special edition of the *International Organization* in 2001, Koremenos, Lipson and Snidal (2001, p. 762) argue that "states use international institutions to further their own goals, and they design institutions accordingly". More recently, Kawasaki (2009) also stated that international institutions are established and designed to allow them to work together for particular reasons. It means institutional design can be a deliberate choice, not a coincidental arrangement, decided by national governments. National governments may design their cooperating institutions according to their need to overcome pre-existing problems and foreseen obstacles. In addition to their influence on institutional design, states' interests can also shape the course of international institutions. A respected scholar of international institutions suggests that the practice of sovereignty by states directly influences the evolution of the institution (Keohane 1988). Thus, states choose or design the type of cooperation framework and may adjust it according to their needs in the course of the cooperation. So, a particular design of an international institution may be maintained to sustain the relations. In addition, the study by Stone, Slantchev, and London (2008) can also be referred to analyse the relations between the enlargement of ASEM and its institutional arrangement. The study argues that big states are in favour of a more institutionalized institution with few partners whereas small states prefer to have less institutionalized framework with a wider set of participants.

The aforementioned institutional approaches are relevant for the focus on the ASEM informal institution and how this characteristic is preferred by Southeast Asian countries. Informality in international relations is not new but it usually takes place as informal agreements between states (Lipson 1991). The ASEM institution is characterized by a remarkable informality which has been written explicitly in various ASEM documents and maintained persistently despite enormous criticism. There must have been a reason for the ASEM founders to choose an informal institution for their relations that may relate to their understanding of ASEM circumstances and their anticipation of uncertainty in global politics. In this case, one can trace the role of ASEAN member countries in the ASEM establishment as the informality of the ASEM institution is similar to that of the ASEAN institution. Acharya and Johnston (2007), Khong and Nesadurai (2007) as well as Kahler (2000) have studied the informal nature of cooperative institutions in Asia. They find that the informal institution is commonly adopted by Asian countries in their regional affairs because the informality enables them to avoid political as well as economic commitments at the cost of their sovereignty; indeed, the underlying objective of Asian states' participation in international institutions is to preserve their sovereignty (Kahler 2000; Khong and Nesadurai 2007).

The informal form of international institutions also reflects a low degree of legalization of the institutions. According to Goldstein et al. (2000), the legalization of international institutions includes the adoption of rules, the specification and accuracy of the rules that govern the institutions, and the establishment of implementing organs to execute the agreed rules. The degree of legalization among existing international institutions is varied because the institutions exist in a particular political context; the existence of the institutions is shaped by world politics (Goldstein et al. 2000). The world politics described by these authors should refer to the practice of political relations among states, such as the objectives of the states to preserve the sovereignty, or the climate of the global political environment. Thus, states may choose not to engage in highly legalized international institutions if such engagement would result in unbearable political cost. In such circumstances, international institutions with a low level of legalization, that is informal institutions, are preferable. Previously, Lipson (1991) had found that participating states may opt for informal arrangements to pursue durable cooperation amidst other obstacles in international affairs. Therefore, the adoption of informality as the design of international institutions may be the result of states' deliberate intention in the initial phase as well as in the course of cooperation based on their perceptions of global and regional political circumstances. This analytical framework is applied in this chapter to analyse the behaviours of East Asian states in maintaining inter-regional relations through ASEM but to keep it as an informal forum and non-binding engagement.

In order to examine the perspective of the Southeast Asian participants regarding the ASEM's institution, this chapter investigates the characteristics of informality that is similar to the ASEAN institution and analyse the possible impacts of the informality on the ASEM longevity. It proceeds in the following order. At the beginning, it analyses ASEM's informal institution, in terms of the meeting style, consensus and non-binding principles. Then, it examines the complexity of region-to-region relations in ASEM, including that caused by the enlargement process, and the benefit of ASEM informal institutions for the inter-regional relations.

ASEM: A SOFT INSTITUTION

This section investigates the informal design of ASEM and asks how the informality has been manifested in the ASEM process. Obstacles to forging international cooperation may vary from free-rider and betrayal to unavoidable uncertainty in global affairs. To be able to pursue their interest in international cooperation, states may design their cooperating institutions in such a way that circumvents those obstacles. According to Lipson (1991), the effect of external upsets and uncertainty can be managed by institutional arrangements. He continues that "[t]he informality of so many agreements illuminates basic features of international politics. It highlights the continuing search for international cooperation, the profusion of forms it takes, and the serious obstacles to more durable commitment" (Lipson 1991, p. 498). Lipson's point, as well as Kawasaki's, and Koremenos, Lipson, and Snidal's points previously mentioned, throw light on understanding why Asian and European states seem to have deliberately designed ASEM as an informal institution.

A study of ASEM documents finds that cooperating partners in ASEM have opted to design the inter-regional forum to be less institutionalized. This choice is depicted in the first ASEM Summit Chairman's Statement, point 18, on the Future Course of ASEM, "The Meeting agreed that inter-sessional activities are necessary although they need not be institutionalised. The meeting furthermore agreed that follow-up actions to be undertaken by the participants to the ASEM will be based on consensus..." (MOFA Thailand 1996). In addition, the background introduction of ASEM, which originally serves as the concept paper of ASEM, states that "The inaugural ASEM is envisaged as an informal gathering of leaders who will be free to discuss any topic of mutual interest..." (MOFA Thailand 1996). The adoption of the informal design by Asian and European leaders in ASEM reflects their understanding of the enormous diversity of ASEM partners as well as the uncertainty in international affairs while determining to forge a durable cooperation through the inter-regional forum.

In the course of building ASEM, however, the Asian and European leaders found the need for a working mechanism. They then suggested a series of inter-governmental meetings and adopted Asia-Europe Co-operation Framework (AECF) in 2000 that includes the working method of the ASEM process. Despite a coordinating mechanism being stipulated in the summit documents and the AECF, the ASEM institution has been kept informal. Therefore, ASEM analysts have identified the ASEM working mechanism as a form of "soft institutionalism" (CAEC 1997, p. 27; Reiterer 2001, p. 18). This soft institution, in which ASEM informality prevails, has been manifested in meeting style as well as in non-binding decisions and consensus.

Informality is the main characteristic of the inter-regional meetings that constitute the ASEM process. This section identifies the ASEM documents that depict the informal setting of ASEM meetings and examines how the informality operates in ASEM forums.

By studying ASEM documents, one can find the written references to the informality of meetings in the ASEM process. The informal characteristic of ASEM meetings is emphasized in the ASEM documents produced at summits. ASEM leaders not only decided that forums would be informal in the initial documents, they also kept reaffirming the ASEM informality principle in further ASEM documents. The second ASEM Summit's Chairman's Statement reconfirms the Chairman's Statement of the Bangkok Summits that ASEM should be kept "as an informal process. ASEM need not be institutionalised. It should stimulate and facilitate progress in other fora; go beyond governments in order to promote dialogue and cooperation" (ASEM Infoboard 2006c, point 3). In addition, at the third ASEM Summit in 2000, ASEM leaders agreed to adopt the AECF to set out the vision, principles, objectives, priorities and mechanisms for future ASEM processes. One of the key principle stated in the AECF is that the ASEM process should be conducted "as an informal process". Indeed, the same sentence states that "ASEM need not be institutionalised. It should stimulate and facilitate progress in other fora". Moreover, the Fifth ASEM Summit Chairman's Statement, Annex 2 on Recommendation for ASEM Working Methods, depicts that, "The benefits of an informal, retreat, open dialogue FMM meeting style are agreed. Officials are to further encourage this style for future foreign ministers meetings" (ASEM Infoboard 2006g).

ASEM and EU websites also highlight the informal nature of ASEM forums. The ASEM official homepage maintained by ASEF, the ASEM Infoboard, declares the informal nature of ASEM. It states that "ASEM is an *informal* process of dialogue and co-operation bringing together the twenty-seven European Union Member States and the European Commission with sixteen Asian countries and the ASEAN Secretariat"(ASEM Infoboard 2006j). Furthermore, EU website also mentions the informality of the ASEM process,

"As an informal process, ASEM has no secretariat" (European Commission 2006*b*).

In practice, the ASEM process takes place as informal dialogues among participants from Asian and EU countries. According to some officials who have attended ASEM forums, in dialogue setting the forums adopt a less fixed agenda (D01; D47). As dialogues, the ASEM forums might not be expected to produce particular targeted outcomes except for building trust and confidence. The purpose of a summit, for example is "to provide leaders with an opportunity to get to know one another" (MOFA Thailand 1996). This aim is supposed to apply to other forums in the ASEM process. As described in Chapter 1, the ASEM process includes various forums and activities in three ASEM tracks: the first track (government-to-government), second track (among business associations, but sometimes also referred to the track for scholars); or third track (people-to-people). Despite tight protocol and security arrangements, ASEM summits are supposed to be conducted as informally as other ASEM forums. The intra-regional coordinating mechanism of the first track, assessed in Chapter 1, does not create formal and strict structures either. The intra-regional coordination is merely a mechanism to reflect ASEM as a meeting between the two regions. Participating officials could present additional agenda or suggest ideas that might not be discussed in the intra-regional coordinating meetings (D48). This informal dialogue among ASEM partners may also take place in other forums. According to interviewee I42, informal communication among ASEM partners at inter-governmental meetings in other forums such as the UN, WTO and UNESCO is the outstanding feature of the inter-regional relations.

ASEM leaders seem to choose the informal nature of the ASEM process to fulfil the aims of ASEM which are, as stated in the introduction of the Chairman's Statement of the first ASEM Summit, "to make leaders to meet and become foundation for future cooperation and to encourage greater understanding and to generate greater trust and confidence..." (MOFA Thailand 1996). This informality within the forums allows leaders and other participants to freely discuss a wide range of topics and explore their common interests. An informal forum is intended to create a relaxed atmosphere for meeting participants and to relieve them of any pressure to achieve any particular goals or commitment. The informality of the meetings can also allow participants to interact more personally, to build relations more comfortably, and to nurture trust and confidence within the phases that are convenient for them.

Those aims seem to have been fulfilled at informal forums conducted by ASEF for people-to-people contacts such as the second Asia-Europe Young

Political Leader Seminar in 2007 and the steering committee meeting of Asia-Europe Youth Network on Sustainable Development in 2008. Participant observations conducted at those two forums witnessed the emergence of friendships as well as free-flowing discussions in which participants identified their shared and non-shared interests in apparently egalitarian and casual ways. The informal arrangement of the forums allows participants to talk more freely, lifting the burden of being the representatives of their countries and interacting at a more personal level.

These observation are supported by interviewees who personally attended ASEM forums of the first and third track respectively,

> Informality of ASEM is good because people can talk easier in less formal setting so communication is more possible. (I46).

> Given the informal process of ASEM, there is no need to have strong common position. [You may] agree for what you can agree and not agree for things you do not or cannot agree. (S53)

In addition to the interaction at ASEM or ASEF forums, coordination in the ASEM process has also been conducted informally. Interviews reveal that collegial consultations and personal communications through telephone, telegram, and email are common in the ASEM process (D01; S20; D48). This informal interaction has allowed more sustainable personal relations to develop and grow (D04; D07; D15; D16; D49; D50).

Given the wide diversity among the ASEM partner countries, ranging from economic advancement to political values and cultural differences, the informal meeting style also contributes to sustaining the ASEM process. The informal interactions such as those in dialogue and collegial interactions provide speed not only to overcome layers of bureaucratic procedures. For example Prime Minister A can directly talk to President B and get more personal views, but also to circumvent their differences. According to Dittmer, Fukui and Lee (2000), informal politics in East Asian countries can result in fast communication and action. In the context of ASEM meetings, the informal arrangement may be aimed to achieve similar rapid communication and reaction. In addition, the dialogue setting allows flexibility in presenting, discussing as well as arguing ideas or issues. This kind of setting may create less pressure for ASEM partners to achieve or even to talk or not to talk about sensitive or critical issues. Indeed, some believe that the informality is beneficial as it allows ASEM participants to communicate openly, to reach understanding and come to a common view (S20; I46). The informal forum with dialogue setting, therefore, serves quite effectively the ASEM purpose to bridge the differences between Asian and European participants. This kind of interaction contributes to sustaining the ASEM process, which may eventually help sustain the ASEM institution.

NON-BINDING PRINCIPLE AND CONSENSUS IN ASEM

The previous section described the informality of ASEM forums which is the first characteristic of ASEM as a soft institution. This part will discuss another form of ASEM informality, the non-binding nature of ASEM decisions and consensus. It first analyses the non-binding nature of ASEM. Second, it identifies the application of this non-binding principle in ASEM documents. Finally, an analysis of correlations between consensus decision making and the informal nature of ASEM is presented to conclude this section.

The non-binding principle is probably the most important binding political decision governing ASEM. Founded initially as an inter-governmental forum, ASEM has been directed mostly by political agreements and disagreements. The first of the ASEM pillars, the political pillar, seems to determine the discourse of Asian-EU states relations in the ASEM process. As described previously and in Appendix I on ASEM structure, ASEM inter-governmental forums (government-to-government meeting such as summits and official meetings) are the main organ of the ASEM process. The most important meetings in the ASEM process are foreign ministers meetings (FMMs), which determine the political dialogue and are responsible for the overall coordination of the ASEM process (ASEM Infoboard 2006e, point 22). This means ASEM has been managed and steered by the political process. So, cooperation in the other two pillars can only be possible when politically approved by the first pillar. An "exit" mechanism such as a non-binding principle may be needed to anticipate problems among ASEM partners (the uncertainty) and to reduce the cost of commitment.

From the official documents, it appears that ASEM could only be established on a non-binding principle. Asian and EU countries have different levels of commitment to regional institutions (He 2004; Fawcett 2004; Fort and Webber 2006). Whereas the European countries have exercised the transfer of partial state sovereignty to regional supranational bodies in the EU system (Moravcsik 1998; Slapin 2008; Hage 2008), maintaining states' sovereignty is a particular characteristic of regionalism in Asia (Higgot and Breslin 2000; Fawcett 2004; Higgot 2006; Beeson 2007, 2009; Khong and Nesadurai 2007). Thus, efforts to undertake cooperation based on formal agreements may incur political and economic costs that will impede the cooperation. Adopting non-binding decisions could be a mechanism to address the lack of political will for ASEM while still pursuing cooperation between Asian and European countries.

ASEM's non-binding principle was established at ASEM's inauguration in 1996. It is depicted in the first ASEM Summit's Chairman's Statement, on the Future Course of ASEM, "The meeting furthermore agreed that follow-up actions to be undertaken jointly by the participants to the ASEM will be based on consensus" (MOFA Thailand 1996). Like the informal setting of ASEM forums, this non-binding principle may be aimed at circumventing the differences among the ASEM partners that were foreseen by the ASEM founders. They seem to build ASEM as a loose institution without any binding mechanisms as a precautionary measure to anticipate differences among ASEM partners in political values, economic aspects and socio-cultural life, to adjust to the "ASEAN way" given that the ASEM Asian side is constituted mainly by ASEAN countries, and to encourage participation of Asian states that remain opposed to a membership with formal and binding commitments.

The non-binding principle of ASEM is applied in documents produced at summits as the summits serve as the highest driver in ASEM (see Appendix I: Structure of ASEM Process). The summit documents are mainly created as the chairman's statement and its annexes. The summit documents seem to be composed in such a way as to avoid binding or compliance; therefore, the chairman's statements always moderate the word "binding". While they employ particularly strong words such as "committed", "determination", "commitment", "support", "strongly agree", "reaffirm" as well as several weak phrases such as "reiterate", "acknowledge", "touch upon", "welcome", "emphasized", "express support", and "willingness to engage", the documents do not include methods of enforcement to guarantee the compliance of "decisions" that are found in the chairman's statements. Below are examples from the Chairman's Statement of the fifth ASEM Summit in 2004:

> 1.2 "…To this end, they agreed to strengthen coordination and cooperation in the context of ASEM dialogue and cooperation and the Asia-Europe partnership."

> 1.3 "…, reaffirmed their strong commitment to multilateralism and…"

> 1.4 "The leaders reiterated their support to the ongoing process of the reform of the United Nations and its principal organs.…" They emphasized that ASEM countries are committed to making utmost efforts to ensure the success of the UNGA High-Level Plenary Meeting in 2005, addressing the implementation of all the commitments of the Millennium Declaration.… They also touched upon the International Criminal Court and agreed to continue dialogue on this issue."

1.5 "… They also welcomed the 'ASEM Declaration on Multilateralism' by the ASEM Foreign Ministers in Kildare, Ireland, in April 2004."

1.9 "The Leaders reaffirm their commitment to the non-proliferation of weapons of mass destruction and their means of delivery, and their determination to deepen ASEM cooperation in this field."

1.12 "The Leaders emphasized the need to reinforce ASEM cooperation in the field of international migration through the concrete actions identified by ASEM senior officials in charge of immigration, and express support for UN efforts in tackle migration issues."

2.3 "The Leaders agreed on the need to intensify and focus ASEM economic activities on enhancing Asia-Europe trade and investment facilitation and promotion; strengthening coordination and cooperation on financial issues…"

3.4 "… they emphasized their commitment to pursue dialogue within the UNESCO in the course of ongoing negotiations on a draft convention on cultural diversity."

4.5 "The Leaders confirmed their support to the Interim Iraqi Government in its effort to ensure security and stability in the country, and their willingness to engage together with the UN and the international community to achieve these goals…" (ASEM Infoboard 2006*f*)

In addition, ASEM leaders seem to avoid commitment to particular initiatives listed in the AECF by using weakly binding words, such as "endorse", as seen from the last point of the second ASEM Summit Chairman's Statement:

Taking forward cooperation on major themes identified at ASEM 1 Bangkok and in line with the priorities outlined in the Asia-Europe co-operation framework, leaders: endorse new initiatives to… (ASEM Infoboard 2006*c*)

Moreover, a Chairman's Statement may consist of a loose commitment to ASEM institutionalization such as the one adopted at the fifth ASEM Summit, below,

6.3 "…They tasked Foreign Ministers and senior officials to study and submit their recommendations on the continued improvement of ASEM institutional mechanism, including the possibility of moving towards an ASEM Secretariat at an appropriate time, and the issue of future membership enlargement …" (ASEM Infoboard 2006*g*)

It is likely that the non-binding words in all those summit documents indicate precautionary actions by the officials to circumvent their compliance obligations as well as to lower their expectation for other parties' compliance.

Despite frequent criticism of the "ASEAN way", EU countries seem to tolerate ASEM adopting a similar principle in composing summit documents. The non-binding mechanism has been criticized as one of the weaknesses of ASEAN as it denigrates the Association's decisions for the sake of its member countries' interests, indicating the lack of political will to support the agreed decisions (Jones and Smith 2007*a*). In addition to the lack of political will, the non-binding principle may be used to avoid unbearable commitments that have been agreed at the summits. Two interviewees suggested that leaders and officials might create commitments in ASEM forums which they would neglect when they had returned to their own countries due to their being overwhelmed by other tasks, leaving those commitments unattended (S19; D62).

Nevertheless, the non-binding principle applied to ASEM's decisions seems to provide flexibility which eventually helps sustain ASEM. Decisions resulting from ASEM summits and forums are usually formulated as chairman's statements, proposals or declarations. According to Lipson (1991), those types of meeting outcomes are informal agreements, less restrictive of heads of state and much less effective in binding national policies (of participating countries) than formal agreements such as treaties. For example, at the second Summit, ASEM leaders agreed to adopt the AECF, but this document does not bind ASEM partners as it merely serves "to guide, focus and coordinate ASEM activities in political dialogue, the economic and financial fields and other areas" (ASEM Infoboard 2006*c*, point 21).

Beside the non-binding principle, ASEM has also adopted another characteristic of ASEAN, particularly in its decision-making mechanism: consensus. ASEM applies consensus in formulating and drafting the chairman's statements of summits and FMMs. In the ASEM working method, it is stated that (emphasis by author):

> (d) In order to gain more time for dialogue the Chair shall be responsible for reflecting fairly the outcome of meetings in short and factual statements. For Summits and Ministers' meetings consensus on Chair Statements (CS) should be reached through close coordination among partners. However, it was confirmed at the meeting that *consensus shall not be interpreted as meaning that texts would be negotiated word for word. Separate negotiated political declarations on specific subjects in addition to chairman's statement, if appropriate, could be issued,* thereby raising the visibility of the issue treated. (ASEM Infoboard 2006*i*)

According to high-ranking officials from ASEAN countries, consensus is the main mechanism of ASEAN decision-making (D03; D06; S20); even though "ASEAN minus X", in which one particular ASEAN member may not agree with general agreements, is now possible (S20). One may argue that ASEM does not necessarily need to have "ASEM minus X" mechanism as the meetings are set as dialogue forums with no obligation or target to overcome specific problems or to make decisions.

In practice, however, consensus is essentially complementary to the non-binding principle. Leaders and officials may be encouraged or persuaded to agree on a particular idea or initiative to achieve consensus. As rewards, they would not be placed under pressure to fulfill the agreement because the decision is not compulsory. Both consensus and non-binding principle seem to be the means to create room for flexibility in the ASEM process.

The outcomes of ASEM forums need to be flexible to give room for relaxing commitments, allowing ASEM partners to adjust or fulfil the decisions based on their political willingness as well as their ability. The impediments to cooperation in ASEM are not only uncertainty, such as the Asian financial crisis and political or security instabilities, but also the varied political, economic and cultural disparities among ASEM partners that range from advanced to less developed countries, and from liberal democratic to authoritarian regimes. In this circumstance, the obstacles of cooperation are not only "the high cost of self-enforcement" and "the danger of opportunism" (Lipson 1991, p. 509) but also the inability to comply with all ASEM decisions. The former obstacles may apply to advanced countries whereas the latter may take place in less developed countries. Thus, ASEM decisions risk not only free riders and betrayal but also the future cost of compliance that ASEM partners may not able to afford economically, politically or socially.

Given the circumstance under which ASEM was established, flexibility resulting from informality seems to be essential for maintaining the support from Southeast Asian countries. The topic will be further analysed in the following section.

INFORMALITY AND SOUTHEAST ASIAN COUNTRIES IN ASEM

The soft institutional arrangement that is manifested in informality may support the longevity of ASEM given the complexity of the inter-regional relations between Asian and EU countries. This section examines the complexity of relations in ASEM before considering that the flexibility resulting from ASEM's soft institution can help sustain the ASEM process.

The region-to-region relations between Asian and European countries in the ASEM framework are rather complex. ASEM partners consist of not only a large number of Asian and European countries but also the variety of attachments of those partner states to each other and to other regional institutions outside ASEM. In addition, the ASEM enlargement in 2004 and 2008 contributes to growing diversities in ASEM.

The ASEM region-to-region arrangement involves a large number of participating countries in Asia and Europe. The number of ASEM partners has grown quite significantly since its first summit. Table 3.1 shows the increase of ASEM partners from 1996 to 2008. The names of those participating countries can be seen in Table 1 in "Introduction".

The growing number of ASEM partners is due to a deliberate enlargement exercise in 2004 and 2006. The first enlargement took place right before the fifth Summit in Hanoi (see Chapter 2); the second enlargement was decided at the sixth Summit in Helsinki and was only executed at the seventh Summit in Beijing. The ASEM enlargement was conducted partially in conjunction with the expansion of members of ASEAN and EU.

Besides this increase in the number of partner countries, the further complexity of relations in ASEM stems from the distinctive diversity embedded in the large number of partner countries. Europe and Asia have

TABLE 3.1
The Increasing Numbers of ASEM Partners, 1996–2008

Summit	ASEM partners from Asia	ASEM partners from Europe	Total number of ASEM partners
First Summit 1–2 March 1996, Bangkok	10	15+1	25+1
Second Summit 3–4 April 1998, London	10	15+1	25+1
Third Summit 20–21 October 2000, Seoul	10	15+1	25+1
Fourth Summit 22–24 September 2002, Copenhagen	10	15+1	25+1
Fifth Summit 8–9 October 2004, Hanoi	13	25+1	38+1
Sixth Summit 10–11 September 2006, Helsinki	13	25+1	38+1
Seventh Summit 24–25 October 2008, Beijing	16+1	27+1	43+2

Note: +1 or +2 refers to non-state partners in ASEM which is the European Commission since 1996 and addition of the ASEAN Secretariat in 2008.

neither geographical proximity nor cultural similarity. Comparing Asians and Europeans regionally, one could easily find the differences that have led to the unparalleled diversity of political and cultural values and interests between countries and peoples of the two regions (CAEC 1997; Segal 1998; Chirathivat et al. 2001). In addition, ASEM consists of an Asian group and a European group that are different internally. Both groups are made up of diverse states with different cultures that have led to dissimilar interests among their members (Palmujoki 1997; Friedberg 2000; Yeo 2000). So, Asia and Europe as regions also pose divergence among their own constituents. The divergence seems much wider among the states in the Asian group whereas the European group is able to build political and economic commonality due to their previous adjustment to EU; the two groups also have different levels of regionalization.

As a result, the complexity of relations in ASEM can predictably occur at two levels: the intra-regional and the inter-regional. At intra-regional level, the ASEM mechanism requires Asian and European states to consolidate and formulate regional standpoints through intra-regional coordination (see Figure 1.2). This intra-regional coordination means another series of difficult processes of negotiations and adjustments horizontally and vertically.

Horizontally, among participating states in each region, compromise and common regional standpoints may be difficult, if not impossible, to achieve. Because of the diverse interests among the Asian countries, the Asian group in ASEM can barely consolidate a common regional position. This reality was revealed in some interviews (D03; J11; S33; S54). Because the European group is integrated in the EU, the European states may be able to build common positions more easily than the Asian group. The European countries in ASEM had already been integrated within the EU with a more institutionalized regionalism while the Asian countries have been involved in a different type of regionalism which is less institutionalized (S22; S32; S34; see also Fawcett and Hurrell 1995; Ruland 2001; Dent 2001; Fawcett 2004; Soesastro 2009). Even ASEAN states, that have been seen as key actors in the Asian side of ASEM and have been perceived as forming the most developed type of regional group outside the EU (Hernandez 2007, p. 9), have had limitations in developing a more institutionalized regional institution despite the recent adoption of the ASEAN Charter. A number of scholars claim that ASEAN is not reliable and not assertive enough to act as an authoritative and effective regional association (Ruland 2001; Haacke 2003; Ojendal 2004). With its seeming incapability to move forward into a higher degree of institutionalization, ASEAN will have to overcome enormous difficulties to incorporate the voices of all Asian states in ASEM.

Vertically, the intra-regional complexity in ASEM derives from the different actors in the ASEM process who include state officials, business people and civil society. Involving those three kinds of actors in ASEM creates enormous difficulties as each of them naturally has their own interest and perspectives. Even though politically sensitive issues may only be handled at an inter-governmental level, difficulties in consolidating decisions can still occur. For example, in the case of the Myanmar problem in the 2004 ASEM enlargement (Chapter 2), the compromise made by the European Council and European Commission aroused criticism from the European Parliament and several non-governmental organizations in EU countries (Burma Campaign UK 2004; EP 2004; IIAS 2004; Vichitsorasatra 2004).

At the inter-regional level, the complexity of relations in ASEM may play out in several ways. First, the complexity at the regional level seems to arise from the fact that the Asian and European states have had different degrees of regionalism in their respective regions. Whereas EU regional interest and position may be formulated in Brussels, the preferences and positions of Asian states could hardly be crystallized due to the absence of a formal regional institution that involves all the Asian partners who are represented in ASEM. This divergent nature at regional level has inevitably resulted in misunderstandings and mismatched expectations between the Asian and European states. Some interviewees such as S36, I45, and I46 reveal examples of such mismatched expectation during ASEM summits between Asian and European participants.

Second, ASEM's inter-regional relations are multidimensional as reflected in the three ASEM pillars: political, economic and cultural. Because of the pre-existing discrepancies among the ASEM partner states, ASEM partners display different capabilities as well as willingness to cope with the phase of the ASEM process. This circumstance could eventually result in the fragmentation of the ASEM responses, movements, or initiatives. In addition, the aspirations and spirit presented in one pillar do not always carry over into other pillars. What happens at ASEM forums in the economic area, for example, may not go in parallel with the political forum. Similarly, an ASEM forum in the cultural field can develop in directions that may be different from those of the political forums. As seen in the Myanmar case during ASEM enlargement (Chapter 1), economic and political interests of the EU in relation to the ASEAN countries have complicated the Europeans' position in ASEM.

Third, ASEM's inter-regional relations have grown in parallel with other engagements that existed before or developed after ASEM's establishment. ASEM leaders and elites claimed that the region-to-region relations are not intended to replace pre-existing bilateral and sub-regional engagements

(Santer 1998). For example, EU member states have still maintained their relations with individual Asian states and with ASEAN. So, ASEM has developed alongside pre-existing institutions such as ASEAN-EU, EU-Japan, EU-Korean, and EU-China (Palmujoki 1997, p. 273; Yeo 2003). Region-to region relations within ASEM are distinct from the previous EU approach to Asian countries that was mainly conducted in bilateral or sub-regional levels. Whereas ASEM region-to-region forums that take place concomitantly with other EU relations with Asian countries may provide a more flexible mechanism for settling issues because it gives another alternative channel of communication (Reiterer 2006; Forster 1999), it can also result in a more complex relationship because the level of engagement with EU or EU countries is not the same among Asian countries.

Fourth, ASEM region-to-region relations have been complicated by the degree of attachment of ASEM partners to different regional initiatives in Asia. The involvement of ASEM partners in Asian regional architecture is set out in Table 3.2.

The complexity of ASEM partners' involvement in these various regional and international institutions vis-à-vis their participation in ASEM may be another significant factor that complicates Asia-Europe relations in ASEM. ASEM partners are involved in different regional and international institutions that may eventually affect their attitude and commitment to ASEM. Table 3.2 shows that it is only with ARF that ASEM has almost common membership. The data depict that whereas almost all ASEM partners are members of international institutions like the UN and WTO, Laos is the only ASEM partner that is not a WTO member, their involvement in regional institutions especially in Asia is rather diverse.

Table 3.2 also indicates that not all ASEM Asian partners are APEC members, let alone all the ASEM EU partners. This circumstance is likely to create confusion as one of the main conceptual objectives of ASEM inception was to balance the U.S. dominance in Asia and Europe (Shin and Segal 1999; CAEC 1997; Bridges 1999) and strengthen the Asia-Europe axis (Hanggi 1999). The data reveal that ASEM partners not only belong to various different regional institutions, particularly in Asia, but are also participants in a substantial number of regional and international institutions. The different levels of ASEM partners' engagement in the regional and international institutions illustrate their divergence in loyalty, preference and probably collaboration or lobbying groups towards those institutions (see layered identities in Asia in Chapter 1). Among this complexity of regional and international relations, their preference and attachment to ASEM is probably also quite varied. Those preferences and attachments may also change

TABLE 3.2
ASEM Partners' Involvement in Selected International Institutions

No.	State	ASEM	ASEAN	APT	ARF	EAS	SARC	APEC	EU	UN	PM UNSC	WTO
1.	Austria	✓							✓	✓		✓
2.	Belgium	✓							✓	✓		✓
3.	Brunei Darussalam	✓	✓	✓	✓	✓		✓		✓		✓
4.	Bulgaria	✓			✓				✓	✓		✓
5.	Cambodia	✓	✓	✓	✓	✓				✓		✓
6.	China	✓		✓	✓	✓		✓		✓	✓	✓
7.	Cyprus	✓			✓				✓	✓		✓
8.	Czech Rep.	✓			✓				✓	✓		✓
9.	Denmark	✓			✓				✓	✓		✓
10.	Estonia	✓			✓				✓	✓		✓
11.	Finland	✓			✓				✓	✓		✓
12.	France	✓			✓				✓	✓	✓	✓
13.	Germany	✓							✓	✓		✓
14.	Greece	✓							✓	✓		✓
15.	Hungary	✓							✓	✓		✓
16.	India	✓			✓		✓			✓		✓
17.	Indonesia	✓	✓	✓	✓	✓		✓		✓		✓
18.	Ireland	✓			✓				✓	✓		✓
19.	Italy	✓			✓				✓	✓		✓
20.	Japan	✓		✓	✓	✓		✓		✓		✓
21.	Laos	✓	✓	✓	✓	✓				✓		✓
22.	Latvia	✓							✓	✓		✓
23.	Lithuania	✓							✓	✓		✓
24.	Luxemburg	✓							✓	✓		✓

25.	Netherlands	✓			✓	✓				✓		✓
26.	Malaysia	✓	✓	✓	✓	✓		✓	✓	✓		✓
27.	Malta	✓			✓					✓		✓
28.	Mongolia	✓	✓	✓						✓		✓
29.	Myanmar	✓	✓	✓	✓	✓	✓			✓		✓
30.	Pakistan	✓								✓		✓
31.	Philippines	✓	✓		✓			✓	✓	✓		✓
32.	Poland	✓			✓				✓	✓		✓
33.	Portugal	✓			✓				✓	✓		✓
34.	Romania	✓			✓					✓		✓
35.	Singapore	✓	✓	✓	✓	✓		✓	✓	✓		✓
36.	Slovakia	✓			✓					✓		✓
37.	Slovenia	✓			✓					✓		✓
38.	Spain	✓			✓				✓	✓		✓
39.	S. Korea	✓	✓	✓	✓	✓		✓	✓	✓		✓
40.	Sweden	✓	✓	✓	✓	✓		✓	✓	✓		✓
41.	Thailand	✓			✓				✓	✓		✓
42.	United Kingdom	✓	✓	✓	✓	✓		✓	✓	✓	✓	✓
43.	Vietnam	✓			✓				✓	✓		✓
44.	Total	43	10	13	40	14	2	10	25	43	3	42

Source: Processed from the ASEM Infoboard 2010; WTO 2008; UN 2006.

over time. This contributes to the complexity of the inter-regional relations between the Asian and European states in ASEM.

While dealing with the layered practical and conceptual complexity in undertaking inter-regional relations, ASEM has had to fulfil seemingly ambitious, but rather loose, expectations since its inception. Point 3 of the Chairman's Statement at the first Summit states that ASEM is to forge "A new comprehensive Asia-Europe Partnership for greater growth…" This partnership aims at strengthening links between Asia and Europe thereby contributing to "peace, global stability, and prosperity" (ASEM Infoboard 2006*b*). Later in the AECF, ASEM aimed to strengthen the linkage between Asia and Europe. So ASEM was intended to bridge Asia and Europe for political dialogue, economic relations and sociocultural cooperation, enhancing those that had already been established in bilateral and EU-ASEAN relations as well as complementing those that could not have been undertaken through pre-existing channels. Thus, expectations for ASEM are high but the inter-regional forum is built on a complex circumstances.

The complexity of the inter-regional relations in ASEM can, however, be circumvented by the informal design of ASEM. Indeed, one of the most important factors that helps the Asian and European countries to maintain ASEM inter-regional relations is its informality. It is likely that Asian and European states have managed to sustain the ASEM process for more than a decade because of the informality. The informality seems to generate a kind of flexibility that enables the Asian and European groups to circumvent the complexity of the inter-regionalism while at the same time allowing Asian leaders to avoid binding commitments.

Data in this study reveal that there are at least two types of benefits that can be observed from the ASEM informality. First, ASEM serves as an informal forum for the development of ideas and the negotiation of positions for both intra-regional and inter-regional purposes. In Westerlund's observation (1999, p. 25), ASEM is a perfect medium for sending political signals and for the concerting efforts' whose results were settled in bilateral contacts. So, what cannot be solved at bilateral level may be perceived differently at regional level, and perhaps can be discussed in an inter-regional forum, or vice versa. Reiterer's study (2006) illustrates how regional and inter-regional forums provided Japan the chances to settle its problems with China and South Korea that could not be settled at the bilateral level. This means ASEM can possibly undertake its task to provide an alternative channel of communication among ASEM partners through either government-to-government dialogue or people-to-people contact. Second, as an informal forum, ASEM seems to provide an opportunity for the process of learning and networking. EU also sees ASEM as a policy-making laboratory (EC 2005) because ASEM provides forums for informal interactions between state and non-state actors which can be used to discuss and sound positions or policies on particular issues. An ASEF staff member pointed out that:

> Besides networks, the ASEF Intellectual Exchange Division provides a forum to "think tank" to discuss and identify strategic issues, contributing to policy making. (I42)

Thus, the ASEM process may serve as learning and adapting forums for Asian and European leaders and elites. ASEM provides what Ofken calls a "collective learning process" (2001, pp. 107–17). The Asians and Europeans pursue their common interests while trying to accommodate other actors' principles and objectives within the institutional framework of ASEM. This process is not always smooth, as reflected, for example in the issue of Myanmar and this has caused some tensions before the 2004 Hanoi Summit (see Chapter 2). Several interviewees express their appreciation for the role played by ASEM in this context:

> [After experiencing ASEF workshop] I think we should have more forums for youth to meet either with the EU or with other Asian fellows so we can grow the understanding toward each other. At the peaceful time, this event is important. (C25)

> ASEM should not [sic] for negotiation neither it for specific project or issues. So it is better to make ASEM as a forum to enhance understanding. Consequently, it is difficult to prove that ASEM has concrete results. (S36)

In addition, the informality can ideally be used by ASEM partners not only to find common interests but also to forge dialogue over their divergent principles and objectives. Through the informal ASEM process and the non-binding principle, the Asian and the European partners in ASEM can have bigger chances to flexibly manage, address and negotiate their dissimilarities and the discrepancies that stem from their different cultures, power, and political-strategic as well as development levels.

The results of the informality, however, have not emerged in some important aspects. It appears that the distance between Asian and European states in terms of interest and culture have not been bridged well (Chapter 1), and the differences in political values are still wide (Chapter 2). In terms of geostrategic link, ASEM, intended to be an Asia-Europe axis to counter the U.S. unilateralism, has not been seen as a serious challenger to the super power. The United States has not only maintained formal defence alliances with Japan, Singapore, Thailand and the Philippines, but has also dragged several Asian and European countries into the "war against terror". Some ASEM partners, such as the United Kingdom and Japan, will not risk their relations with the United States for the sake of the Asia-EU alliance (S33; S68; S71). Therefore, the trust could rarely emerge, especially in the first ASEM track. Perhaps, the need to build trust is another reason for ASEM to maintain its informal institutional framework.

For Southeast Asian countries, the informality of ASEM has created benefits. The informal arrangement of ASEM institutions has facilitated the East Asian states to feel that they are on the same side of ASEM without binding them. This feeling is needed more by the Southeast Asians than their partners in the Northeast Asia. As Stone, Slantchev and London (2008) argue, small countries would prefer shallow cooperation with a wider participation and multilateral institutions. The Southeast Asian countries have supported the enlargement process in ASEM and remain opposed to a more institutionalized ASEM.

INFORMAL INSTITUTION TO SUPPORT ASEM LONGEVITY

Despite criticism of its shortcomings and of its unclear future path, ASEM has survived. ASEM has evolved in slow motion and taken a flexible path amidst the challenges from the internal dynamics in Asia and Europe as well as from the external pressure from global politics and economic environment. Like other regional institutions such as ASEAN, APEC, and even the EU, ASEM is not immune from weaknesses and cannot satisfy all people. However, the criticisms fail to appreciate the richness of the soft institution of the ASEM as a useful framework to mitigate the distance divergent Asian and European states and regions.

The nature of ASEM's constituents and their principles and objectives, as well as the institution's own characteristics, thus, result in a complex set of relationships that bring significant impacts in terms of interactions and in institutions. Because of the different needs of its constituents, ASEM has had to be operated through a loose mechanism. The difficulties in accommodating and negotiating principles and objectives of the various constituents from both regions have resulted in the need for the flexibility which can be accommodated by the informality of ASEM's institution. Consequently, the ASEM institution has become less institutionalized, has unclear priorities, and lacks binding commitments. Nevertheless, as a process, ASEM reflects what Ofken writes as a "collective learning process" (2001, pp. 107–17). The Asians and Europeans pursue their common interests while trying to accommodate other actors' principles and objectives. This process is not always smooth, such as in the case of Myanmar's accession that almost ended ASEM before the 2004 Hanoi Summit.

The informality of the ASEM institution reflects a number of characteristics that seem to suit the needs of Southeast Asian countries. First, the informal ASEM institution does not require a high political cost that may undermine the sovereignty of its Asian partners. One interviewee commented that

> Given the informal process of ASEM, there is no need to have strong common position. [You may] agree for what you can agree and not agree for things you do not or cannot agree. (S53).

Secondly, the informal setting of the ASEM forums accommodates the cooperative culture of the East Asian countries in general and of the ASEAN members in particular, which, according to Acharya and Johnston (2007) emphasizes the process of region-building more than the institution building, aiming at the process rather than the outcomes. To borrow the words of two interviewees,

> Informality of ASEM is good because people can talk easier in less formal setting so communication is more possible. (I46)

> ASEM gives platform for Asian region building because ASEM process is merely informal. (S53)

Third, the informality in the ASEM process provides a conducive environment for more collegial relations among participants. This equality is one of the principles of ASEAN that has been accommodated by ASEM. A number of interviewees pointed out that informal interactions in the ASEM process allow more sustainable personal relations to develop and grow (D04; D07; D15; D16; D49; D50). Fourth, the informality in ASEM forums allows flexibility for participants to talk, discuss, and argue in less protocol-bound circumstances which is more appropriate for sensitive or critical issues. Some interviewees argued that the informality is beneficial as it allows ASEM participants to communicate openly and to find understanding and common views (D01; C10; S20; I46; D47). Thus, the informality of ASEM works well from the perspective of Southeast Asia.

It is understandable that there are concerns about ASEM of being weak and merely a "talk shop" because of its principles of informality and non-binding decisions. These "perceived" weaknesses, however, appear to be some of the factors that prevent ASEM from breaking up due to being too tied down by institutionalization. The ASEM soft institutional characteristics are embedded in the informal procedures and non-binding principles. The informality provides more room for the ASEM partners, whose differences are so broad and deep, to stay in the forum.

Hence, this chapter reveals that from the institutionalists' perspectives, the ASEM informal institution has two dimensions. First, the informality suits the needs of the Southeast Asian countries whose the cooperating culture is in favour of a soft institution with flexible procedures and non-binding commitments. This circumstance, in turn, maintains the participation of the ASEAN countries in the ASEM process and, therefore, supports the ASEM longevity. Second, the ASEM informality provides flexible framework for ASEM partners that have such different diversities inter-regionally as well as intra-regionally. The flexibility has likely helped maintain the existence of ASEM.

CONCLUSION
ASEM Has Delivered Significant Benefits to Southeast Asian Countries

The existence and significance of ASEM as a forum for inter-regional relations between Asia and Europe is little appreciated in both regions, and even less in the rest of the world. Within Asia, only a small number of state officials and non-official actors have any real understanding of, or engagement with, ASEM. Nevertheless, ASEM has survived and even enlarged. Most Asian leaders have continued to attend the ASEM summits despite the frequent failure of their European counterparts to attend with a complete team and despite little attention being given to this inter-regional institution. Why is this? What has ASEM delivered to its Asian partners? If the sceptics and critics are right about ASEM's weaknesses, why has it been maintained? This puzzle provides the rationale for this investigation into why and how ASEM has sustained, from the Southeast Asian perspectives, given the challenges in maintaining multidimensional relations and the inter-regional character of ASEM. This concluding chapter brings together the various strands of the overarching arguments in this study, and in so doing seeks to make a contribution to the literature of ASEM.

Whereas other studies of ASEM have indicated the challenges and what have been perceived as failures of these inter-regional relations, a distinctive feature of this study is its focus precisely on the question of why ASEM has endured as long as it has. Scholarly articles and reports during the initial years of ASEM mostly consist of the excitement and hopes for the new framework of relations written in neoliberal perspectives or historical–cultural points of view (Stokhof and van der Velde 1999; CAEC 1997; Dent 1997/1998). The positive tone, however, largely disappeared and was replaced by the negative assessments and criticisms of ASEM when the relevance of the inter-regional relations seemed to wane after the Asian financial crisis (Dent 1999; Forster 1999; Richards and Kirkpatrick 1999). In addition, the relevance of ASEM was questioned after the attack on U.S. territory in 2001. The overwhelming influence of the United States was able to persuade almost all international institutions, including ASEM, to devote their attention to security issues and the global campaign against what the United States termed "terrorism". Terrorism became the main issue in the fourth ASEM Summit in 2002 in Copenhagen and ASEM leaders' position to cooperate to combat terrorism was placed as the first point in the Chairman's Statement (ASEM 2006*f*). Subsequently, scholars developed another critique beyond its failure to take root as a strong framework of economic cooperation after the Asian financial crisis. They questioned the relevance of ASEM as a new partnership to counter the United States (Dent 2001, 2004; Dosch 2001; Ruland 2001; Loewen 2007). This coincided with the resurgence of neo-realist analysis in the international relations literature more generally. Nevertheless, a number of scholars have studied ASEM from other dimensions. Their explorations have added to the understanding of ASEM in terms of its institution (Loewen 2007; Reiterer 2004, 2006, 2009; Yeo 2004; Kaiser 2004; Japan and Finnish Ministries of Foreign Affairs 2006) as well as its place in regional identity building in Asia (Lee and Park 2001; Gilson 2002, 2005; Yeo 2003; Gilson and Yeo 2004). A study of why ASEM has worked for Southeast Asian countries or what are the perspectives from Southeast Asian countries about the longevity of ASEM had not been undertaken seriously. These gaps in the literature create the opportunities for further studies, and this thesis is a response to that need. Its focus has been on investigating ASEM's longevity from the Southeast Asian perspective and it has used the existing literature to formulate the working hypotheses to guide the initial phase of the research process, especially in developing the scheme for interviews.

This study has attempted to consider ASEM in terms of inter-regional and not just "inter-national" relations, an approach commended by some previous scholars (Gilson 2002; Reiterer 2006), as well as in the post-colonial framework. This approach has the potential to use ASEM as a laboratory of Asia-Europe relations. This thesis, however, focuses on the Southeast Asian perspectives, especially in its relations with the longevity of ASEM, because Southeast Asian behaviour in international relations is distinctive; the Asian approach to negotiation and cooperation is different from the non-Asians. Nevertheless, the results of this study can be considered for some thoughts under the inter-regionalism and the post-colonial studies as seen later.

The relevance and significance of this study of ASEM's longevity from the Southeast Asian perspective derives from several considerations. To begin with, this research strengthens the study of ASEM by incorporating the insights of involved or relevant actors through broad-ranging in-depth interviews. The interviews with various actors across Southeast Asian countries are valuable resources to be put side by side with the secondary data and to be analysed using an interpretive method.

In addition, the ASEM inter-regionalism is a new practice in international relations. The inter-regionalism of ASEM is also distinctive because it excludes the United States and it brings together the ASEAN countries with the Northeast Asian countries as an Asian group to meet and coordinate collectively with another regional group (the EU countries). The investigation of ASEM from the Asian perspectives reveals the opportunities and challenges to the relations, as well as forming better observations on this kind of relations. This research highlights the role of ASEM's inter-regionalism in the development of an intra-regional grouping while at the same time providing empirical evidence of the influence of the European integration over other regions. This investigation contributes in this way to an understanding of the role of external powers such as the EU in constructing a regional identity in East Asia.

At its heart, this study examines three types of possible benefits of ASEM to Southeast Asian countries that might help to build support from the ASEAN countries, which, in turn, explain ASEM longevity. Because of the quite different nature of each of these possible dimensions of national benefit, a different analytic framework has been needed for each. This kind of approach throws light on a more comprehensive understanding of international phenomena such as ASEM for two reasons. First, the issue of regional institutions such as ASEM and its longevity is a complex discourse, and no single analytical framework can provide a complete answer to the puzzle raised in this study. Second, the perspectives of Southeast Asian officials and non-officials regarding ASEM are varied, ranging from identity building to concern about the Europeans' interventions in human rights practices in Asia, to the frustration as well as advocation for the informality of the ASEM institution. There is no analytical framework that by itself can explain those perspectives. Nevertheless, the use of the three frameworks in this study does not aim at paradigmatic unity. Although mixing the three frameworks is theoretically not possible, applying — in parallel — each of them to analyse the most relevant or suitable issues can reveal a more complete analysis because the three analyses may be complementary to each other in explaining the main question in this thesis.

Finally, this research focuses on the relations between states' interests versus their need for cooperation that eventually shape the course of international institutions including inter-regional forums such as ASEM from the perspectives of state and non-state actors. The focus on how states exercise their power in international institutions is not new, but this study explores the use of an inter-regional institution (ASEM) by the Southeast Asian countries in two directions: towards the external actors (EU countries) and towards other regional countries in East Asia. By incorporating the views from non-state actors, this study considers not only the government-to-government relations but also people-to-people relations in ASEM to reveal what functions and interests ASEM has served for the Southeast Asian countries and participants.

The data for this thesis were collected through: documentary study; news study; two participant observations; and eighty-two in-depth interviews with officials, scholars, journalists, business people, and civil society in Indonesia, Malaysia, Singapore, Thailand, and Japan. Although these four kinds of data include meeting records, secondary data, news, observable facts, and transcripts of the interviews, this thesis is mainly driven by the interview data. The application of the inductive method in this study allows the data to be explained by the most relevant framework of analysis borrowed from the international relations discipline.

The limitations of this study are acknowledged. Because of familiar research constraints of time and funding associated with such a large multi-country topic, the focus has been on Southeast Asia, and even here it has not been feasible to cover all Southeast Asian countries equally. Nor could participant observation be extended to cover the ASEM summits. Nevertheless, this thesis provides a much fuller empirical grounding for deeper understanding of inter-regional relations between Asia and Europe in ASEM than has previously existed, particularly in terms of what ASEM has delivered for Southeast Asian countries. This, in turn, sheds light on the longevity of ASEM from the Southeast Asian perspectives.

The richness of the in-depth interview data could be translated into contextual insights with the help of the interpretive approach. The benefit in using this approach is enhanced by the fact that the researcher comes from a country in Southeast Asia, and this has helped her capture the insights from Southeast Asia and convey the perspectives based on the understanding of the context from which those perspectives have come.

However, the application of the interpretive approach in this study faces the inevitable challenge of possible researcher-induced bias. The difficulty is to find the right balance between recognizing the researcher's prior beliefs that can enrich inference making during the analysis, and preventing those beliefs from colouring the research in a judgmental way. To find a reasonable balance, this research took two steps: first, complementing the findings from the interview data and the participant observations, which unavoidably include subjective perceptions and opinions either from interviewees or from the researcher, with other types of data such as documents, news, and the academic literature. Secondly, instead of focusing on only data that comfortably supports the working hypotheses, the study has also addressed alternative views and analysed how such views emerged. The alternative views in this research are addressed in several parts in Chapters 1 to 3. By applying these two strategies, this book has tried to take advantage of the interpretive approach while controlling its weakness.

This study identifies three dimensions that explain what ASEM has delivered to the Southeast Asian countries: the relations between ASEM and the development of an Asian identity; the foreign policy advantage that can be pursued in the ASEM process; and the preference of Southeast Asians for the ASEM informal institution. The following sections explain each of the three dimensions. It is followed by further discussion over the findings of the book.

RELATIONS BETWEEN ASEM AND SOUTHEAST ASIAN COUNTRIES

This book reveals three possible explanations to answer what ASEM has delivered to the Southeast Asian countries: the relations between ASEM and the development of an Asian identity; the use of ASEM for foreign policy advancement by ASEAN member countries; and the maintenance of informality in the ASEM institution.

First, ASEM is a useful forum for Southeast Asian leaders and meeting participants due to its role in facilitating the development of an Asian regional identity or identities. ASEM has not only brought Asia closer to Europe through more frequent meetings and interactions in government-to-government as well as people-to-people forums, but also helped shape Asian identities among ASEM Asian partners, placing the Southeast Asian countries in the same regional group with the Northeast Asian countries. The ASEM process has managed seven summits for Asian and European leaders and numerous meetings of state apparatus, the private sector, and civil society. With three tracks of interactions and through political dialogues, economic cooperation, and sociocultural interactions, the ASEM process offers plenty of opportunities to develop the "we" feeling among Asian officials and non-officials. The broader channels of communication and interactions in the ASEM process have made it possible for state and non-state actors from East Asia to become much more familiar with each other. However, the inter-regional mechanism in ASEM or ASEF forums has sometimes developed into dynamics and, in some cases, crises through which the Asian participants position themselves as "Asian" vis-à-vis their European counterparts. To put it differently, ASEM takes part in social construction to create a stronger voice of Asian regional identity.

As shown in Chapter 1, the role of ASEM in the construction of Asian identity is mainly highlighted by those who are involved directly in the ASEM process or who have personally attended ASEM or ASEF forums such as state officials and non-officials from civil society. This thesis argues that the opportunities to meet counterparts from other East Asian countries is a significant factor that allows the Asian participants to share the regional awareness and to build the regional identity as the forums allow interactive socialization with Asian and European counterparts. The forums have improved chances for the Asian participants to communicate and interact, facilitating the "meeting of hearts and minds", a cognitive process that encourages the development of inter-subjective understandings among them.

In ASEM and ASEF forums, cognitive processes among Asian participants occur in two ways: by determining their concept of self as part of the Asian group and by comparing their Asian positions with those of their European counterparts. The communication and the socialization in the ASEM and ASEF forums inform perceptions, concerns, and intentions of other Asian fellows, making them even closer and more familiar with each other. At the same time Asian participants also compare and contrast their interests with their European counterparts. The cognitive process during the communication and interaction with the European participants helps the Asian participants to identify the similarities or differences between their concerns and interests and those of the European group (interviews with C24, C25, D50 S52 and D48). The process brought about awareness among the Asian people that they were different from the European people and that they shared more similarity with other Asians. Subsequently, they felt more comfortable among the Asians than among the Europeans.

The growth of regional consciousness and collective intentionality for Asian identity was strengthened, even to those who had not intended to build a "coalition", by the behaviours of European counterparts in the forums: first, by European critical assessment of Asian political affairs, especially those dealing with practices of human rights. Political values are the most sensitive issues in Asia and Europe relations so it would naturally provoke polarization. Second, the interview data demonstrates the significance of European distant attitudes in meetings and the way they are grouped among themselves in triggering reactions by Asian participants.

Another factor that contributes to strengthen Asian identity building in the ASEM process is cultural closeness and acquaintance among the ASEM partners from the Southeast and Northeast Asian countries. The inter-subjective cultural affinity (Ruggie 1998*a*) and the colonial memory that creates a "psychic unity" (D21) have made the Asian participants at ASEM or ASEF forums prefer to affiliate themselves to other Asian partners.

Thus, the sense of shared identity among the Asian participants in the ASEM process has been generated by cognitive processes and the collective experience in ASEM or ASEF forums. Those forums are in fact the social forums in which Asian participants are involved in an active process to understand and interpret about "us" and the "other".

Because the communication and interactions among Asian state and non-state actors were undertaken differently in term of frequency and intensity, it is inevitable that there have been various layers of identities among the Asian leaders and participants. In the ASEM process, the Southeast Asian participants bear at least three identities: their nation-state, ASEAN, and Asia; whereas Northeast Asian participants hold two: their nation-state and Asia. The existence of layered identities among the Asian participants of the ASEM or ASEF forums has caused some doubts about the existence of Asian identity or identities. The frequently asked question is, "Which identity?" However, the layered identity in Asia is unavoidable as a consequence of the dynamics of the region. The fact that there are several layers of identities among Asian participants does not mean the identities do not exist. The existence of Asian layered identities is obvious in the ASEM process. Indeed, the pre-summit meeting mechanism of ASEM (Figure 1.3) which consists of the intra-Asia coordinating meetings among ASEAN countries and among non-ASEAN countries reinforces the grouping within the ASEM Asian side. The intra-Asian meeting mechanism reflects the expansion of identities among Asian participants that is also identical with their cognitive institutions (Ruggie 1998*b*): nation-states, ASEAN, and APT (which is also equal with the ASEM Asian side[1] (Figure 1.3).

In short, the channels of communication and interaction in the ASEM process were available when the Southeast Asian countries were developing their Asian regional consciousness and building the sense of regional identity with the Northeast Asian countries in the 1990s and 2000s. This ideational function of ASEM is complementary with other regional channels such as APT and EAS. Thus, ASEM has helped facilitate the development of Asian identity or identities through the frequent social interactions among leaders and participants. The sense of regional awareness resulting from the cognitive process and collective experience in the ASEM process, in turn, has been used by the Southeast Asian countries for other forums. Despite ASEM's low profile in Asian regionalization, leaders from Southeast Asian countries keep attending ASEM summits which in itself contribute to the longevity of ASEM.

Second, this book argues that ASEM has strategically benefited the Southeast Asian countries because the inter-regional institution seems to be an important forum to pursue foreign policy advantages for the ASEAN members. This conclusion is suggested based on the interview results and other supporting data particularly that on Myanmar's accession to ASEM and the application of the framework of the strategic usage of international institutions by states. The case study of Myanmar's admission to ASEM highlights not only a discrepancy in Asia-Europe political values but also the ability of ASEAN countries and China to take advantage of European economic interest for their political purposes. As Chapter 2 has shown, Asian-EU countries' disagreement on Myanmar's admission before the fifth ASEM Summit in Hanoi in 2004 led to a deadlock of the ASEM process and posed the most serious threat to the ASEM continuity. ASEAN countries were more confident about articulating and pushing an Asian position supportive of Myanmar's accession to ASEM, because of both the delicate relations between Japan and China, and China's willingness to endorse ASEAN's position. ASEAN countries were able to forge a collaborative effort with China in this case through the coordination mechanism in the ASEM process that facilitates intra-regional meetings before the region-to-region meetings.

In line with the arguments of Simmons and Martin (1998, 2002) who perceive international institutions as strategic tools by states rather than as a medium for cooperation, the data from interviews and news suggested that ASEAN countries and China have used ASEM to gain political advantages over the EU countries. Whereas they had failed to negotiate their support for Myanmar in the ASEAN-EU forum, ASEAN countries obtained a stronger political bargaining power vis-à-vis the EU counterparts because of China's support. For China, its support for the ASEAN position in the process of Myanmar's admission to ASEM seems to relate to its strategy to build closer relations with the countries in Southeast Asia and to reaffirm its relations with Myanmar amid its competition with India to approach the Myanmar military regime.

China's presence in ASEM seems to enhance not only the position of the Asian side but also the importance of ASEM. This research does not investigate in-depth the role of China in ASEM but data from interviews suggest that China's participation in ASEM is a very significant power that not only makes the EU countries value ASEM but also attracts other Asian countries to maintain the inter-regional forum. The attendance of forty-three Asian and EU leaders in the seventh ASEM Summit hosted by China in 2008, the first time EU leaders attended ASEM summit almost in full[2] after the inaugural summit, indicates that China is a very, if not the most, attractive partner in ASEM.

Thus, despite its neglected position in regional affairs, ASEM seems to have delivered strategic advantages — of a traditional *realpolitik* type — for ASEAN countries and China. ASEAN countries treat ASEM not only as an additional forum to address issues that cannot be tackled in ASEAN-EU forum but also to play a stronger role in regional decision making. In addition, China has appeared to be the magnet of ASEM that attracts Asian and European countries to stay in ASEM. Despite China's interest in using ASEM for its own foreign policy advantage, its commitment and participation in the ASEM process has contributed to ASEM's longevity. The theme of the ASEM summit in Beijing 2008, which was *Vision and action: Towards a win-win solution*, clearly shows that China has an interest in supporting ASEM and to transfer the "talk-shop" into action without underplaying its interests. ASEM has survived because the Asian countries still perceive it as a forum worth maintaining for the advancement of their traditional interest in foreign policies. This pursuit of the traditional power games such as the one shown in the Myanmar case is likely to be one of the reasons why the Asian countries maintain ASEM.

Third, this study argues that ASEM's institutional design has worked comfortably for the Southeast Asian countries. There are several studies from institutional theorists, which provide useful guidance for situating questions about the institution of ASEM. This perspective draws on institutional theorists (Lipson 1991; Koremenos, Lipson, and Snidal 2001; Kawasaki 2009) who argue that institutional design can be a deliberate choice of states to achieve particular outcomes. States may choose or design the type of their cooperation framework, and may adjust it, according to their need in the evolution of their cooperating institution. Accordingly, the adoption of informality for international institutions could possibly be the result of states' deliberate intention in the initial phase as well as in the course of cooperation. Stone, Slantchev and London (2008) have also argued that small states' behaviour in international institutions would prefer shallow cooperation with wide participants. These perspectives shed light on the behaviour of the Asian states in general and Southeast Asian countries in particular to maintain the inter-regional relations through ASEM but keep it as an informal forum and non-binding engagement.

Chapter 3 reveals that during ASEM's initial years, the Southeast Asian leaders who initiated ASEM seemed to foresee the complexity of intra-regional relations that they designed ASEM's mechanism to be flexible. The difficulties in accommodating and negotiating principles and objectives of various constituents from both regions required flexibility in the ASEM process. Because of the different needs of its constituents, ASEM has had to be operated through a loose mechanism. For the inter-regional relations to survive, the ASEM institution had to become less institutionalized and avoid binding commitment.

ASEM has survived despite the complexity of the inter-regional relations. ASEM's longevity seems to be supported by its soft institutional arrangement that takes place as an informal ASEM process with non-binding decisions. Some people may see these aspects as hampering ASEM's development to a higher level of institutionalization but the informality creates flexibility for ASEM partners to counter the complexity. ASEM's soft institution helps ASEM partners, whose differences are so various and wide, to learn and negotiate. With the growing number of ASEM partners, the soft institutional design may be even more necessary and pivotal to make ASEM acceptable to all partners.

Institutional informality has been a significant factor contributing to ASEM's longevity. As one of the interviewees commented, "Currently, [there is] no pressing need to strengthen Asia-EU relations, [It is] only a goodwill diplomacy" (S68). Nevertheless, given the soft institutional arrangement of ASEM, maintaining the inter-regional relations is not costly. Owing to the non-binding principle, ASEM does not require significant political and financial commitments.

Despite widespread neglect and even disdain, ASEM has various functions that complement with other regional initiatives and bilateral relations between Asia and Europe and among Asian states. ASEM is a low-cost diplomatic channel between Asia-Europe and/or among Asian countries that does not need a lot of investment from participating countries; yet it can be a valuable instrument in a time of crisis. Compared with the potential intangible linkages that ASEM can activate in times of crisis, maintaining ASEM appears to be significantly less costly than terminating it. One of the interviewees commented that,

> Nobody wants to be seen as a bad guy who kills ASEM. It started as dialogue but now A-E need more than dialogue. ASEM may stay there to add to other channels [of communication], merely as a low cost channel with no binding policy. [The] Asian and European countries will tackle serious issues in other forums. They can be bilateral, ASEAN-EU, China-EU [forums]. ASEM is a low cost forum so nothing wrong to maintain it in case we need it sometime in the future. (S31)

Data gathered for this study reveals that ASEM institution has been built in accordance with the needs of the Southeast Asian countries, that is, inter-regional relations managed by an informality and non-binding principle. The Southeast Asian countries seem to influence ASEM with these institutional characteristics that are similar to those of their regional institution, ASEAN. This factor, in turn, helps maintain ASEAN countries' acceptance and support to ASEM. In addition, the ASEM institution contributes to its longevity because of two considerations. First, the informality of the ASEM institution, a soft institution, creates flexibility for ASEM, allowing the inter-regional forums to accommodate the wide diversity, varying interests, and different capabilities of its partners. Second, ASEM's soft or informal institutional arrangement seems to reduce the cost of maintaining cooperation through region-to-region relations between the Asian and European states while opening up opportunities for the two regions to develop different kinds of strategic relations.

In this light, it can be seen that ASEM has produced benefits for the Southeast Asian group. There is no intention here to overstate these gains; they are modest, but they are not insignificant. They also help explain why Southeast Asian governments continue their engagement with ASEM despite the multiplicity of other forums that have sprung up.

In sum, for Southeast Asian leaders not only are there some genuine — if modest — gains to be had from maintaining ASEM, doing so avoids the costs likely to be associated with terminating it. It is an efficient form of diplomacy. ASEM has survived because Asian and European countries still perceive it as a forum worth maintaining. ASEAN countries treat ASEM as additional forum to address issues that cannot be tackled in other forums. The fact that ASEM has been established also helps sustain it. Thus, maintaining ASEM is more useful than superseding it.

LEARNING FROM SOUTHEAST ASIAN
PERSPECTIVES ABOUT ASEM

The previous section has elaborated the findings of this book. They provide some opportunities for further analysis. This section tries to place those findings in a broader context because the observations of the Southeast Asian perspectives about ASEM can reveal regional dynamics in Asia and the potency of (East) Asia as a regional entity.

First, the development of identity building in Asia may be better facilitated in informal settings, be it in regional institutions or in the arrangement of meetings. This notion that has been built throughout this study can be useful in the study of identity building. The informality is needed to help a more interactive socialization among Asian leaders and people because only in such circumstances can the cognitive process among meeting participants create a more genuine openness, which turns to acquaintance, then perhaps trust and inter-subjective understanding. It is hard to be attached to other people if there is no genuine conversation and interaction. Informality provides more room for Asian leaders and participants to establish more solid human relations that are necessary for the feeling of a group, the identification to a particular identity, to develop. It will be interesting to observe to what extent the informality helps facilitate the development of regional awareness among Asian participants in comparison with the pressure of external factors such as EU participants. Nevertheless, a combination of those two factors has apparently been obtained from the ASEM process by Southeast Asian participants with their counterparts from the Northeast Asian countries that allow them to develop an Asian identity.

The significance of the informal setting to help develop regional identity could be an interesting consideration in the context of EU studies too, especially in regard to the EU's efforts to develop European citizenship. The EU countries are known for their preference for formal institutions in managing cooperation (Fawcett and Hurrell 1995; Palmujoki 1997; Ruland 2001; Fawcett 2004) and a number of interviewees reveal the informality of ASEM caused widespread scepticism among the European elites (S19; S36; I42). It will be an advantage for EU to learn to understand the benefits that come from the informality of ASEM's institution in regard to the development of shared regional awareness and identity building. The advantage of an informal setting can shed light on the context of Europe where the European Commission took a top-down, legal-formal approach in using cultural policy and political symbolism to develop the notion of EU citizenship (Shore 2000) and where the causal relations between European identities and EU institutions have been questioned (Risse 2005).

Second, informality is important and necessary to keep institutions going. Lipson (1991) is correct in arguing that to sustain cooperation, flexibility is needed, and informality is a way to create this flexibility in international or regional institutions. The flexibility is needed because the challenges to cooperation are too big while direct, short-term, concrete outcomes may not be secured (Lipson 1991). In ASEM, the challenges are the diversity of its partners and the difference in Asia and Europe in their cooperation culture and approaches. Without informality, ASEM may not have survived at all, much less embarked on its membership enlargements.

The preference for informality over formalization can also reveal the operation of the Asian cooperation culture. The informality of ASEM's institution is influenced by ASEAN's institution that has been brought by the Southeast Asian countries to ASEM. The ASEM's institution, after all, is also the result of political calculation among the Asian countries and the compromise between its Asian and European partners. This is in line with Goldstein, Kahler, Keohane and Slaughter (2000) who perceive that the level of the legalization of institutions is shaped by political dynamics. For Southeast Asian countries, the process is more important than short-term material gains as they emphasize more the process of confidence and trust building. The criticisms of ASEM informality such as Jones and Smith (2007a, b) seem to overlook the Asian cooperative culture that emphasizes "region building" rather than "institution building" (Acharya and Johnston 2007) and the preservation of sovereignty of the involved countries (Kahler 2000; He 2004; Khong and Nesadurai 2007). In the context of regional institutions, whether such formality and institutional building approach can create the "real" region is still in doubt (Hettne and Soderbaum 2002). The bottom line is, with the informal institution, actors may achieve goals that cannot otherwise be achieved. Thus, the informal institution should not be underestimated, as something significant may emerge from it; after all, formal relations usually start with informal contacts.

An implication of this study is that it is better to let ASEM evolve at a pace acceptable to the partners in both regions — which, in practice, probably gives greater weight to those who want to move less quickly. Enforcing a movement of legalization or creating a higher level of institutionalization may not help in sustaining the ASEM process. As Chapter 1 has shown, the trust has not yet become robust between the Asian and the European groups. From the East Asian perspective, cooperation cannot genuinely develop without such trust. The European leaders who were absent from the summits have, in fact, suffered from the exclusion from the opportunities to build trust with their Asian counterparts. While criticizing the ineffectiveness of ASEM forums and the inability of ASEM to bring about concrete material gains, and not bothering to attend the summits, European leaders actually miss a chance to approach Asian leaders in a more genuine way. Asian leaders, officials and scholars seem to have understood the short-term, materialistic reasons behind the frequent absence of the European leaders and very critical to this behaviour (D02; D17; S35; D48; D50). In addition, the underlying reason for the Southeast Asian countries' aversion to formal and binding institutions is to protect their sovereignty (Kahler 2000; He 2004; Acharya and Johnston 2007). As ASEM was created with the purpose of improving the understanding between the two regions, as stated in the Chairman's Statement of the first ASEM Summit (ASEM 2006*b*), this inter-regional institution should be left as it is; as the forum to build the inter-subjective understandings that may in turn create trust among its partners. The trust built through the ASEM process may be transferred to a more concrete cooperation projects in other forums.

Third, the benefits that the Southeast Asian countries have extracted from their region-to-region relations with the EU countries in ASEM can help explain the relations between the two regions in the post-colonial context. This study has revealed that the colonial memories have, in subtle and little noticed ways, united a majority of the Southeast and Northeast Asian countries within ASEM. In addition, the interaction with the European participants in the ASEM process, particularly in regard to the European distant attitude and criticisms of the Asian political values and practices, has exacerbated the Asian perception of the past in which the exploitative nature of European colonialization is remarkable. The shared awareness of the past regarding European colonialism and the limited success of the trust building between the Asians and the Europeans in the ASEM process, can underplay the efforts to recover the linkage between peoples in the two regions.

The potency of the Southeast Asian states and China to take collective actions is also an interesting issue for post-colonial studies as the former colonized countries in Asia usually perceive themselves as the victims of Western colonialization and as marginalized states. Observing the power relations between the two regions is particularly interesting in the current context where the "under-developed" Asians have become the global economic power houses, whereas the European countries have seemed to be losing their ground in the global arena. It is not only crucial to observe how the former colonized Asian countries and the former colonial powers in Europe cope in the period that has been perceived as the global power shifting but also important to observe how the Asian states adjust the pressure to take global "responsibility" and how the European states deal with the possibility of being "subordinate". Will the Europeans play their "old games" of divide and rule with the Asian powers to avoid losing their "traditional" power?

Thus, this study can enrich post-colonial scholarship by revealing two findings: first, that the common perception about the continuity of the European exploitative nature in the post-colonial period is one of the factors that united the Asian participants in the ASEM process; second, the pressure from the EU countries in the inter-regional relations has encouraged the Asian participants to take collective action vis-à-vis the European counterparts.

Fourth, inter-regional relations, such as in ASEM, can represent an important pattern of global affairs in the future. More than encouraging a diverse region such as East Asia to form collective actions, the inter-regionalism of the ASEM forums can create a regional entity that can challenge prevailing patterns of global politics. The region-to-region relations in ASEM have created such circumstance that is conducive enough not only for Asian region-building but is also a meaningful political action, for example as the Asian countries have shown in the Myanmar case.

Such inter-regional relations can be an important focus in international relations studies. This is because not only has the end of the Cold War removed structural barriers for regional dialogue and provided a more favourable environment for regionalism (Buzan 1991; Katzenstein 2000; Fawcett 2004) but also in the future, regions may evolve as global actors (Dosch 2001; Katzenstein 2006; Hurrell 2007). Therefore, inter-regionalism may become an important model of interaction in the world. By definition, inter-regionalism is different from the Westphalia international system that highlights the state-to-state relations. In practice, as shown in this study, the region-to-region relations are even more complex than state-to-state relations as they deal with intra-regional as well as extra-regional dynamics. So, whereas state-to-state relations is perceived as two-level games between international bargaining and domestic politics (Putnam 1988; Moravcsik 1993, 1997), the region-to-region relations can actually be four-level games in which the intra-regional bargaining and inter-regional dynamics intervene between global pressure and domestic politics. In addition, the region-to-region relations are different from bloc-versus-bloc relations that prevailed during the Cold War. Currently, the study, as well as the practice, of inter-regionalism has only been limited to EU-Asian in ASEM and EU-Mercusor. This study can help set the path for future studies of the inter-regional paradigm as it provides insights into the Southeast Asian side of ASEM's inter-regionalism.

Finally, Asian countries can be a powerful international actor if they can work together. This research reveals that under the inter-regional framework, with togetherness and "cheap" investment, Asian countries could dictate the meeting agenda and take a leading role over their European counterparts, who less than a century ago were still the colonial rulers in most of ASEM's Asian countries. The experience that Asian countries have gained in ASEM can make them more confident to take up further challenges, such as soliciting common Asian positions on global issues such as climate change and restructurization. Asian common positions will be important in an era where the global power is shifting, that is followed by responsibilities shifting, to Asia. If they can build more solid common positions, the Asian countries may be able to undertake the global responsibilities in their own term and ways. The analysis in this study reveals that the Southeast Asian countries can be the force behind such Asian movements.

In closing, the main question that emerges in contemplating the future of ASEM is whether the argument developed here about ASEM's utility in the past will continue to hold true after the absorption of new members such as Pakistan, India and Mongolia — and even more so, Russia, Australia, and New Zealand. These effects will likely take some years to emerge. It would also be fascinating to extend the scope of this study to include a detailed investigation of ASEM's utility to the whole Asian countries in ASEM or to European countries. Exploring such issues are the opportunities for future research but the Epilogue may put forward some latest developments in this context.

Notes

1. As stated in Chapter 1, the focus of this thesis is the ASEM process from 1996 to 2008 when the ASEM Asian side merely consisted of ASEAN countries, China, Japan, and South Korea.
2. The U.K. Prime Minister is the only head of state of major European countries who did not attend the Beijing Summit in 2008. Indeed, apart from the ASEM inaugural summit in 1996, British top leaders only attended the second summit in London in 1998 when the United Kingdom was the host.

EPILOGUE
Southeast Asia and
ASEM after 2008

As a social construction, Asian identity has not yet appeared as a solid single collective intention, but the process of interactive construction of identity has taken place among Asian elites and people in ASEM from 1996 up to 2008. ASEM took part in this process as a social arena for socialization among Asian participants. Nevertheless, since 2008 ASEM has experienced the second and third enlargements[1] which change the Asian group in ASEM. In 2008, India, Pakistan, and Mongolia became new partners of ASEM, followed by Russia, Australia, and New Zealand in 2010 (see Map 2). These developments brought some consequences not only to ASEM as an inter-regional institution but also to the Asian group in ASEM and to the Southeast Asian countries.

First, the accession of India, another rising state in Asia, can provide another source and power to the Asian group in ASEM. Accordingly, the Asians' bargaining power vis-à-vis the European counterparts could increase. Nevertheless, the involvement of India also creates challenges for the Southeast Asian countries since India has been perceived as a competitor to China and because the country has had strained relations with Pakistan. The Southeast Asian countries have to manage their relations with India in such a way in order not to jeopardize their relations with China and Pakistan. The consolidation of the Asian group in ASEM and the enhancement of their regional identity in ASEM are arguably even more complex and harder as the group now includes more countries and two distinctive cultures, China and India.

Second, the ASEM enlargement in 2010 that accepted the accession of Russia, Australia, and New Zealand also brings some other challenges. The challenges can be referred back to the research question in this thesis: Will ASEM still work for Asian countries after the 2010 enlargement? The challenges arise from two facts that Russia becomes the first non-EU country in ASEM and Australia has sometimes tried to identify itself as an Asian country, but the position of this country in the Asian group has been frequently questioned, not only by some Asian countries but also within its own domestic political debates. The three newcomers have been categorized as "others" due to confusion — and rejection — to place them in either Asian or European group. This third category creates a question in regard to the ASEM inter-regional arrangement as to where to place them in pre-summit coordinator meeting. More substantially, the last accession can also influence the solidarity in the Asian side of ASEM. There are at least two factors that can indicate that Australia may not add to the strength of the Asian group in ASEM. Australia shared more values with the European countries than with the Asians. These values include support for liberal democracy and environment protection. The second is that since 31 October 2011, EU-Australia has embarked a negotiation for a treaty-level framework agreement as the two parties aim to establish free trade agreements. This new development shows that EU and Australia has had special relations that they may bring to ASEM.

It will be interesting to observe whether the findings of this research, that address the utility of ASEM from the (Southeast) Asian perspectives, still apply if the ASEM's Asian group includes the new accessed countries. This will be a topic for future research, together with an inquiry to investigate how ASEM has worked for the European countries.

Note

1. The first enlargement was in 2004 with the accession of three Asian and ten European countries. See Chapter 1.

REFERENCES

Acharya, Amitav. *The Quest for Identity: International Relations of Southeast Asia*. Oxford: Oxford University Press, 2000.

———. "The Social Construction of Regions: Insights from Southeast Asia". In *Regionalism in Asia and Europe and Implications for Asia-Europe Relations*, edited by ASEF University. Singapore: Asia Europe Foundation, 2004.

———. *Constructing a Security Community in Southeast Asia: ASEAN and the Problem of Regional Order*. London: Routledge, 2009.

——— and A. Johnston. "Comparing regional institutions: An introduction". In *Crafting Cooperation: Regional international institutions in comparative perspectives*, edited by A. Acharya and A. Johnston. Cambridge: Cambridge University Press, 2007.

Agence France Press (AFP). "EU work for compromise to resolve Myanmar row". 4 September 2004 <http://global.factiva.com/aa/default.aspx?pp=print&hc=Publication> (accessed 6 February 2009).

Aggarwal, V. and M. Koo. "Beyond network power? The dynamics of formal economic integration in Northeast Asia". *Pacific Review* 18, no. 2 (2005): 189–216.

ASEM Education Secretariat 2010. "Members". <http://www.asem-education-secretariat.org/en/12183/> (accessed 17 May 2010).

Asian Development Bank (ADB). *Emerging Asian regionalism: A Partnership for shared prosperity*. Manila: Asian Development Bank, 2008.

Asia-Europe Foundation (ASEF). *The Asia-Europe Roundtable: Regions in Transition*. Singapore: Institute of Southeast Asian Studies, ASEF, and Friedrich Ebert Stiftung, 2001.

———. *The 10th of ASEF: Voices from Asia & Europe*. Singapore: Asia-Europe Foundation, 2007.

———. "Themes and projects", 2009 <http://www.asef.org/index.php?option=com_project&Itemid=75> (accessed 20 October 2009).

————. "Themes and projects", 2012 <http://www.asef.org/index.php?option=com_project&Itemid> (accessed 10 June 2012).

Asia-Europe Meeting Infoboard (ASEM Infoboard). "About ASEM — Overview". Asia Europe Meeting, 2006*a* <http://www.aseminfoboard.org/page.phtml?code=About> (accessed 8 November 2007).

————. "Chairmans_statement_asem_1". Asia Europe Meeting, 2006*b* <http://www.aseminfoboard.org/content/documents/chairmans_statement_asem_1.pdf> (accessed 8 November 2007).

————. "Chairmans_statement_asem_2". Asia Europe Meeting, 2006*c* <http://www.aseminfoboard.org/content/documents/chairmans_statement_asem_2.pdf> (accessed 28 April 2010).

————. "Chairmans_statement_asem_3". Asia Europe Meeting, 2006*d* <http://www.aseminfoboard.org/content/documents/chairmans_statement_asem_3.pdf> (accessed 8 November 2007).

————. "Asia-Europe Cooperation Framework (AECF) 2000". Asia Europe Meeting, 2006*e* <http://www.aseminfoboard.org/About/AECF2000/> (accessed 8 November 2007).

————. "Chairmans_statement_asem_4". Asia Europe Meeting, 2006*f* <http://www.aseminfoboard.org/content/documents/chairmans_statement_asem_4.pdf> (accessed 8 November 2007).

————. "Chairmans_statement_asem_5". Asia Europe Meeting, 2006*g* <http://www.aseminfoboard.org/content/documents/chairmans_statement_asem_5.pdf> (accessed 8 November 2007).

————. "Chairmans_statement_asem_6". Asia Europe Meeting, 2006*h* <http://www.aseminfoboard.org/content/documents/chairmans_statement_asem_6.pdf> (accessed 8 November 2007).

————. "Working Methodology". Asia Europe Meeting, 2006*i* <http://www.aseminfoboard.org/page.phtml?code=AboutWorkingMethodology> (accessed 8 November 2007).

————. "About ASEM". Asia Europe Meeting, 2006*j* <http://www.aseminfoboard.org/page.phtml?code=About> (accessed 8 November 2007).

————. "ASEM in brief". Asia Europe Meeting, 2006*k* <http://www.asem6.fi/what_is_asem/asem_in_brief/en_GB/asem_in_brief/> (accessed 17 October 2006).

————. "Structure". Asia Europe Meeting, 2007 <http://www.aseminfoboard.org/About/Structure/structure.pdf> (accessed 7 November 2007).

————."ASEM 7 Chair-Statement". Asia Europe Meeting, 2008 <http://www.aseminfoboard.org/content/documents/ASEM7_Chair-Statement.pdf> (accessed 20 June 2009).

————. "ASEM Partners". Asia-Europe Meeting, 2010 <http://www.aseminfoboard.org/page.phtml?code=Partners> (accessed 28 January 2010).

Asia-Europe Network. "EU emissary seeks Myanmar-ASEM compromise". 2004

<http://www.asia-europe network.org/index2.php? option=com_content&do_pdf =1&id=159> (accessed 8 February 2009).

Asia-Europe Vision Group (AEVG). "For a better tomorrow: Asia-Europe Partnership in the 21st Century". Asia Europe Meeting, 1999 <www.igenet.com/files/AEVG-Report.doc> (accessed on 28 April 2010).

Asia Times, 25 July 2003 <http://www.asiantribune.com/oldsite/show_news. php?id=9929>.

Association of the Southeast Asian Nations (ASEAN). "Framework Agreement on Comprehensive Economic Co-Operation Between ASEAN and the People's Republic of China, Phnom Penh, 4 November 2002". 2002 <http://www. aseansec.org/13196.htm> (accessed 28 April 2010).

―――. "Excerpts from the Joint Communique of the 36th ASEAN Ministerial Meeting, Phnom Penh, 16–17 June 2003". 2003*a* <http://www.aseansec. org/14876.htm> (accessed 10 November 2009).

―――. "Instrument of Accession to Treaty of Amity and Cooperation in Southeast Asia, 8 October 2003". 2003*b* <http://www.aseansec.org/15271.htm> (accessed 10 November 2009).

―――. "Excerpts from the Joint Communique of the 37th ASEAN Ministerial Meeting, Jakarta, 29–30 June 2004". 2004 <http://www.aseansec.org/16265. htm> (accessed 10 November 2009).

―――. "Forging closer ASEAN-China economic relations in the twentieth-first century: A Report Submitted by the ASEAN-China Expert Group on Economic Cooperation, October 2001". 2009*a* <http://www.aseansec.org/ newdata/asean_ chi.pdf> (accessed 10 November 2009).

―――. "ASEAN: Overview". 2009*b* <http://www.aseansec.org/64.htm> (accessed 10 January 2010).

―――. "ASEAN Charter". 2009*c* <http://www.aseansec.org/21861.htm> (accessed 20 April 2010).

Association of the Southeast Asian Nations (ASEAN) Vietnam. "Vietnam in ASEM". 2010 <http://asean2010.vn/asean_en/news/18/2DA79E/VIETNAM-IN-ASEM> (accessed 27 April 2010).

Ba, A. "China and ASEAN: Renavigating relations for a 21st-century Asia". *Asian Survey* 43, no. 4 (2003): 622–47.

Bangkok Post. "ASEM to avoid mention of Burma". 6 September 2004 <http://www. karen.org/news2/messages/153.html> (accessed 12 February 2009).

Beeson, M. *Regionalism and Globalization in East Asia: Politics, security and economic development*. New York: Palgrave Macmillan, 2007.

―――. *Institutions of the Asia-Pacific: ASEAN, APEC and beyond*. London: Routledge, 2009.

Bersick, S. "The ASEM regime and its participants' interests". *Asia Europe Crosspoints*, 2002 <http://tni.org/archives/act/4334> (accessed 27 April 2010).

————. "Inter-regional cooperation beyon ASEM @10: Responding to rising extremism and resurging nationalism". *Panorama* 1 (2007): 63–74.

————. "China and ASEM: Strengthening multilateralism through inter-regionalism". In *The Eurasian space: Far more than two continents*, edited by W. Stokhof, P. van der Velde and Yeo L.H. Leiden: IIAS, 2004.

————. "Review". In *The Asia-Europe Meeting: Engagement, enlargement and expectations*, edited by Yeo L.H. and W. Hofmeister. *Asia Europe Journal* 8 (2010): 441–42.

Boyd, A. "EU's Myanmar move risks ASEM ties". *Asia Times Online*, 11 August 2004 <http://www.atimes.com/atimes/Global_Economy/FH11Dj01.html> (accessed 12 February 2009).

Bretherton, C. and J. Vogler. *The European Union as a global actor*. London: Routledge, 2006.

Bridges, B. "Europe and the Asian Financial Crisis". *Asian Survey* 39, no. 3 (1999): 456–67.

British Broadcasting Corporation (BBC). "EU attempts to dampen Burma row". 13 July 2004 <http://news.bbc.co.uk/2/hi/asia-pacific/3888673.stm> (accessed 6 February 2009).

Burma Campaign UK. "EU lets Burma into ASEM". 2004 <http://www.burmacampaign.org.uk/> (accessed 28 December 2007).

Buzan, B. *People, states and fear: The national security problem in international relations*. Brighton: Harvester Wheatsheaf, 1991.

Caballero-Anthony, M. "Evolving regional governance in East Asia: From ASEAN to an East Asian Community". In *Governance and Regionalism in Asia*, edited by Nicholas Thomas, pp. 32–65. Oxford and New York: Routledge, 2009.

Chalermpalanupap, T. "Institutional reform: One charter, three communities, many challenges". In *Hard Choice: Security, democracy, and regionalism in Southeast Asia*, edited by D. Emmerson. Stanford: Walter H. Shorenstein Asia-Pacific Research Center, 2009.

China View. 26 August 2004 <http://news.xinhuanet.com/English/2004-08/26/content_1890571.html> (accessed 6 February 2009).

Chirathivat, S., F. Knippping, P. Lassen and Chia S.Y., eds. *Asia-Europe on the eve of the 21st century*. Bangkok: Centre for European Studies, Chulalongkorn University, 2001.

Corbett, J. and E. Fitriani. "Australian perspectives on the road map towards East Asian economic integration". *APEC Economies Newsletter* 12, no. 5 (June 2008).

Council for Asia-Europe Cooperation (CAEC). *The rationale and common agenda for Asia-Europe cooperation: CAEC task force reports*. Tokyo: Japan Centre for International Exchange (JCIE), 1997.

————. "The Council for Asia-Europe Cooperation (CAEC)". 1999 <http://www.caec-asiaeurope.org/IE/What/index.html> (accessed 9 May 2006).

Curley, M. and N. Thomas. *Advancing East Asian Regionalism*. London: Routledge, 2007.

Daily Telegraph. "Backing for Burma", 21 July 2004 <http://global.factiva.com/aaa/default.aspx?pp=Print&hc=Publication> (accessed 6 February 2009).

Daily Times. 1 September 2004 <http://www.dailytimes.com.pk/default.asp?page=story_1-9-2004_pg4_12> (accessed 6 February 2009).

Darby, P. "Pursuing the political: A postcolonial rethinking of relations international". *Millennium: Journal of International Studies* 33, no. 1 (2004): 1–34.

Dent, C. "The ASEM: Managing the new framework of the EU's economic relations with East Asia". *Pacific Affairs* 74, no. 1 (1997/1998): 25–52.

———. *The European Union and East Asia: An economic relationship*. London: Routledge, 1999.

———. "ASEM and 'Cinderella complex' of EU-East Asia economic relations". *Pacific Affairs* 70, no. 4 (2001): 495–516.

———. "The Asia-Europe Meeting and inter-regionalism: Toward a theory of multilateral utility". *Asian Survey* 44, no. 2 (2004): 213–36.

———. *New Free Trade Agreements in the Asia Pacific*. New York: Palgrave Macmillan, 2006.

Dieter, H. and R. Higgott. "Exploring alternative theories of economic regionalism: From trade to finance in Asia cooperation?". *Review of International Political Economy* 10, no. 3 (2003): 430–54.

Dittmer, L., H. Fukui and P. Lee, eds. *Informal politics in East Asia*. Cambridge: Cambridge University Press, 2000.

Dosch, J. "The ASEAN-EU relations: An emerging pillar of the new international order?". In *Asia-Europe on the eve of the 21st century*, edited by S. Chirathivat, F. Knippping, P. Lassen and Chia Siow Yue. Bangkok: Centre for European Studies, Chulalongkorn University, 2001.

———. "The impact of EU-enlargement on relations between Europe & East Asia". *Asia-Europe Journal* 5, no. 1 (March 2007): 33–50.

Edwards, G. and E. Regelsberger, eds. *Europe's global links: The European Community and inter-regional cooperation*. New York: St. Martin's Press, 1990.

Emmerson, D., ed. *Hard Choices: Security, democracy and regionalism in Southeast Asia*. Stanford: Walter H. Shorenstein Asia-Pacific Research Center, 2009.

European Commission (EC). "Towards a new Asia strategy". Brussels, 13 July 1994, COM (1994) 314 final, European Union (EU) <http://ec.europa.eu/external_relations/library/publications> (accessed 10 October 2008).

———. "Perspectives and Priorities for the ASEM Process (Asia Europe Meeting) into the new decade". Commission Working Document, Brussels, 18 April 2000 COM (2000) 241 final, European Union (EU) <http://ec.europa.eu/external_relations/asia/docs/index_en.htm> (accessed 17 April 2010).

———. "Europe and Asia: A Strategic Framework for Enhanced Partnerships". Brussels, 4 September 2001, COM (2001) 469 final, European Union (EU) <http://ec.europa.eu/external_relations/asia/docs/index_en.htm> (accessed 17 April 2010).

———. "A new partnership with South East Asia". Brussels, COM (2003)

399/4, European Union (EU) <http://ec.europa.eu/external_relations/library/publications/09seaen.pdf> (accessed 10 October 2008).

——. "The ASEM Process: Background Documents". European Union (EU), 2005 <http://ec.europa.eu/comm/external_relations/asem/asem_process/backg_process.htm> (accessed 16 May 2006).

——. *10 Years of ASEM: Global Challenges — Joint responses.* Luxembourg: European Commission, 2006*a*.

——. "The ASEM Process". European Union (EU), 2006*b* <http://ec.europa.eu/comm/external_relations/asem/asem_process/index_process.htm> (accessed 20 November 2007).

——. "The EU's relations with Asia: overview". European Union — External relations, 2007 <http://ec.europa.eu/external_relations/asia/index.htm> (accessed 19 March 2008).

——. "ASEM 6". 2007b <http://ec.europa.eu/external_Relations/ase/Asem_summits/asem6/Asem6_list_innitiative.pdf> (accessed 20 November 2007).

——. "EU-China Relations: Chronology". European Union (EU), 2009*a* <http://ec.europa.eu/external_relations/china/docs/chronology_2009_en.pdf> (accessed 9 November 2009).

——. "EU bilateral trade and trade with the world: Asian ASEM countries". European Union (EU), 2009*b* <http://trade.ec.europa.eu/doclib/docs/2006/september/tradoc_113472.pdf> (accessed 14 May 2010).

European Commission (EC) — External Relations 2009. "EU-China Relations: Chronology". European Union (EU) <http://ec.europa.eu/external_relations/china/docs/chronology_2009_en.pdf> (accessed 9 November 2009).

European Parliament (EP). "European Parliament resolution on the situation in Burma/ASEM". EP1999 – 2004 — Session document, European Union (EU), 13 September 2004. B6-0046/2004, <http://www.europarl.europa.eu/sides/getDoc.do?type=MOTION&reference=P6-RC-20040046&language=EN> (accessed 6 February 2009).

EU Business, 28 June 2004.

Evans, T. and P. Wilson. "Regime theory and the English School of international relations: A comparison". *Millennium: Journal of International Studies* 21, no. 3 (1992): 330.

Fatchett, D. "Setting the Agenda for ASEM 2: From Bangkok to London via Singapore". In *ASEM: A window of opportunity*, edited by W. Stokhof and P. van der Velde. London: Kegan Paul International, 1999.

Fawcett, L. "Exploring regional domains: A comparative historical regionalism". *International Affairs* 80, no. 3 (2004): 429–47.

—— and A. Hurrell, eds. "Introduction". In *Regionalism in world politics: Regional organization and international order*, edited by L. Fawcett and A, Hurrell. Oxford: Oxford University Press, 1995.

Fitriani, E. "Asian perceptions about the EU in the Asia-Europe Meeting (ASEM)". *Asia Europe Journal* 9, no. 1 (2011): 55–68.

Foot, R. "China in the ASEAN Regional Forum: Organizational Processes and Domestic Modes of Thought". *Asian Survey* 38, no. 5 (1988): 425–40.

Forster, A. "The European Union in South-East Asia: Continuity and change in turbulent times". *International Affairs* 75, no. 4 (1999): 743–58.

Fort, B. "Can Asia and Europe Co-operate? Enhancing Asia-Europe Co-operation through the Framework of ASEM". Speech at the International Conference EU-Asia Relations: A critical review, organized by the Contemporary Europe Research Centre, University of Melbourne, in partnership with the European Institute for Asian Studies, Brussels, 27–28 March 2008.

———— and D. Webber. "Evaluating the EU-ASEM relationship: A negotiated order approach". *Journal of European Public Policy* 7, no. 5, special issue (2000): 787–805.

———— and D. Webber, eds. *Regional integration in East Asia and Europe: Convergence or divergent?* London: Routledge, 2006.

Fouquet, D. "ASEM IV in Copenhagen seeks to establish identity". *EURAsia Bulletin* 6, nos. 7 and 8 (2002): 3–4.

Friberg, E. "Burma/Myanmar and ASEM enlargement 2004: What lessons from Cambodia & ASEAN Enlargement in 1997?". *EIAS Policy Brief* 04, no. 03 (2004). European Institute for Asian Studies <http:// www.eias.org> (accessed 6 February 2009)

Friedberg, A.L. "Will Europe's past be Asia's future?". *Survival* 42, no. 3 (Autumn 2000): 147–59.

Fukui, H. "Introduction: On the significance of informal politics". In *Informal politics in East Asia*, edited by L. Dittmer, L. Fukui and P. Lee. Cambridge: Cambridge University Press, 2000.

Gilson, J. "Japan's role in the Asia-Europe Meeting: Establishing an interregional or intraregional agenda?". *Asian Survey* 39, no. 5 (1999): 735–52.

————. *Asia Meets Europe: Inter-Regionalism and the Asia-Europe Meeting.* Cheltenham: Edward Elgar, 2002.

————. "New Interregionalism? The EU and East Asia". *European Integration* 27, no. 3 (2005): 307–26.

————. "Strategic regionalism in East Asia". *Review of International Studies* 33 (2007): 145–63.

———— and Yeo L.H. "Collective identity-building through trans-regionalism: ASEM and East Asian regional identity". In *The Eurasian space: Far more than two continents*, edited by W. Stokhof, P. van der Velde and Yeo L.H. Singapore: Institute of Southeast Asian Studies and International Institute for Asian Studies, 2004.

Goldstein, J., M. Kahler, R. Keohane and A. Slaughter. "Introduction: Legalization and the World Politics". *International Organization* 54, no. 3 (2000): 385–99.

Guardian. "Britain and France fall out over seat at forum for Burma". 2004 <http:// www.guardian.co.uk/world/2004/aug/27/burma.france> (accessed 6 February 2009).

Haacke, J. "ASEAN's diplomatic & security culture: A constructivist assessment". *International Relations of the Asia-Pacific*, no. 3 (2003): 57–87.

———. "Myanmar and ASEAN". *Adelphi Papers* 46, no. 381 (2006): 41–60.

Hage, F. "Who decides in the Council of the European Union?". *Journal of Common Market Studies* 46, no. 3 (2008): 533–58.

Hanggi, H. "ASEM and the construction of the New Triad'. *Journal of the Asia Pacific Economy* 4, no. 2 (1999): 56–80.

———. "Regionalism through inter-regionalism: East Asia and ASEM". In *Regionalism in East Asia: Paradigm shifting*, edited by F. Liu and P. Régnier. London: RoutledgeCurzon, 2003.

He, B. "East Asia ideas of regionalism: A normative critique". *Australia Institute of International Affairs* 58, no. 1 (2004): 105–25.

He, K. "Institutional balancing and international relations theory: Economic interdependence and balance of power strategies in Southeast Asia". *European Journal of International Relations*, no. 14 (2008): 489–518.

Hendriks, C. "Praxis stories: Experiencing interpretive policy research". *Critical Policy Analysis* 1, no. 3 (2007): 278–300.

Hernandez, C. "Institutional building through an ASEAN Charter". *Panorama* 1. Singapore: Konrad Adenauer Stiftung, 2007.

Hettne, B. and F. Soderbaum. "Theorizing the rise of regionness". In *New regionalism in the global political economy*, edited by S. Breslin, C. Hughes, N. Phillips and B. Rosamond. London: Routledge, 2002.

Higgot, R. "The political economy of globalization in East Asia: the salience of 'region building' ". In *Globalization and the Asia-Pacific: Contested territories*, edited by Olds et al. Warwick Studies in Globalization Series. London: Routledge, 1999.

———. "The theory and practice of region: The changing global context". In *Regional integration in East Asia & Europe: Convergence or divergence?*, edited by B. Fort and D. Webber. London: Routledge, 2006.

——— and S. Breslin. "Studying regions: learning from the old, constructing the new". *New Political Economy* 5, no. 3 (2000): 333–52.

Hughes, C. "Japan's policy towards China: Domestic structural change, globalisation, history and nationalism". In *China, Japan and Regional Leadership in East Asia*, edited by C. Dent. Cheltenham: Edward Elgar, 2008.

Hund, M. "From 'neighbourhood watch group' to community: The case of ASEAN institutions and the pooling of sovereignty". *Australian Journal of International Affairs* 56, no. 1 (2002): 99–122.

Hundt, D. and R. Bleiker. "Reconciling colonial memories in Korea and Japan". *Asian Perspectives* 31, no. 1 (2007): 69.

Hurrell, A., ed. "Regionalism in theoretical perspectives". In *Regionalism in world politics: Regional organization and international order*, edited by L. Fawcett and A. Hurrell. Oxford: Oxford University Press, 1995.

————. "One world? Many world? The Place of regions in the study of international society". *International Affairs* 83, no. 1 (2007): 127–46.

International Institute of Asian Studies (IIAS). "ASEM_enlargement". 2003 <http://www.iias.nl/asem/ASEM_enlargement.html> (accessed 28 October 2009).

————. "European Parliament solution on Burma". 2004 <http://www.iias.nl/asem/discussion/EPresolutionBurma_March_2004.pdf> (accessed 28 October 2009).

Islam. "Tackling the challenge of global governance". *ASEM visibility team 2010 online publication*. Brussels: European Commission, 2010.

Jabri, V. "Solidarity and sphere of culture: The cosmopolitan and the postcolonial". *Review of International Studies* 33 (2007): 715–28.

James, H. "Myanmar's international relations strategy: The search for security". *Contemporary Southeast Asia* 26, no. 3 (2004): 530–53.

Japan and Finnish Ministries of Foreign Affairs. "ASEM in its tenth year: Looking back, looking forward". Research report, Tokyo and Stockholm, 2006.

Jervis, R. "Realism, game theory, and cooperation". *World Politics* 40, no. 3 (April 1988): 317–49.

Jones, D. and M. Smith. "Making process, not progress; ASEAN and the evolving East Asian regional order". *International Security*. Singapore: CSIS, 2007*a*.

————. "Constructing communities: The curious case of East Asian regionalism". *Review of International Studies* 33 (2007*b*): 165–86.

Journal of East Asian Studies. "Roundtable: Peter J. Katzenstein's contributions to the study of East Asian regionalism". *Journal of East Asian Studies* 7 (2007): 359–412.

Kahler, M. "Legalization as strategy: The Asia-Pacific case". *International Organization* 54, no. 3 (2000): 549–71.

Kaiser, K. "The necessity for cooperation". In *Asia and Europe: The necessity for co-operation*, edited by K. Kaiser. Tokyo: Council for Asia-Europe Cooperation (CAEC), 2004.

Kaldor, M., M. Martin and S. Selchow. "Human security: A new strategic narrative for Europe". *International Affairs* 83, no. 2 (2007): 273–88.

Katzenstein, P. *Asian Regionalism*. Ithaca: East Asia Program, Cornell University Press, 2000.

————. "East Asia beyond Japan". In *Beyond Japan: The dynamics of East Asian regionalism*, edited by P. Katzenstein and T. Shiraishi, pp. 1–36. Ithaca: Cornell University Press, 2006.

———— and T. Shiraishi. "Introduction". In *Beyond Japan: The dynamics of East Asian regionalism*, edited by P. Katzenstein and T. Shiraishi. Ithaca: Cornell University Press, 2006.

Kawasaki, T. "Neither skepticism nor romanticism: The ASEAN regional Forum as a solution for the Asia-Pacific Assurance Game". In *Theorizing Southeast Asian relations: Emerging debates*, edited by A. Acharya and R. Stubbs. New York: Routledge, 2009.

Kent, A. "China's international socialization: The role of international organizations". *Global Governance* 8 (2002): 343–64.

Keohane, R. "International institutions: Two approaches". *International Studies* 32 (1988): 379–96.

Khong, Y. and H. Nesadurai. "Hanging together, institutional design, and cooperation in Southeast Asia: AFTA and ARF". In *Crafting Cooperation: Regional international institutions in comparative perspectives*, edited by A. Acharya and A. Johnston. Cambridge: Cambridge University Press, 2007.

Kim, H. "Korea Country Report". In *ASEM in Its Tenth Year: Looking Back, Looking Forward*, edited by Yamamoto and Yeo. Tokyo: Japan Center for International Exchange (JCIE), 2006.

King, G., R. Keohane and S. Verba. *Designing social inquiry*. New Jersey: Princeton University Press, 1994.

Kivimaki, T. "Europe and Asian international cooperation". *Asia-Europe Journal* 5, no. 3 (2007): 303–15.

Koh, T. "Opening remarks in the inaugural Asia-Europe lecture in Singapore on 13 January 1998". In *Asia and Europe: The Road from Bangkok to London and Beyond*, by J. Santer. Singapore: Asia-Europe Foundation, 1998.

Koremenos, B., C. Lipson and D. Snidal. "Rational design of international institutions". *International Organization* 55, no. 4 (2001): 761–99.

Kratochwil, F. and J. Ruggie. "International organization: A state-of-the-art or an art of the state". *International Organization* 40, no. 4 (1986): 424–46.

Kuik, C. "Multilateralism in China's ASEAN Policy: Its evolution, characteristics & aspirations". *Contemporary Southeast Asia* 27, no. 1 (2005): 102–22.

Kwa Chong Guan. "The historical setting". In *Europe and the Asia Pacific*, edited by H. Maull, G. Segal and J. Wanandi. London: Routledge, 1998.

Lall, M. "Indo-Myanmar relations in the era of pipeline diplomacy". *Contemporary Southeast Asia* 28, no. 3 (2006): 424–46.

Lee, C. "Searching for an economic agenda for the 3rd ASEM Summit: Two scenario". Korean Institute for International Economic Policy (KIEP) Working Paper 99-31, 1999.

Lee, J. and J. Park. "The role of regional identity in Asia-Europe relations with special reference to ASEM". *Global Economic Review* 30, no. 3 (2001): 19–33.

Leifer, M. "The ASEAN peace process: A category mistake". *Pacific Review* 12, no. 1 (1999): 25–38.

———. "The quest for identity: International relations of Southeast Asia". *Pacific Review* 14, no. 3 (2001): 499–504.

——— and S. Djiwandono. "Europe and Southeast Asia". In *Europe and the Asia Pacific*, edited by H. Maull, G. Segal and J. Wanandi. London: Routledge, 1998.

Letta, C. *ASEM's Future*, vol. 1. Bologna: Lo Scarabeo Editrice, 2002.

Li, H. and Zheng Y. "Re-interpreting China's non-intervention policy towards Myanmar: Leverage, interest and intervention". *Journal of Contemporary China* 18, no. 61 (2009): 617–37.

Li, M. "Explaining China proactive engagement in Asia". In *Living with China*, edited by S. Tang. New York: Palgrave Macmillan, 2009.

Ling, H. *Post colonial international relations: Conquest and desire between Asia and the West*. Houndmills: Palgrave Macmillan, 2002.

Lipson, C. "Why are some international agreements informal?". *International Organization* 45, no. 4 (1991): 495–535.

Liu, F. and P. Régnier. "Prolog: Whiter regionalism in East Asia?". In *Regionalism in East Asia: Paradigm Shift?*, edited by F. Liu & P. Régnier. London: Routledge Curzon, 2003.

Loewen, H. "East Asia and Europe — partner in global politics?". *Asia-Europe Journal* 5, no. 1 (2007): 23–31.

MacAskill, E. and E. Gentleman. "Britain and France fall out over seat at forum for Burma". *Guardian*, 27 August 2004 <http://www.guardian.co.uk/world/2004/aug/27/burma.framce/print> (accessed 6 February 2009).

MacIntyre, A, T. Pempel and J. Ravenhill. "East Asia in the wake of financial crisis". In *Crisis as catalyst: Asia's dynamic political economy*, edited by A. MacIntyre, T. Pempel and J. Ravenhill. Ithaca: Cornell University Press, 2008.

Manea, M. "Human rights and the inter-regional dialogue between Asia and Europe: ASEAN-EU relations and ASEM". *Pacific Review* 21, no. 3 (2008): 369–96.

Maull, H., G. Segal and J. Wanandi. "Preface". In *Europe and the Asia Pacific*, edited by H. Maull, G. Segal and J. Wanandi. London: Routledge, 1998.

McCarthy, S. "Burma and ASEAN". *Asian Survey* 48, no. 6 (2008): 911–35.

McMahon, J. "ASEAN and Asia-Europe Meeting: Strengthening the Europeaan Union's Relationship with South-East Asia?". *European Foreign Affairs Review* 3 (1998): 233–51.

Ministry of Foreign Affairs of Finland (MOFA Finland). *ASEM 6: Overview and report*. Helsinki, 2006.

Ministry of Foreign Affairs of Japan (MOFA Japan). 2010 <http://www.mofa.go.jp/POLICY/economy/asem/asem4/overview.html> (accessed 26 April 2010).

Ministry of Foreign Affairs of People's Republic of China (MOFA PRC). "China's Participation in APEC's Important Activities", 2000. <http://www.mfa.gov.cn/eng/wjb/zzjg/gjs/gjzzyhy/2604/t15266.htm> (accessed 6 November 2009).

Ministry of Foreign Affairs of the Kingdom of Thailand (MOFA Thailand). "The First ASEM", 1996. <http://asem.inter.net.th/asem-info/background.html> (accessed 27 November 2007).

Moravcsik, A. "Integrating International and Domestic Theories of International Bargaining". In *Double-Edged Diplomacy: International Bargaining and Domestic*

Politics, edited by P. Evans, H. Jacobson and R. Putnam. Berkeley: University of California Press, 1993.

———. "Taking Preferences Seriously: A Liberal Theory of International Politics". *International Organization* 51, no. 4 (1997): 513–53.

———. *The choice for Europe: Social purpose and state power from Messina to Maastricht.* Ithaca: Cornell University Press, 1998.

Murphy, A. and B. Welsh. *Legacy of engagement in Southeast Asia.* Singapore: Institute of Southeast Asian Studies, 2008.

Nabers, D. "The Social construction of the international institutions: The case of ASEAN + 3". *International Relations of the Asia-Pacific* 3 (2003): 113–36.

Nguyen, D., Nguyen T. and P. Duong, eds. *Asia-Europe cooperation and the role of Vietnam.* Hanoi: Vietnam Academy of Social Science and European Studies Programme, 2004.

Ofken, N. "ASEM: time for an overhaul". In *Asian-European perspectives: Developing the ASEM process*, edited by W. Stokhof and P. van der Velde. Richmond: Curzon Press, 2001.

Ojendal, J. "Back to the future? Regionalism in South-East Asia under unilateral pressure". *International Affairs* 80, no. 3 (2004): 519–33.

Pablo-Baviera, A. "Regionalism and community building in East Asia". In *Advancing East Asian regionalism*, edited by M. Curley and N. Thomas. London: Routhledge, 2007.

Palmujoki, E. "EU-ASEAN relations: reconciling two different agendas". *Contemporary Southeast Asia* 19, no. 3 (1997): 269–85.

———. *Regionalism and Globalism in Southeast Asia.* New York: Palgrave, 2001.

Pempel, T. "Restructuring regional ties". In *Crisis as catalyst: Asia's dynamic political economy*, edited by A. Macintyre, T. Pempel and J. Ravenhill. Ithaca: Cornell University Press, 2008.

Percival, B. *The dragon looks south: China and Southeast Asia in the new century.* London: Praeger Security International, 2007.

Pereira, R. "The Helsinki Summit and the future course of ASEM". *Asia Europe Journal* 5, no. 1 (2007): 17–22.

Petersen, N. "ASEM: Realizing the potential for the next millenium". In *Asian-European perspectives*, edited by W. Stokhof and P. van der Velde. Richmond: Curzon Press, 2001.

Petersson, M. "Myanmar in EU-ASEAN relations". *Asia-Europe Journal* 4, no. 4 (2006): 563–81.

Pitsuwan, S. "Foreword". In *Hard Choices: Security, democracy and regionalism in Southeast Asia*, edited by D. Emmerson. Stanford: Walter H. Shorenstein Asia-Pacific Research Center, 2009.

Putnam, R. "Diplomacy and Domestic Politics: The Logic of Two-Level Games". *International Organization* 42, no. 3 (1988): 427–60.

Ravenhill, J. "East Asian regionalism: Much ado about nothing?". *Review of International Studies*, no. 35 (2009): 215–35.

————— and Yang, J. "China's move to preferential trading: A new direction in China's diplomacy". *Journal of Contemporary China* 18, no. 58 (2009): 27–46.

Ravi, S., B. Goh and M. Rutten. "Introduction". In *Asia in Europe, Europe in Asia*, edited by S. Ravi, M. Rutten and B. Goh. Leiden: IIAS, 2004.

Reiterer, M. "ASEM-The Third Summit in Seoul 2000: A roadmap to consolidate the partnership between Asia and Europe". *Europe Foreign Affairs Review*, no. 6 (2001): 1–30.

—————. *Asia-Europe: Do they meet?* Singapore: Asia-Europe Foundation, 2002*a*.

—————. "The Asia Europe Meeting (ASEM): The importance of the Fourth ASEM Summit in the light of 11 September". *European Foreign Affairs Review* 7 (2002*b*): 133–52.

—————. "ASEM: Value-added to International relations and to the Asia-Europe relationship". In *The Eurasian space: Far more than two continents*, edited by W. Stokhof, P. van der Velde and Yeo L.H. Leiden: IIAS, 2004.

—————. "Inter-regionalism as a new diplomatic tool: the EU & East Asia". *European Foreign Affairs Review* 11 (2006): 223–43.

—————. "Asia-Europe Meeting (ASEM): Fostering a multipolar world order through inter-regional cooperation". *Asia Europe Journal* 7, no. 1 (2009): 179–96.

Reus-Smit, C. "Constructivism". In *Theories of international relations*, by S. Burchill et al. 4th ed. New York: Palgrave Macmillan, 2009.

Richards, G. and C. Kirkpatrick. "Reorienting interregional cooperation in the global political economy: Europe's East Asia Policy". *Journal of Common Market Studies* 37, no. 4 (1999): 683–710.

Risse, T. "Neofunctionalism, European Identity, and the Puzzles of European Integration". *Journal of European Public Policy* 12 (2005): 291–309.

Rose, C. *Sino-Japanese Relations: Facing the Past, Looking to the Future?* London: Routledge Curzon, 2005.

Rothermund, D. "Cultural partnership between Asia & Europe". In *Asia-Europe on the eve of the 21st century*, edited by S. Chirathivat, F. Knippping, P. Lassen and Chia S.Y. Bangkok: Centre for European Studies, Chulalongkorn University, 2001.

Rowse, B. "Quiet diplomacy expected to resolve ASEAN-EU spat over ASEM summit". 21 March 2004 <http://www.aseansec. org/afp/29.htm> (accessed 9 February 2009).

Ruggie, J. "What Makes the World Hang Together? Neo-Utilitarianism and the Social Constructivist Challenge". *International Organization* 52, no. 4 (1998*a*): 855–85.

—————. *Constructing the world polity*. London: Routledge, 1998*b*.

Ruland, J. "The EU as an inter-regional actor: The Asia-Europe Meeting". In *Asia-Europe on the eve of the 21st century*, edited by S. Chirathivat, F. Knippping, P. Lassen and Chia S.Y. Bangkok: Centre for European Studies, Chulalongkorn University, 2001.

————. "East Asian regionalism: From stagnation to reinvent". *European Journal of East Asian Studies* 4, no. 2 (2005): 149–76.

Saberwal, S. "Civilizational encounters: Europe in Asia". In *Asia in Europe, Europe in Asia*, edited by S. Ravi, M. Rutten and B. Goh. Leiden: IIAS, 2004.

Sakuwa, K. "A not so dangerous dyad: China's rise and Sino-Japanese rivalry". *International Relations of the Asia-Pacific* 9 (2009): 497–528.

Santer, J. "Asia and Europe: The road from Bangkok to London and beyond". The Inaugural Asia-Europe Lecture, President of the European Commission, Singapore, 13 January 1998.

Saw S., Sheng L. & Chin K. "An overview of ASEAN-China relations". In *ASEAN-China relations: Realities and prospects*, edited by Saw S., Sheng L. and Chin K. Singapore: Institute of Southeast Asian Studies, 2005.

Schmit, L. "The ASEM process: New rules for engagement in a global environment". In *Asian-European perspectives*, edited by W. Stokhof and P. van der Velde. Richmond: Curzon Press, 2001.

Searle, J. *The construction of social reality*. New York: Free Press, 1995.

Segal, G. "Asia and Europe: Societies in transition — A new ASEM agenda: A report on the British Council's meeting, 19–22 March 1998". *Pacific Review* 11, no. 4 (1998): 561–72.

Shambaugh, D. "China Engages Asia: Reshaping the Regional Order". *International Security* 29, no. 3 (2004): 64–99.

Shin, D. and G. Segal. "Getting serious about Asia-Europe security cooperation". In *ASEM: A window of opportunity*, edited by W. Stokhof and P. van der Velde. London: Kegan Paul International, 1999.

Shore, C. *Building Europe: The Cultural Politics of European Integration*. London: Routledge, 2000.

Simanjuntak, D. "The search for regional architecture: The role of ASEAN as strange attractor". Speech at the High-level Conference on Asian Economic Integration: Vision of a New Asia, organized by Research and Information System (RIS), Tokyo, 18–19 November 2004.

Simmons, B. and L. Martin. "Theories and empirical studies of international institutions". *International Organizations* 52, no. 4 (1998): 729–57.

————. "International Organizations & Institutions". In *Handbook of international relations*, edited by W. Carlsnaes, T. Risse and B. Simmons. London: Sage, 2002.

Singh, B. "ASEAN's Perceptions of Japan: Change and Continuity". *Asian Survey* 42, no. 2 (2002): 276–96.

Slapin, J. "Bargaining Power at Europe's Intergovernmental Conferences: Testing Institutional and Intergovernmental Theories". *International Organization* 62 (2008): 131–62.

Smith, S. "New approaches to international theory". In *The globalization of world politics: An introduction to international relations*, edited by J. Baylis and S. Smith. Oxford: Oxford University Press, 1997.

Soesastro, H. "ASEM: Towards an exciting inter-regional journey". In *The Seoul 2000 Summit: The way ahead for the Asia-Europe partnership*, edited by C. Lee. Conference Proceeding, 00-03. Seoul: Korea Institute for International Economic Policy (KIEP), 2000.

————. "Knowledge and regional community building". Graduation Speech, Australian National University, Canberra, Australia, 17 July 2009.

Soesastro, H. and S. Nuttall. "The institutional dimension". In *The rationale and common agenda for Asia-Europe cooperation: CAEC task force reports*, by Council for Asia-Europe Cooperation (CAEC). Tokyo: Japan Centre for International Exchange (JCIE), 1997.

Sohn, I. "Learning to co-operate: China's multilateral approach to Asian financial co-operation". *China Quarterly* 194 (2008): 309–26.

Solingen, E. "ASEAN, quo vadis? Domestic coalitions and regional Co-operation". *Contemporary Southeast Asia* 21, no. 1 (1999): 30–53.

Stokhof, W. "Bringing the communities together: What can be done?". In *ASEM: A window of opportunity*, edited by W. Stokhof and P. van der Velde. London: Kegan Paul International, 1999.

———— and P. van der Velde, eds. *ASEM: A window of opportunity*. London: Kegan Paul International, 1999.

———— and P. van der Velde, eds. *Asian-European perspectives: Developing the ASEM process*. Richmond: Curzon Press, 2001.

————, P. van der Velde and Yeo L.H., eds. *The Eurasian space: Far more than two continents*. Leiden: IIAS, 2004.

Stone, R., B. Slantchev and T. London. "Choosing How to Cooperate: A Repeated Public-Goods Model of International Relations". *International Studies Quarterly* 52 (2008): 335–62.

Stubbs, R. "ASEAN Plus Three: Emerging East Asian regionalism?". *Asian Survey* 42, no. 3 (2002): 440–55.

————. "Meeting the challenge of regional-building in ASEAN". In *Contemporary Southeast Asia*, edited by M. Beeson. 2nd ed. London: Palgrave Macmillan, 2009.

Taipei Times. 23 June 2004, <http://www.taipeitimes.com/News/world/archives/2004/06/23/2003176189> (accessed 6 February 2009).

Tang, S. "Introduction: Understanding 'Living with China'". In *Living with China: Regional states and China through crises and turning points*, edited by S. Tang, M. Li and A. Acharya. New York: Palgrave, 2009.

Terada, T. "The birth & growth of ASEAN+3". In *Regional integration in East Asia and Europe: Convergence or divergence?*, edited by B. Fort & D. Webber. London: Routledge, 2006.

Tilman, O. *Southeast Asia and the enemy beyond: ASEAN's perceptions of external threats*. Boulder: Westview Press, 1987.

Togo, K. "Japan and ASEM". In *The Eurasian space: Far more than two continents*, edited by W. Stokhof, P. van der Velde and Yeo L.H. Leiden: IIAS, 2004.

United Nations (UN). "Member states of the United Nations". 2006 <http://www.un.org/en/members/index.shtml> (accessed 28 January 2010).

University of Helsinki Network for European Studies. *ASEM in its tenth year: Looking back, looking forward.* Helsinki: University of Helsinki, 2006.

Vichitsorasatra, N. "A Burmese test for the future of ASEM". *BurmaNet News*, 3 August 2004 <http://six.pairlist.net/pipermail/burmanet/20040803/000507.html> (accessed 6 February 2009).

Vietnam Development Gateway. "Vietnam: An Active Member of ASEM". <http://www.vietnamgateway.org/asem/economic1.html> (accessed on 26 April 2010).

Vietnam News. 9 August 2004 <http://patrick.guenin2.free.fr/cantho/ vnnews/ asem.htm>.

Westerfield, B. "EU to do Myanmar/Burma deal". *EU Politics News — the Parliament. com,* 2004 <http://www.eupolitix.com/latestnews/news-article/newsarticle/eu-to-donbspmyanmarbu...> (accessed 6 February 2009).

Westerlund, P. "Strengthening Euro-Asian relations: ASEM as a catalyst". In *ASEM: A window of opportunity,* edited by W. Stokhof and P. van der Velde. London: Kegan Paul International, 1999.

Wirth, C. "China, Japan, and East Asian regional cooperation: the views of 'self' and 'other' from Beijing and Tokyo". *International Relations of the Asia-Pacific* 9 (2009): 469–96.

Wiessala, G. *Catalysts and inhibitors: The role and meaning of human rights in EU-Asia relations.* CERC Working Papers Series, no. 1/2007. Melbourne: University of Melbourne, 2007.

World Trade Organization (WTO). "Understanding the WTO: The organization members and observers". 2008 <http://www.wto.org/english/theWTO_e/whatis_e/tif_e/org6_e.htm> (accessed 28 January 2010).

World News. 2 July 2004.

Xiao, R. "Between adapting and shaping: China's role in Asian regional cooperation". *Journal of Contemporary China* 18, issue 59 (2009): 303–20.

Xinhua. 2004 <http://english.peopledaily.com.cn/200407/07/ print20040707148810.html>.

Yahuda, M. "Sino-Japanese relations: Partners and rivals". *Korean Journal of Defense Analysis* 21, no. 4 (2009): 365–79.

Yawnghwe, H. "ASEM's Expansion: Solving the Burma/Myanmar Dilemma". ASEM News July 2004 <http://www.iias.nl/asem/discussion/Harn_Burma_Dilemma_ASEM_News.pdf> (accessed 10 February 2009).

Yeo, L. "The Bangkok ASEM and the future of Asian-Europe Relations". *Southeast Asian Affairs 1997*, pp. 33–44. Singapore: Institute of Southeast Asian Studies, 1997.

———. "ASEM: looking forward". *Contemporary Southeast Asia* 22, no. 1 (2000): 113–44.

————. *Asia and Europe: The development and different dimensions of ASEM*. London: Routledge, 2003.

————. "Dimension of Asia-Europe cooperation". *Asia Europe Journal* 2 (2004): 19–31.

————. "Taking stock of ASEM@10". *Panorama* 1 (2007): 75–82.

———— and W. Hofmeister, eds. *The Asia-Europe Meeting: Engagement, enlargement and expectations*. Singapore: EU Center, 2010.

Zhang, Y. "China & Europe". In *Europe and the Asia Pacific*, edited by H. Maull, G. Segal and J. Wanandi. London: Routledge, 1998.

Zhao Gancheng. "Assessing China's Impact on Asia-EU relations". In *ASEM: A window of opportunity*, edited by W. Stockhof and P. van der Velde. London: Kegan Paul International, 1999.

Zhimin, C. "NATO, APEC and ASEM: Triadic Interregionalism and Global". *Asia Europe Journal* 3, no. 3 (2005): 361–78.

Appendix I: Structure of the ASEM Process

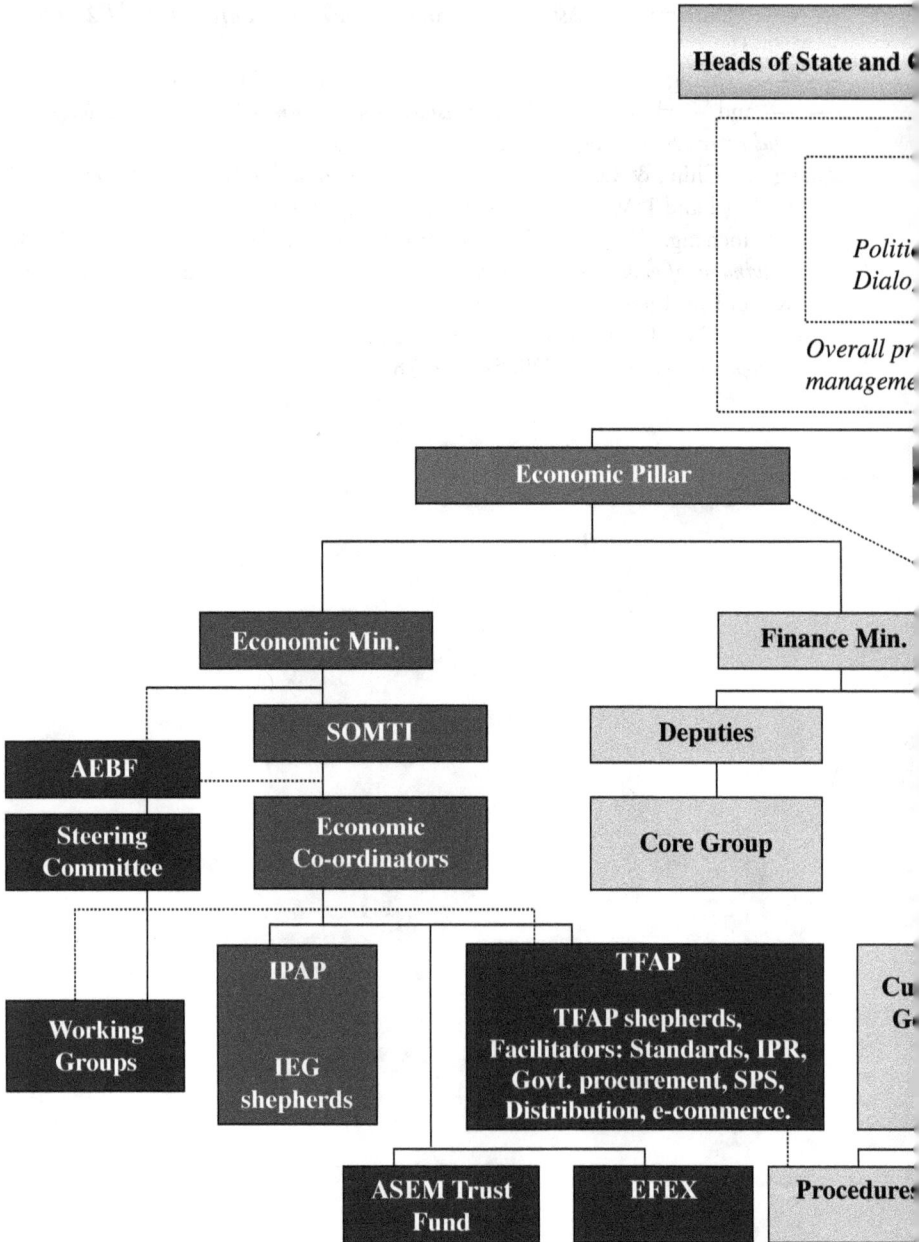

Source: ASEM Infoboard 2007, Asia Europe Meeting, <http://www.aseminfoboard.org/About/Structu

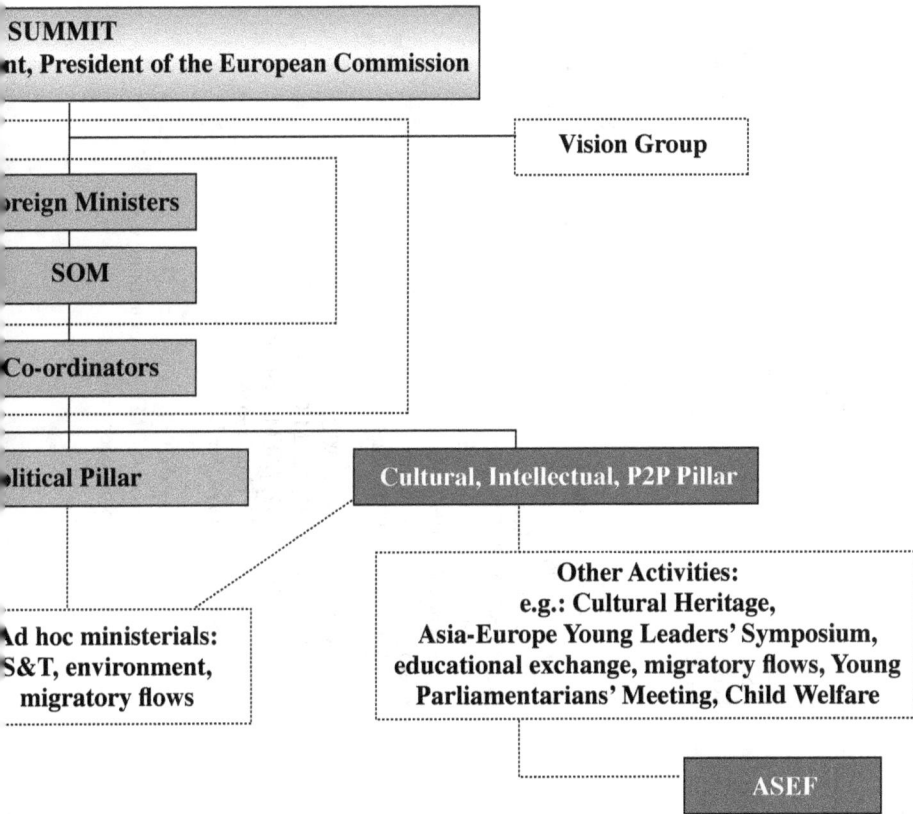

SUMMIT
nt, President of the European Commission

Vision Group

reign Ministers

SOM

Co-ordinators

litical Pillar

Cultural, Intellectual, P2P Pillar

Other Activities:
e.g.: Cultural Heritage,
Asia-Europe Young Leaders' Symposium,
educational exchange, migratory flows, Young
Parliamentarians' Meeting, Child Welfare

Ad hoc ministerials:
S&T, environment,
migratory flows

ASEF

ctors-
the

on

rcement

Acronyms:
AEBP: Asia-Europe Business Forum
ASEF: Asia-Europe Foundation
EFEX: European Financial Expertise Network
IPAP: Investment Promotion Action Plan
IPR: Intellectual Property Rights
S&T: Science and Technology
SOM: Senior Officials Meeting
SOMTI: Senior Officials' Meeting on Trade and Investment
SPS: Sanitary-Phytosanitary Standards
TFAP: Trade Promotion Action Plan

e.pdf> (accessed 7 November 2007).

Appendix II: The Development of the ASEM Process, 1996–2010

Year	Asian coordinators	ASEM Pre-summit official meetings	Culminating events (ASEM Summits)
1994–1996	ASEAN: Singapore (then Thailand as the host country) Non-ASEAN: Japan (CAEC 1997)	3 Senior Official Meetings (SOMs) from mid-1995 between Senior Official of ASEAN countries and the EU (Yeo 2003)	First Summit 1–2 March 1996, Bangkok
1996–1998	ASEAN: Singapore Non-ASEAN: Japan (CAEC 1997)	ASEM Coordinators' Meeting: • 15 June 1996, Rome • 11 July 1996, Singapore • 22 July 1996, Jakarta • 24 January 1997, Jakarta • 26 July 1997, Kuala Lumpur • 28 September 1997, Makuhari • 13 January 1998, Tokyo • 16–17 March 1998, Bangkok Working Group Meeting (WGM): • 7–8 February 1997, ASEM Customs (EWG) • 21–11 March 1997, ASEM Customs (PWG) • 30 April 1997, for Finance MM • 3–4 September 1997, for Finance MM Senior Official Meeting (SOM) • 25 July 1996 Brussels (SOMTI-1): examining ways to promote economic cooperation	Second Summit 3–4 April 1998, London

1998–2000	• 20 December 1996 (SOM-1), Dublin • 11–12 February 1997 (SOM-2), Singapore • 5–6 June 1997 (SOMTI-2), Tokyo • 26 September 1997, Hong Kong • 30 October 1997, Luxemburg • 5–6 February 1998 (SOMTI-3), Brussels • 19–20 February 1998 (SOM-3), London • 2 April 1998 (SOM-4), London Ministerial Meeting (MM): • 30 January 1997 first Economic MM, Makuhari, Japan • 14–15 February 1997 first Foreign MM Singapore (17 February: Foreign MM launched ASEF) • 25 April 1997 (Economic MM Coordinator preparatory Meeting) the Hague • 7 June 1997 (Economic MM Coordinator preparatory Meeting), Tokyo • 19 September 1997, first Finance MM, Bangkok, Thailand ASEM Coordinators' Meeting: • 26 July 1998, Manila, Philippines • 29 January 1999, Berlin, Germany Working Group Meeting (WGM): • 5 October 1998, Finn Officials' Core Group Meeting, Washington, DC • 18 December 1998, Financial Deputies' Meeting, Vienna, Austria	Third Summit 20–21 October 2000, Seoul
ASEAN: Thailand Non-ASEAN: Korea (Kim 2006, p. 62) (Reiterer 2001, p. 6)		

continued on next page

Appendix II — cont'd

Year	Asian coordinators	ASEM Pre-summit official meetings	Culminating events (ASEM Summits)
		• 18 December 1999, Financial Deputies' Meeting, Vienna, Austria	
		• 14 September 2000, Financial Deputies' Meeting, France	
		Senior Official Meeting (SOM):	
		• 5–6 March 1998 (SOMTI-3), Brussels, Belgium	
		• 24 July 1998 (SOMTI Coordinators Meeting), Bangkok, Thailand	
		• 27–28 October 1998 (SOM IV), Bangkok, Thailand	
		• 27 November 1998 (SOMTI Coordinators Meeting), Geneva, Switzerland	
		• 11–13 February 1999 (SOMTI), Singapore	
		• 27–28 March 1999 (SOM), Berlin, Germany	
		• 7–8 July 1999 (SOMTI V), Brussels, Belgium	
		• 2–4 November 1999 (SOM), Finland	
		• 2–3 May 2000 (SOM), Lisbon, Portugal	
		• 12–13 May 2000 (SOMTI), Seoul, Korea	
		• 18–20 September 2000 (SOM), Seoul, Korea	
		Ministerial Meeting (MM):	
		• 9–10 October 1998 Economic MM, Berlin, Germany	
		• 15–16 January 1999, second Finance MM, Frankfurt, Germany	

- 28–29 March 1999, second Foreign MM, Berlin, Germany
- 9–10 October 1999, second Economic MM, Berlin, Germany
- 14–15 October 1999, firsr Science and Technology MM, Beijing, China

Fourth Summit
22–24 September 2002, Copenhagen

2000–2002

ASEAN: Vietnam (Vietnam Development gateway 2010; ASEAN Vietnam 2010)

Non-ASEAN:

Ministerial Meeting (MM):
- January 2001, third Finance MM, Kobe
- May 2001, third Foreign MM, Beijing, China
- September 2001, third Economic MM, Hanoi, Vietnam
- January 2002, first Environment MM, Beijing, China
- June 2002, fourth Foreign MM, Madrid, Spain
- September 2002, fourth Economic MM, Copenhagen, Denmark

2002–2004

ASEAN: Vietnam (ASEAN Vietnam 2010)

Non-ASEAN: Japan (MOFA-Japan 2010)

ASEM Coordinators' Meeting (CM):
- 28–29 January 2003, Brussels, Belgium
- 7–8 July 2003, Tokyo, Japan
- 25 February 2003, Economic CM, Tokyo, Japan
- 14 April 2003, Economic CM, Brussels, Belgium
- 16 January 2004, Dublin, Ireland
- 5 March 2004, Economic CM, Hanoi, Vietnam
- 5 March 2004, Economic CM, Dublin, Ireland
- 10 March 2004, Hanoi, Vietnam
- 9 July 2004, Tokyo, Japan
- 6–7 October 2004, Hanoi, Vietnam

Fifth Summit
8–9 October 2004, Hanoi

continued on next page

Appendix II — *cont'd*

Year	Asian coordinators	ASEM Pre-summit official meetings	Culminating events (ASEM Summits)
		Working Group Meeting (WGM):	
		• 6 May 2003, first Meeting of Taskforce for Closer Economic Partnership, Madrid, Spain	
		• 7–8 June 2003, ASEM Deputy Finance Ministers' Meeting, Bali, Indonesia	
		• 8–9 September 2003, second Meeting of Taskforce for Closer Economic Partnership, Tokyo, Japan	
		• November 2003, third Meeting of Taskforce for Closer Economic Partnership, Frankfurt, Germany	
		• 12–13 March 2004, ASEM Task Force Economic pillar, Bangkok, Thailand	
		• 11–12 March 2004, fourth Meeting of Taskforce for Closer Economic Partnership, Bangkok, Thailand	
		• 17 May 2004, fifth Meeting of Taskforce for Closer Economic Partnership, Barcelona, Spain	
		Senior Official Meeting (SOM):	
		• 6 June 2003, SOMTI, Paris	
		• 13–14 November 2003, Informal SOM, Rome	
		• 2–3 March 2004, Asian SOM, Vietnam	
		• 16 April 2004, ASEM SOM on preparation of Foreign MM, Kildare, Ireland	
		• 24 April 2004, ASEM Core Group Meeting, Washington DC	

2004–2006

ASEAN: Indonesia

Non-ASEAN: Korea (Ministry of Foreign Affairs of Finland 2006)

- 29–30 June 2004, SOMTI, Qing Dao, China
- 5 October 2004, Hanoi, Vietnam

Ministerial Meeting (MM):

- 5–6 July 2003, fifth Finance MM, Bali, Indonesia
- 23–24 July 2003, fifth Foreign MM, Bali, Indonesia
- 23–24 July 2003, fifth Economic MM, Dalian, China
- October 2003, second Environment MM, Lecce, Italy
- December 2003, first Culture MM, Beijing, China
- 17–18 April 2004, sixth Foreign MM, Kildare, Ireland

ASEM Coordinators' Meeting:

- 20–21 January 2006, Jeju Island, Korea
- 21–22 May 2006, Singapore
- 18–19 June, Hämeenlinna, Finland

Working Group Meeting (WGM):

- 20–21 April 2006, ninth ASEM Customs Enforcement Working Group (EWG), Seoul, Korea
- 21–22 May, Openended WGM, Singapore
- 30 June, Intellectual Property Protection, Bangkok, Thailand

Senior Official Meeting (SOM):

- 8 March 2006, Vienna, Austria
- 18–19 June, Hämeenlinna, Finland
- 9 September, Helsinki, Finland

Sixth Summit 10–11 September 2006, Helsinki

continued on next page

Appendix II — cont'd

Year	Asian coordinators	ASEM Pre-summit official meetings	Culminating events (ASEM Summits)
		Ministerial Meeting (MM): • 6–7 May 2005, seventh Foreign MM, Kyoto, Japan • 25–26 June 2005, sixth Finance MM, Tianjin, China • June 2005, second Culture MM, Paris, France • 16–17 September 2005, sixth Economic MM, Rotterdam, the Netherlands • 8–9 April 2006, seventh Finance MM, Vienna, Austria • 3–5 September 2006, Labour MM, Berlin, Germany	
2006–2008	SOM Coordinators: Japan, Vietnam Econ. Coordinators: Japan, Vietnam IEG sherpers: Indonesia, Japan (ASEF Infoboard, 2007) Asian Coordinators: ASEAN: Brunei Non-ASEAN: China	Working Group Meeting (WGM): • 12–13 November 2007, SOM Custom, Yokohama, Japan • 19–26 November 2007, SOM Immigration, Seoul, Korea • 3–4 June 2008, SOM Labor, Geneva, Switzerland • 30 June–1 July 2008, first ASEM Social partners Forum, Brussels, Belgium • 11–12 December 2006, Kuopio, Finland, fifth ASEM Meeting for Directors General on Migratory, Kuopio, Finland Senior Official Meeting (SOM): • 29–30 October 2007, Guilin City, China • 17 December 2007, SOMTI, Lisbon, Portugal	Seventh Summit 23–24 October 2008, Beijing

- 2–3 March 2008, Ljubljana, Slovenia
- 15–16 April 2008, SOMTI, Maribor, Slovenia
- 12–13 June 2008, Bandar Seri Begawan, Brunei
- 29–30 June 2008, Beijing, China

Ministerial Meeting (MM):
- 30 November–1 December 2006 ICT MM Hanoi, Vietnam
- 23–26 April 2007, third Environment MM Copenhagen, Denmark
- 28–29 May 2007, eighth Foreign MM, Hamburg, Germany
- 29 October–1 November 2007, Small and Medium Enterprises MM, Beijing/Qingdao, China
- 21 April 2008, third Culture MM, Kuala Lumpur, Malaysia
- 5–6 May, first Education MM, Berlin
- 16 June 2008, eighth Finance MM, Jeju Island, Korea
- 13–15 October 2008, second Labour MM, Bali, Indonesia

ASEAN Coordinators' Meeting:
- 6–7 September 2010, Seoul, Korea
- 2 October 2010, Brussels, Belgium

Working Group Meeting (WGM):
- 6–7 May 2010, fourth Meeting of the ASEM WG on Customs Matters (AWC), Hanoi, Vietnam

2008–2010   ASEAN:

Non-ASEAN:

Eighth Summit
4–5 October 2001,
Brussels

continued on next page

Appendix II — *cont'd*

Year	Asian coordinators	ASEM Pre-summit official meetings	Culminating events (ASEM Summits)
		Senior Official Meeting (SOM):	
		• 25 January 2010, Madrid, Spain	
		• 5–6 May 2010, Phnom Penh, Cambodia	
		• 13–15 July 2010, Brussels, Belgium	
		• 3 October 2010, Brussels, Belgium	
		Ministerial Meeting (MM):	
		• 17–18 April 2010, ninth Finance MM, Madrid, Spain	
		• 17 April 2010, Finance Department Meeting, Madrid, Spain	
		• 9–10 September 2010, fourth Culture MM, Poznan, Poland	
		Thematic Forums:	
		• 24 March 2010, Working for More Effective Global Governance, Brussels, Belgium	
		• 29 March 2010, second ASEM Social Partners' Forum, Brussels, Belgium	
		• 29–31 March 2010, High-level Forum on Employment and Social Issues, Brussels, Belgium	
		• 30 March 2010, Asia-Europe Learning Mutually, Tokyo, Japan	

continued on next page

- 7–9 April 2010, sixth ASEM Interfaith Dialogue, Madrid & Toledo, Spain
- 15–17 April 2010, second Preparatory Meeting for the fourth ASEM Cultural MM, Solo, Indonesia
- 15–16 April 2010, ASEM Outlook Workshop, Brussels, Belgium
- 26–27 April 2010, Overcoming the Financial Crisis, Nha Trang, Vietnam
- 28–29 April 2010, Workshop on Coordinating Cultural Activities for the Enhancement of ASEM Visibility, Ha Long City, Vietnam
- 4–5 May 2010, ASEM Seminar on Piracy at Sea, Brussels, Belgium
- 4–5 May 2010, ASEM Conference on Forest, Forest Governance and Forest Products, Phnom Penh, Cambodia
- 5 May 2010, ASEM Customs Trade Day, Hanoi, Vietnam
- 6–8 May 2010, ASEM Forum 2010 on Green Growth and Small and Medium Enterprises, Seoul, Korea
- 19 May 2010, Seminar on the Enforcement of IPRs, Prague, Czech Republic
- 26–27 May 2010, second ASEM Development Conference, Yogyakarta, Indonesia
- 10–11 June 2010, eighth ASEM Conference on Counter-Terrorism, Brussels, Belgium
- 14 June 2010, Employment High-level Forum, Geneve, Switzerland

Appendix II — *cont'd*

Year	Asian coordinators	ASEM Pre-summit official meetings	Culminating events (ASEM Summits)
		• 5–7 July 2010, ASEM Forum on Sustainable Food Security, Ho Chi Minh City, Vietnam	
		• 7–9 July 2010, tenth Informal seminar on Human Rights 'Gender Equality', Manila, Philippines	
		• 12–13 July 2010, Public Conference on EU-Asia Inter-regional Relations, Brussels, Belgium	
		• 6–7 September 2010, first ASEM Climate Change Forum, Ha Long City, Vietnam	
		• 26–28 September 2010, Asia-Europe Parliamentary Meeting (ASEP), Brussels, Belgium	
		• 27–28 September 2010, Workshop Social Protection Floor and Informal Economy, Nice, France	
		• 1 October 2010, ASEM People's Forum, Brussels, Belgium	
		• 2–5 October 2010, Asia-Europe People Forum (AEPF), Brussels, Belgium	
		• 2–3 October 2010, ASEF Connecting Civil Societies of Asia and Europe, Brussels, Belgium	
		• 3 October 2010, ASEF Editors' Roundtable, Brussels, Belgium	
		• 4 October 2010, Asia-Europe Business Forum (AEBF), Brussels, Belgium	

Sources:

ASEAN Vietnam 2010, "Vietnam in ASEM", <http://asean2010.vn/asean_en/news/18/2DA79E/VIETNAM-IN-ASEM> (accessed 27 April 2010).

ASEM Infoboard, <http://www.aseminfoboard.org /Calendar /Officials Meetings/> (accessed 26 April 2010 and 4 December 2011).

Council for Asia-Europe Cooperation (CAEC), *The Rationale and Common Agenda for Asia-Europe Cooperation: CAEC Task Force Reports* (Tokyo: Japan Centre for International Exchange, 1997).

European Commission, 2007b, <//ec.europa.eu /external_ Relations/ase/Asem_summits/asem6/Asem6_list_innitiative.pdf> (accessed 20 November 2007).

Gilson, *Asia Meets Europe: Inter-Regionalism and the Asia-Europe Meeting* (Cheltenham: Edward Elgar, 2002).

Kim Heunghong, "Korea Country Report", in *ASEM in Its Tenth Year: Looking Back, Looking Forward*, edited by Yamamoto and Yeo (Tokyo: Japan Center for International Exchange, 2006).

Ministry of Foreign Affairs of Finland, "Calendar of ASEM Events", 2006, <:\QO_ASVASEM \"CALENDAR OF ASEM EVENTS 2006 2007 DOC.>

Ministry of Foreign Affairs of Japan (MOFA Japan), <http://www.mofa.go.jp/POLICY/economy/asem/asem4/overview.html> (accessed 26 April 2010).

Yeo Lay Hwee, *Asia and Europe: The Development and Different Dimensions of ASEM* (London: Routledge, 2003).

Vietnam Development Gateway, "Vietnam — An Active Member of ASEM", <http://www.vietnamgateway.org/asem/economic1.html,> (accessed 26 April 2010).

Appendix III: Agenda and Issues around ASEM Summits, 1996–2010

Summit	Agenda	Issues	Outcomes of the Summit
First Summit 1–2 March 1996, Bangkok, Thailand	Strengthening links between Asia and Europe for peace, global stability, and prosperity	Europe-Asia partnership for greater growth	Chairman's statement: 1. Towards a common vision for Asia and Europe 2. Fostering political dialogue 3. Reinforcing economic cooperation 4. Promoting cooperation in other areas 5. Future course of ASEM a. An Asia-Europe Business Forum to hold its inaugural meeting France in 1996. b. Asia-Europe Foundation (ASEF) to be established in Singapore to promote exchange between think-tanks, people, and cultural groups.
Second Summit 3–4 April 1998, London, UK	Reaffirming on the partnership between Asia and Europe to carry the ASEM process forward.	The financial crises in Asia dominated the second ASEM Summits	A. Chairman's statement: 1. Developments in the two regions 2. Fostering political dialogue 3. Reinforcing economic cooperation 4. Promoting cooperation on global issues 5. Promoting cooperation in social and cultural issues 6. Taking forward the ASEM process B. Asia-Europe Cooperation Framework

Third Summit 20–21 October 2000, Seoul, Korea	Leaders reaffirmed their commitment to strengthening the Asia-Europe partnership. Leaders are to look at the proposal of the Asia-Europe Cooperation Framework (AECF). Issues: extending cooperation to include science and technology field	1. The heightening of North Korean nuclear issues (Reiterer, 2001) 2. Prolonged impacts of the financial crisis in East Asian countries (Reiterer, 2001) 3. EU have just launched a new regional currency, Euro	A. Chairman's statement: 1. Developments in the two regions 2. Fostering political dialogue 3. Reinforcing cooperation in economic and financial fields 4. Promoting cooperation in other areas, including social and cultural issues 5. Taking forward the ASEM process B. Seoul Declaration for the peace on Korean Peninsula
Fourth Summit 22–24 September 2002, Copenhagen, Denmark	Issues: review Asia-Europe Cooperation Framework (AECF) 2000; extending cooperation to include environment and migration	The heightening of "war against terrorism"	A. Chairman's statement: 1. Political dialogue on the challenges of the twenty-first century 2. Unity in diversity 3. Recent regional developments 4. Closer economic partnership 5. HRD, social cohesion and environmental cooperation 6. Deepening ASEM cooperation B. Political declaration for the peace on Korean Peninsula C. Declaration on cooperation against international terrorism

continued on next page

Appendix III — cont'd

Summit	Agenda	Issues	Outcomes of the Summit
Fifth Summit 8–9 October 2004, Hanoi, Vietnam	Theme: "Further Revitalising and Substantiating the Asia-Europe Partnership".	EU resentment on Myanmar participation in ASEM but ASEAN insisted the inclusion of Myanmar as the consequence of ASEAN enlargement	A. Chairman's statement: 1. Deepening political dialogue 2. Closer economic partnership 3. Expanding and strengthening cooperation in other fields 4. Recent regional developments 5. Taking the ASEM process forward 6. ASEM enlargement B. Recommendation for strategy and sustainability of ASEF C. Recommendation for ASEM working methods D. ASEM work program 2004–2006
Sixth Summit 10–11 September 2006, Helsinki, Finland	Theme: "10 Years of ASEM: Global Challenges -Joint Responses" Issues: support for the multilateral international system, security threats, including health threat, energy security, intercultural dialogues	1. "Premature fatigue" on ASEM. 2. China's outstanding development and energy needs. 3. The robust development of minilateral and bilateral FTAs in Asia.	A. Chairman's statement: 1. 10 years of ASEM 2. Regional developments 3. Strengthening multilateralism and addressing security theats 4. Globalization and competitiveness 5. Sustainable development 6. Dialogue among cultures and civilization 7. Asia-Europe Foundation 8. The future of ASEM

Summit	Theme	Context	Outcomes
			B. ASEM 6 Declaration on climate change
			C. Helsinki Declaration on the future of ASEM
Seventh Summit 24–25 October 2008, Beijing, China	Theme: "Vision and Action: Towards a Win-Win Solution"	1. Financial crisis in the USA 2. China's economic prowess	A. Chairman's statement: 1. Promoting political dialogue 2. Advancing economic cooperation 3. Driving sustainable development 4. Furthering social and cultural exchanges 5. The future of ASEM 6. New initiatives 7. Issue based Leadership programmes B. Beijing Declaration on sustainable development C. Statement of the seventh Asia-Europe meeting on the International Financial Situation
Eighth Summit 2010, Brussels, Belgium	Theme: "Greater well-being and more dignity for all citizens"	1. New accession of Russia, Australia and New Zealand 2. Financial crisis in the USA and Eurozone 3. Maritime security	A. Chairman's statement: 1. Towards more effective global economic governance 2. Advance on the path of sustainable development a. Economic development b. Social cohesion c. Environment protection 3. Global issues in focus a. Piracy at sea

continued on next page

Appendix III — *cont'd*

Summit	Agenda	Issues	Outcomes of the Summit
			b. Fighting terrorism and combating transnational organized crime
			c. Disaster prevention and disaster relief
			d. Human security
			e. Human rights and democracy
			f. Dialogue of cultures and civilizations
			g. Reform of the UN system
			h. Nuclear non-proliferation and disarmament
			4. Regional Issues
			5. People to people, visibility, and future of ASEM
			B. Brussels Declaration on more effective global economic governance

Source: ASEM Infoboard <http://www.aseminfoboard. org/page.phtml?code=Summits> (accessed 10 July 2006, 12 March 2009, and 4 December 2011).

INDEX

ABOUT THE AUTHOR

Evi Fitriani is Head of the International Relations Department, Faculty of Social and Political Sciences, University of Indonesia (FISIP UI). She is also the co-founder of the university's Master Program of European Studies as well as the ASEAN Study Center of FISIP UI. Since 2012, she has been the Indonesian Country Coordinator of the Network of East Asian Think Tanks (NEAT), a second track of the ASEAN Plus Three countries. She was trained in international relations studies in Indonesia, the United Kingdom, the United States, Australia, Japan, Sweden, the Netherlands and Hungary.

Evi has written numerous books and journal and newspaper articles on topics related to Indonesian foreign policy, ASEAN, Asia Pacific regionalism, and Asia-Europe relations. Her ongoing research includes the issues of irregular migrants between Indonesia and Australia, border issues in Southeast Asia, Indonesia's foreign policy, and EU-ASEAN relations.

She recently co-edited a book entitled *Governance on Extractive Industries: Assessing National Experiences to Inform Regional Cooperation in Southeast Asia* (2014) and *Indonesia-Malaysia Relations: Scholars' Views from Both Sides* (forthcoming). She is also the editor of *Australia dan Negara-Negara Pasifik Selatan: Observasi dan Pandangan dari Indonesia* (2012) and *Hubungan Indonesia-Malaysia dalam perspektif sosial, budaya, politik dan media: Kasus perbatasan dan pekerja migrant* (2012). She co-authored *Europe in Emerging Asia* (forthcoming), to be published by Rowman and Littlefield. She is also the editor of *Global*, a journal on international relations published by the International Relations Department of the University of Indonesia.

Dr Fitriani is married and has two daughters. Her hobbies include travelling, cooking and gardening.

E-mail contact: evi.fitriani09@ui.ac.id or evi.fitriani@gmail.com.

www.ingramcontent.com/pod-product-compliance
Lightning Source LLC
Chambersburg PA
CBHW050443280326
41932CB00013BA/2227